# FINANCIAL ACCOUNTING WITH CORPORATE GOVERNANCE FOR NON-ACCOUNTING STUDENTS

## JOHN HENEGHAN

GILL & MACMILLAN

Gill & Macmillan
Hume Avenue
Park West
Dublin 12
with associated companies throughout the world
www.gillmacmillan.ie

© 2006 John Heneghan

ISBN-13: 978 0 7171 4032 9
ISBN-10: 0 7171 4032 6

Index compiled by Cover to Cover
Print origination in Ireland by O'K Graphic Design, Dublin

# FINANCIAL ACCOUNTING WITH CORPORATE
# GOVERNANCE FOR NON-ACCOUNTING STUDENTS

*To my wife Beatrice and our children Jim, Fiona and Emma*

## Support Material for

## FINANCIAL ACCOUNTING WITH CORPORATE GOVERNANCE FOR NON-ACCCOUNTING STUDENTS

by John Heneghan

Dynamic and easy to use online support material for this book is available at
www.gillmacmillan.ie/lecturers and www.gillmacmillan.ie/student

Provides **lecturers** with:
- PowerPoint presentation slides
- sample exam questions with suggested answers
- web links, including link to IBM Financial Analysis site
- paper entitled 'Corporate Governance & Compliance' written by the author.

To access lecturer support material on our secure site:
1) Go to www.gillmacmillan.ie/lecturers
2) Log on using your username and password. If you don't have a password, register online and we will email your password to you.

Provides **students** with:
- web links, including link to IBM Financial Analysis site
- paper entitled 'Corporate Governance & Compliance' written by the author.

To access student support material:
1) Go to www.gillmacmillan.ie/student
2) Click on the link for Student Support material.

# TABLE OF CONTENTS

# Foreword

When I started out studying business, a close relative suggested that I study accounting, as it would keep me in the 'mainstream of business'. This advice was bolstered further by my first accounting lecturer, who described accounting as the 'language of business'. It is due to the positive impact of these insights early on that I acquired a sense of a world beyond the mechanics, where both the accountant and non-accountant determine whether the financial statements reflect the 'true and fair' state of affairs. A good few years later, I now know how crucial this determination is to directors, shareholders, bankers, suppliers, employees and the Revenue Commissioners. It is the reliance on accounting information by others that makes the study of accounting so important.

Accounting rules are generally referred to as **regulations** and these have evolved over many decades of practice. In more recent years **legislation**, much of it driven by EU directives, further influences the social construction of these rules. And yet, in the last few years, scandals at Enron, WorldCom and Parmalat (to name just a few), which splashed across the front pages and the TV screens (and indeed Ireland's own tribunals), beg the question – *what happened to the rules?* This is why a third element, **corporate governance**, must be added to the study of accounting rules. In a dynamic economy, it is the quality and integrity of information that inspires investors to invest, businesses to trade with each other and entrepreneurs to start enterprises. Good governance demands strong oversight of how a business entity is run, so that others can rely on the integrity of the financial information reported. The people at Enron appear to have known the fundamentals of accounting; to borrow R.D. Laing's insight, what they did *not* understand was the difference between fear of nothing and having nothing to fear.

From the outset, this book strives to integrate corporate governance into the accounting process, which in turn demands that the student look beyond the mere mechanics of the debits and credits. Accounting reflects relationships: between the business and its customers, its suppliers, its bank and its staff; and its fiscal responsibility to the community and society in which it operates. This social responsibility, and its ability to hold businesses accountable, is part of what makes accounting a social science.

The accounting environment today is dynamic. As Anne Brady of the Dublin accounting firm Anne Brady McQuillans DFK puts it: 'The biggest challenges for accountants today are cash flow, staffing, profitability and compliance. Running a business is more complex than ever before, mainly because of increased regulation. This brings with it a need for good corporate governance and enterprise risk management.' In their publication *Corporate Governance in Irish Hospitals*, the accounting firm PricewaterhouseCoopers suggests that the Directors' Report should contain 'a review of the transactions and financial position of the organisation and an explanation of the salient features of the accounts. This review should enable the reader to appreciate the significance of any surpluses or deficits disclosed in the financial statements and the purposes for which the organisation's assets are being held.' These opinions signal the motivation for highlighting corporate governance early on, and integrating its key concepts throughout the book. To become an accounting professional usually requires formal studies that begin with the fundamentals and progress through intermediate stages before completing a number of advanced courses. Studying this textbook will prepare the student or executive to understand a financial report. It will also provide the first step for those who may aspire to preparing this financial information themselves – future accountants.

The book is divided into three parts. Part I (Chapters 1 to 4) introduces the student to the accounting process and applies the principles over the accounting cycle. Part II (Chapters 5 to 8) examines the accrual basis of accounting and applies it to the corporate entity. The student is also introduced to group accounting in order to provide an understanding of the effect of corporate acquisitions in today's economy. The final chapter here addresses the cash flow statement. In Part III (Chapters 9 to 12) the student is provided with the requisite tools in analysis of financial accounting information and an exposure to the internal control system (ICS). The nature of corporate governance is explored and its integral role in accounting is underlined with the inclusion of the audit process in the final chapter.

I am grateful to all those who, over the years, shared their work and teaching experiences with me, both in Ireland and in the United States. My alma mater, Seton Hall University in New Jersey, allowed me to lecture part-time in the Accounting Department for a number of years. I will never be able to fully repay them for all that was done for me there. At the University of Limerick, the teaching and research work of my colleagues in the Department of Accounting and Finance at the Kemmy Business School is always an inspiration. And lastly, I am delighted to acknowledge the management and staff at Gill & Macmillan, and in particular Marion O'Brien, who first proposed the idea of this book and whose diplomatic skills and tenacity saw it through to completion.

John Heneghan
Department of Accounting & Finance
Kemmy Business School
University of Limerick
January 2006

## REFERENCES

Laing, R.D., *The Politics of Experience and the Bird of Paradise*, Harmondsworth: Penguin Books 1967.

PricewaterhouseCoopers, *Corporate Governance in Irish Hospitals*, Dublin: Healthcare Advisory Services 2005.

Interview with Anne Brady, Partner, Anne Brady McQuillans DFK, Dublin.

# Acknowledgements

The following provided many of the key professional signposts to me, leading to completion of this book:

Alfred Basile, Vice President, The Wall Street Group, Jersey City, New Jersey; Jack M. Ciattarelli, President and CEO, Advanced Studies in Medicine, New Jersey; Randy Cochran, Director, Institute of Management and Administration, New York; Joan Coll, Professor of Management, Seton Hall University, New Jersey; Vincent Crowley, Collins Crowley Solicitors, Dublin; Jim Dalton, Lecturer in Marketing, Kemmy Business School, University of Limerick; Peggy Davis (RIP), Athletic Department, Seton Hall University, New Jersey; Robert Davis, Sr., Irish American Cultural Institute, New Jersey; John P. Deehan (RIP), Professor of Accounting, Seton Hall University, New Jersey; Karen Foley, formerly Vice President Human Resources, HUBCO, New Jersey; Jessie Frick, Frick Realty, New Jersey; Timothy Gearty, Becker Conviser Fox Gearty, CPA Review, New Jersey; Jack Hampton, KPMG Professor of Business, St. Peter's College, New Jersey; Thomas Hopkins, Allied Irish Banks, Bank Centre, Dublin; Thomas Mathews, Treasurer, Spenser Savings Bank, New Jersey; Philip McGee, President, The Wall Street Group, New Jersey; W.P. (Brod) McHale (RIP), formerly Executive Director, Allied Irish Finance, Dublin; O. Vincent McNany (RIP), formerly Chairman, Yorkwood Savings Bank, New Jersey; Owen V. McNany, President, McLand Realty Management, New Jersey; Patti McNany, McLand Realty Management, New Jersey; Regina Michel (retired), Executive Vice President, New Jersey Bell, New Jersey; John Moon, Head Track Coach, Seton Hall University, New Jersey; Ulrich Muckenberger, Professor, Hochschule für Wirtschaft und Politik, Hamburg, Germany; John Mulvihill (RIP), Electronic Information & Education Services of New Jersey; Kenneth T. Neilson, Chairman, President and CEO, Hudson United Bankcorp, New Jersey; Loman O'Byrne, CEO, South Dublin Enterprise Board, Dublin; David O'Donnell, Intellectual Capital Ireland, Limerick; Philip O'Regan, Head, Accounting & Finance, Kemmy Business School, University of Limerick; Jack Shannon, Lecturer in Law, Seton Hall University, New Jersey; John Tomlinson, President, First Consumer Mortgage Inc., New Jersey; Robert Villeneuve, Director General, Association Européenne de l'excellence Territoriale, Paris, France; Thomas Wester, Partner McDermott and McGee Attorney at Law, New Jersey; and my parents, Jim and the late Mary Heneghan.

# 1
# *Accounting: Its Role and Environment*

**C O N T E N T S**

# INTRODUCTION

What is accounting? There is a perception that accountants deal mostly with numbers, so it may surprise many that a more appropriate definition is that accounting is the language of business, complete with its own vocabulary and dedicated to effective communication. Certainly the recording and classifying of data demands considerable number crunching, the results of which are often pages containing columns of numbers. Yet when it is understood that this data has been transformed into financial information to allow users to make informed decisions, we can then appreciate that accounting is a critical communicative process as well.

How businesses are structured, how they make decisions and what they report comes under the heading of **corporate governance**. In recent years the general public has received a negative view of corporate behaviour and of the accounting profession by virtue of fraud perpetrated by Enron and WorldCom in the US, and in Europe, Ahold and Parmalat stand charged. Of further significance was the demise of the accounting giant Arthur Andersen, the independent auditor of Enron's financial accounts. Reliance on what companies report about their financial picture and the audit of that picture by the independent auditor is at the heart of corporate governance (Higgs 2003). Accordingly, governance is a major concern for both preparers and users of financial information.

This chapter will give you an overview of the field of accounting, its environment and its means of communication. The concept of corporate governance is also examined and how good accounting is a requirement for good governance is explained.

## OBJECTIVES

**When you have finished this chapter, you will be able to:**
- understand the role of accounting and its environment
- identify financial statements and their uses and users
- understand what corporate governance is.

# HISTORY AND DEVELOPMENT

People have always needed to record events. Archaeologists discovered clay tablets in Iran and Iraq that were used as crude records 5,000 years ago. From around that time the number of settled communities increased and the volume of trade grew accordingly throughout the Middle East. This made it necessary to find some way to record business transactions. By the first century BC, accounting for wealth was so common that the Romans created a word to describe a person who recorded such accounts: the word '**auditor**' is still in use today.

## Historical role: Addressing a social need

From this brief overview of its origins, you can see that accounting emerged very early in history. Once people began to organise themselves, they discovered that they needed accounting information for social control. Thus, accounting for events arose because it met a basic social need.

Social needs also influenced how accounting changed and developed, as accountants changed their systems to accommodate social change. Elementary issues such as wages, benefits and safety for staff, buying and purchasing, paying taxes and safeguarding the environment represent direct interaction with society and must be accounted for responsibly. Accounting provides the internal control systems to track these transactions and must constantly adapt and update them to keep pace with a changing society.

Perhaps the most important consequence of recording financial events is that those with responsibility for recording the figures also play a key role in the allocation of wealth (O'Regan 1998). For example, accountants define and calculate profit, one of the criteria for defining wealth today. In this context, accounting takes on a much greater significance, and those involved in business and management must understand the principles it is based on.

## Early modern developments

Modern accounting and bookkeeping began in the late Middle Ages, when increased trade made it necessary to account for profit and wealth. Gradually, accounting procedures became standardised. In Venice in 1494, a local monk and friend of Leonardo da Vinci, **Fra Luca Pacioli**, produced a text, *Summa de Arithmetica*, that outlined the mechanics of the bookkeeping system that had been used for decades in and around Venice. Over five centuries later, this system is still the basis of modern bookkeeping.

Until the eighteenth century, most businesses were small, family-run concerns with simple accounts and ledgers. With the onset of the Industrial Revolution came much larger businesses that needed more complex recording systems. New business entities called **limited companies** emerged, owned by a number of people called shareholders. Because it was impossible for all shareholders to manage these limited companies, they usually appointed directors to manage the company on their behalf. This need for representation to oversee the running of the business reflects the genesis of the corporate governance issue today – appointing others to act on your behalf and according to your wishes.

This arrangement often meant that the shareholders did not know what was happening in their companies – the classic governance concern – so the financial statements summarising the company's performance became very important. Shareholders needed to receive the statements and understand them to find out how their own company was performing. As we will see later, financial statements prepared annually, together with an annual general meeting organised by the directors, go a long way toward informing shareholders. The arrangement continues to be an uneasy one for shareholders, as they often find that directors do not always act according to their (shareholders') wishes.

## The information age

As the need for financial information increased, the role of accounting and the accounting profession became even more important in modern society. Accounting is now seen as vital to any free enterprise culture, providing important financial data. The advent of computers and information technology has made accounting even more significant. Although we have traced the origins of modern bookkeeping back to the fifteenth century, today's technology may suggest advances in accounting that are more than just incremental. For instance, the creation of a new internet language called **XBRL (extensible business reporting language)** will allow users to electronically 'reach in' to a company's accounting system and attain financial information (DiPiazza and Eccles 2002). The participants will be able to reduce their costs of gathering information in such a set-up. As with all information, its quality is only as good as the degree of effort and honesty brought to bear on its production.

However, financial data is a universal language that is understood in any country, and due to its ease of transfer, it has become one of the most powerful means of communication in the world.

---

### Self-Assessment Questions 1

1. Explain why it is essential for modern business managers and owners to be familiar with accounting data.

2. Explain why the appointment of directors did not eliminate all the concerns of shareholders. Can you detect what may be the genesis of the corporate governance issue today?

---

## ACCOUNTING: PROVIDING FINANCIAL INFORMATION

Accounting is the mechanism that ultimately provides us with reliable financial information. The needs for and uses of this information are best understood when the following questions are posed:

- How do you start a business?
- How do you make it grow?
- How do you determine whether your business is making money?
- How do you finance expansion?

- How do you convince the bank to lend you money?

These questions are clearly the concern of business decision makers who understand that business decisions require financial information. Accounting, then, is an information system that:

- identifies
- collects
- describes  } data and communicates it as financial information.
- records
- processes

This data is the result of transactions identified as economic events pertaining to an entity, be it a business or a non-profit organisation, and provided to those users who have a need or a right to know.

This last statement implies that accounting is not merely a collection of activities, but rather a discipline possessing its own rules, regulations, vocabulary and users.

## The environment of accounting

We live in a service-oriented society and accounting is a service activity. Its workplace or environment exists on a number of key pillars:

*See Forms of Business Organisation below.*

- **Accounting entities:** The businesses or organisations found in society that accounting serves and whose events and activities are captured by the accounting process.
- **Economic events:** The types of events or transactions that can be identified by accounting.
- **Financial description:** This refers to the way in which these events are described.
- **Users:** The beneficiaries of the processing and communicating of the information.

*We'll look at the users and uses of financial statements later.*

- **Accounting rules:** The rules or guides that enhance the preparation and presentation of information.

Financial information is primarily reflected in financial statements that endeavour to present the economic events affecting an entity, regardless of what form the business takes.

## Forms of business organisation

A new business may organise itself into any one of three forms:

- **Sole proprietorship:** A business owned by one person.

- **Partnership:** A business owned by more than one person.
- **Limited company**: A business organised as a separate legal entity owned by shareholders.

The choice of which form to use will depend on many factors, some of which we can categorise as advantages and disadvantages.

|  | Sole proprietorship | Partnership | Limited company |
|---|---|---|---|
| Advantages | <ul><li>Easy to establish.</li><li>Controlled by owner.</li><li>Tax advantages.</li></ul> | <ul><li>Easy to establish.</li><li>Shared control.</li><li>Broader skills.</li><li>Tax advantages.</li></ul> | <ul><li>Easy to transfer ownership.</li><li>Easier to raise funds.</li><li>No personal liability.</li></ul> |
| Disadvantages | <ul><li>Owner is personally liable for debts of the business.</li></ul> | <ul><li>Owners are personally liable for debts of the business.</li></ul> | <ul><li>Issuing shares gives up ownership.</li></ul> |

## Areas of accounting

Growth in businesses, particularly in the services sector, is reflected in the evolving accounting environment. Entrepreneurial effort and knowledge-based economies demand specialised assistance from the accounting profession. These forces have spawned a number of new disciplines which have become stand-alone professions in their own right. Thus, today we can describe accountancy or the accounting profession as including the following.

- **Auditing** deals with examining accounts and reporting on them rather than preparing accounts. Auditors are hired as independent accountants to complete an audit of a company's books.
- **Financial accounting** is concerned with recording, processing and presenting financial information in the form of financial statements (discussed below). A financial accountant is in the employ of a business and the statements prepared are reviewed by internal users (management) and external users (lenders and creditors).
- **Financial management** involves establishing financial plans based on strategic objectives. It is a more senior management role than that of the accountant who prepares the financial statements.

- **Management accounting** is very similar to financial accounting, but is concerned with providing information to managers to help them run the business. Management accountants may determine how much it costs to make a product or what kinds of discounts a business can afford to attract sales.
- **Taxation** is a highly complex discipline that is a mixture of accounting and law. Such is the complexity and the changing nature of tax law that many accountancy firms have departments specialising in taxation.

The distinctions between areas of accounting are not as clear-cut as the descriptions above might suggest, but they certainly reflect the evolving nature of the profession as it meets the demands of business. Roles in accounting departments have evolved and may be separate or combined, depending on the company size.

The role of the controller is usually responsible for the accounting system and its processes. The treasurer's role makes sure that relationships with banks and other fund sources are maintained. The chief financial officer (CFO) may be responsible for all of these roles, but primarily will set policy for the finances and accounting operations of the company.

FIG. 1.1: VARIOUS ROLES FOR AN ACCOUNTANT (ADAPTED FROM HAMPTON 1982)

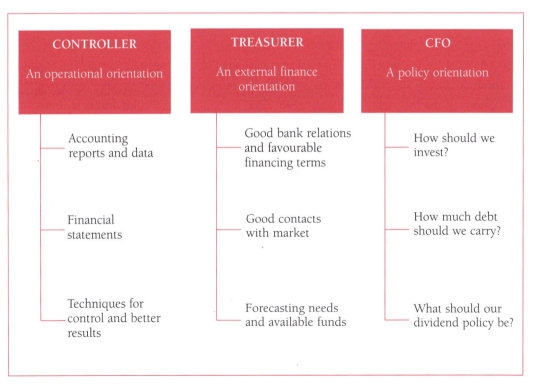

## THE FINANCIAL STATEMENTS

For many in the accounting and financial world, their involvement with accounting ends once financial statements are presented to the relevant users. For others, however, the financial statements represent the beginning of their professional work and the genesis of far-reaching decision making. Thus, it is appropriate not only to discuss what these statements are, but also to understand who the users are.

From a corporate governance perspective, it is important to understand that the preparation of the financial statements is the responsibility of the management of the business.

The three main statements are the:

- income statement
- balance sheet
- cash flow statement.

There are many rules and concepts to be applied as to how these are created. The function of these financial statements is to provide a continual history of the resources and obligations of the business (Hawkins 1998). We will study those rules and principles, and by applying them consistently from one year to the next, we can determine any emerging trends, such as increasing or decreasing sales.

### The income statement

Also known as the **profit and loss account** (P&L).

The income statement reflects the performance of an entity **over a period of time**. It pulls together all the revenues and all the expenses for the period, be it a month or a year, to determine whether the business made a profit or a loss. This result, coming at the end of a period, is the essence of performance. The following is a typical layout for the income statement.

**Boot and Polish Ltd**
**Income statement for the year ended 31 December 2006**

| | | |
|---|---:|---:|
| Sales | | 33,700 |
| Opening stock | 3,200 | |
| Add purchases | 24,490 | |
| | 27,690 | |
| Less closing | 2,390 | |
| Cost of sales | | 25,300 |
| Gross profit | | 8,400 |
| | | |
| Operating expenses: | | |
| Wages | 3,385 | |
| Rent | 1,200 | |
| Miscellaneous expenses | 365 | |
| | | 4,950 |
| Net profit | | 3,450 |

- The annual reports of Irish companies will use any one of the following terms: **profit and loss account**, **profit and loss statement**, **income statement**.
- Notice that it states in the heading 'for the year ended', which is in keeping with our definition of the income statement.
- Expenses are broken into cost of sales and operating expenses. This allows for greater control and understanding of costs.

The top line, or sales, may also be called revenue or turnover. Revenue and sales feature mostly in reports of US companies, while turnover usually features in UK and Irish statements.

## The balance sheet

This statement reflects the financial position of an entity **at a point in time**. It captures the resources owned by the business (these resources are referred to as **assets**) and it also captures the business's obligations (referred to as **liabilities**).

This is understood better with the following simple but fundamental equation:

$$\text{assets} + \text{liabilities} = \text{shareholders' equity}$$

The description **trading, profit and loss account** is often used for the statement of a sole trader.

The term 'shareholders' equity' is often referred to by a number of different terms, such as:
- net worth
- owners' equity
- shareholders' funds and reserves
- capital and reserves.

How well the resources (listed in the balance sheet) were used is reflected in the income statement – did the business make a profit or not?

Stating this a little differently:

$$\text{assets} - \text{liabilities} = \text{shareholders' equity}$$

Or in intuitive terms:

*From what we own (assets), take away what we owe (liabilities) and we are left with our net worth (equity).*

The balance sheet for Boot and Polish Ltd will look like this for the same period.

---

**Boot and Polish Ltd**
**Balance sheet as at 31 December 2006**

| | € | € |
|---|---|---|
| **Fixed assets:** | | |
| Motor van | | 3,400 |
| | | |
| **Current assets:** | | |
| Stock | 2,390 | |
| Debtors | 1,840 | |
| Cash | 1,760 | |
| | 5,990 | |
| | | |
| **Current liabilities:** | | |
| Creditors | 2,700 | |
| Net current assets | | 3,290 |
| | | 6,690 |
| | | |
| **Share capital and reserves:** | | |
| Common stock | | 1,000 |
| Retained profit at 1 Jan 2006 | 1,240 | |
| Add net profit | 3,450 | |
| Retained profit at 31 Dec 2006 | | 4,690 |
| | | 5,690 |
| | | |
| **Long-term liability:** | | |
| Loan | | 1,000 |
| | | 6,690 |

---

- The assets are divided into **fixed** (held in the business over a number of years) and **current** (used up and replenished repeatedly within a one-year period).
- The least liquid assets are listed first, followed by the most liquid.
- The share capital and reserves reflect what is owed by the business to the shareholders. It may seem strange to say that the business owes money to its owners, but as we'll learn later, there is a concept or rule in accounting called the **entity concept** which requires that the accounts of the business be kept separate from those of the owner.
- Following on from the above and using the accounting formula discussed earlier:
  assets = liabilities + shareholders' equity
  6,690 = 1,000 + 5,640

  While the trade creditors are liabilities, accounting practice lists them as **netted against** the assets.

- Notice how profit from the income statement flows into the balance sheet to provide the retained profits up to the end of the year.

> **Liquid** means how close it is to being cash or being turned into cash.

### Self-Assessment Question 3

1. Differentiate between the profit and loss account and the balance sheet.

### The cash flow statement

This is a financial statement that provides information about the cash inflows (receipts) and cash outflows (payments) over a period of time. This statement provides answers to the following important questions:
- Where did cash come from during the period?
- How was cash used?
- What explains the change in the cash balance from that at the beginning of the year to the balance at the end of that same period?

Because cash is an entity's most important resource, users pay particular attention to the cash flow statement. We'll examine this statement in depth in Chapter 8; until then we will study just the income statement and the balance sheet over the next few chapters. Completing Self-Assessment Question 4 should further your understanding of the difference *and* link between the two statements.

## Self-Assessment Question 4

1.  Modern Engineering Ltd began operations on 1 January 2005. On completion of its first year in business (31 December 2005), the following information became available. As the company is a service entity, there is no stock held for resale and the listing of the expenses is straightforward.

| | |
|---|---|
| Revenues | 47,000 |
| Debtors | 14,000 |
| Creditors | 13,000 |
| Rental expense | 19,000 |
| Loan (short term) | 15,000 |
| Share capital | 20,000 |
| Equipment | 26,000 |
| Insurance expense | 11,000 |
| Office supplies | 11,000 |
| Office supplies expense | 2,000 |
| Cash | 12,000 |

Prepare an income statement and a balance sheet using this information for the year ended 31 December 2005.

Note: Office supplies is a current asset, and later, when they are used up, they are expensed, at which point they become office supplies expense.

## Users and uses of financial statements

Users of accounting information can be broadly defined as **internal** and **external** users.

### INTERNAL USERS

Internal users of financial information are the managers who plan, organise and run a business. They will want to know:

- if there is enough cash for Friday's payroll
- if suppliers can be paid on time
- the cost to produce each unit of product
- which product line is the most profitable.

The accounting process provides these users with internal reports that will facilitate comparisons, projections, forecasts and what-if scenarios that will assist in making operating decisions.

## EXTERNAL USERS

There are several types of external users:

- **Shareholders:** Owners of businesses who buy, sell or hold shares (stock) in the business. They are not normally involved in running the business.
- **Financial analysts:** Individuals who use accounting information to advise existing or potential shareholders. They are regarded as sophisticated users.
- **Creditors:** These are suppliers of goods and services and bankers who use accounting information to determine the risk of extending credit or lending money. They are particularly interested in the availability of cash and the value of assets given as security against loans.
- **Regulators:** Although it is more precise to refer to them as legislators, Irish business has to deal with two regulators. **The Office of the Director of Corporate Enforcement (ODCE)** has responsibility for compliance with company law and possesses the legal power to restrict or disqualify a company director (Companies Act 2001, Section 40). **The Irish Auditing and Accounting Supervisory Authority (IAASA)** is authorised to 'supervise how the accountancy bodies regulate and monitor' their members and 'to monitor whether the accounts' of companies comply with corporate law (Companies Act 2003, Section 8).

  To use the vernacular, when considered jointly, the ODCE and IAASA represent the 'new sheriff in town'.

  We will examine the powers of these two bodies in greater depth later, but suffice it to say for now that the ODCE and IAASA are expected to make their presence felt, particularly with errant company directors and accountants. They are the key drivers of good governance among companies in Ireland.
- **Revenue Commissioners:** They will want to know if the business has complied with the tax laws.
- **Trade unions:** As representatives of employees, they will want to know if the business can pay an increase in wages and benefits.
- **Pressure groups:** These emanate out of the **general public** and may use accounting information to pressure companies into changing their operating practices. Such developments have prompted companies to acknowledge the concerns of the public by including a report on **corporate social responsibility** within their annual reports.

### Self-Assessment Question 5

1.  What questions might each of the following decision makers have that could be answered with financial information: (a) bank manager (b) investor (c) trade unionist (d) Revenue Commissioner?

## CORPORATE GOVERNANCE

In prior sections, we were introduced to the elements of accounting and were given a sense of accounting's role in business. Yet those with even a remote interest in business are familiar with the many scandals that have come to light in recent years. In most of these cases there were the usual signs of bad governance, such as fraudulent reporting, a domineering CEO and auditors who seem to have missed vital clues of trouble. Whether you intend pursuing a career in the profession or wish to enhance your decision making as a businessperson, it is crucial to appreciate that others rely fully on reported financial information (Cadbury 2002). Seeing to it that reliable accounting information is produced is the goal of **corporate governance.** (This point is demonstrated in all chapters up to Chapter 10, where governance is examined in depth.) Before proceeding, a brief discussion of accounting in the context of governance is warranted.

### What is corporate governance?

There are a number of definitions of corporate governance. The Organisation for Economic Co-operation and Development (OECD 1999) describes it as 'a set of relationships between a company's board, its shareholders and other stakeholders. It also provides the structure through which the objectives of the company are set, and the means of attaining those objectives, and the monitoring of performance.'

In 1993, the Public Oversight Board defined corporate governance as 'those oversight activities undertaken by the board of directors and audit committee to ensure the integrity of the financial reporting process.' Although the accounting professional establishes the structure and mechanics of the accounting system, it is the directors who are responsible for the **oversight** of the systems. As stated earlier, the directors of the company are also legally responsible for the preparation of the financial statements.

### Reporting and disclosure

We have already introduced the financial statements that are included in a company's annual report for review by external users. The statements are the culmination of hundreds of thousands of transactions of many medium-sized businesses (transactions in the millions for larger companies) and sheer common sense would suggest some very reasonable questions:

- Have all transactions been captured?
- Are there controls in place to prevent fraud?
- Can we rely on the information reported?
- Do the directors understand what is going on in the company and how is this achieved?
- If the company is the defendant in a lawsuit, has that been disclosed?

It is fair to say that unless users can rely on the reported financial information, financial analysis (see Chapter 9) will be meaningless.

## Controls and oversight

Directors of companies are required by law to oversee the running of their entities. This oversight duty entails:

- installing and maintaining an internal control system
- processing transactions accurately and on a timely basis
- reporting the true and fair view of the company's financial health.

They must also appoint an independent auditor to review and test the control systems and to report whether the resulting financial picture does indeed reflect the true and fair view. This report is completed on behalf of the shareholders. Whether they and all other users can rely on the reported information is a pertinent question for the student commencing accounting studies. The bookkeeping duties that we start with eventually give way to including judgment (and prudence) in completing the financial statements. It will become apparent that even with the best control system in place:

- mistakes are still possible
- fraud is difficult to prevent if there is collusion among staff
- auditors risk a conflict of interest that threatens their independence.

If we add to this the roles of the ODCE and IAASA to oversee the overseers, as it were, it means that **accounting and corporate governance are inseparable**. The student of accounting must grasp this point at the outset.

## Self-Assessment Question 6

1. How are the internal control system and the oversight role understood in accounting? Make sure that you include the relevant players involved.

## CHAPTER REVIEW

In this chapter we established the need for useful and reliable information and for a system that will communicate that information effectively. Accounting is made up of users and rules that facilitate the capture of economic events in a systematic fashion, allowing business and non-business organisations to grow and prosper.

We discussed the three types of business organisations (sole proprietorship, partnership, limited company) and the advantages and disadvantages of each. The accounting profession has evolved into a number of related disciplines to service the needs of these organisations: auditing, financial management, managerial accounting or taxation services. Professionals must demonstrate the highest standards of integrity and expertise if they are to command the respect of all users, both internal and external.

For presenting actual accounting information, we introduced the three statements that most concern us:

- the income statement reflects the performance of an entity over a period
- the balance sheet reflects the financial position at a point in time
- the statement of cash flow provides important information about the movements in raw cash during a period.

Corporate governance reflects the oversight of accounting systems, a legal duty carried out by company directors. This entails:

- installing and maintaining an internal control system
- processing transactions accurately and on a timely basis
- reporting the true and fair view of the company's financial health.

The creation of the ODCE and IAASA to ensure that directors and auditors comply with company law and accounting regulation demonstrates that accounting and governance are intertwined.

You should now have an understanding of the key parts of the accounting environment where information is communicated to users, information that is regarded as reliable and useful for decision making.

## SELF-ASSESSMENT QUESTION ANSWERS

### SAQ 1

1. Accountants in today's society control financial information that is, in many senses, the life blood of commerce. As a result, they can have a lot of power because the decisions they make, such as how to calculate profit, affect the many different users of accounting data. These decisions also affect those who control society's wealth. Therefore, it is

essential for modern business managers to be familiar with accounting data. In today's information age, where those who control information find themselves in an even more powerful position than before, it is critical that there is oversight of accounting systems.

2. When companies were formed by shareholders, they appointed managers or directors to run the businesses, preferring to have somebody else worry about day-to-day operations. However, the owners found themselves uninformed about the business they owned. The introduction of financial statements went a long way towards redressing the lack of information, but the gulf has essentially continued through to today. The governance problem is that directors may not act according to the wishes of the owners, nor fully inform the owners of all details.

## SAQ 2

1. We define accounting as an information system because it systemically identifies, describes and then records data concerning an entity's activities and processes it into financial information so that users can make informed judgments about the business.

2. The pillars of the accounting environment are accounting entities, economic events, financial descriptions, users and accounting rules.

3. The three forms of business are sole proprietorship, partnership and limited company.

## SAQ 3

1. The income statement (sometimes called the P&L) contains the revenues and the expenses that are used to calculate a profit or loss. The balance sheet contains the resources (assets) and the obligations (liabilities) of the business. The income statement reflects the performance of the business over a period of time, whereas the balance sheet reflects the financial position of the business at a point in time.

## SAQ 4

### Modern Engineering Ltd
Profit and loss statement for the year ended 31 December 2005

| | | |
|---|---|---|
| Revenue | | 47,000 |
| Less expenses: | | |
| Rent | 19,000 | |
| Insurance | 11,000 | |

| | | |
|---|---:|---:|
| Office supplies | 2,000 | |
| Total expenses | | 32,000 |
| Net profit | | 15,000 |

## Modern Engineering Ltd
### Balance sheet as at 31 December 2005

| | € | € |
|---|---:|---:|
| **Fixed assets:** | | €26,000 |
| **Current assets**: | | |
| Debtors | 14,000 | |
| Office supplies | 11,000 | |
| Cash | 12,000 | |
| | 37,000 | |
| **Less current liabilities** | | |
| Creditors | 13,000 | |
| Loans | 15,000 | |
| | 28,000 | |
| | | 9,000 |
| **Net assets** | | **35,000** |
| | | |
| **Financed by:** | | |
| Capital | 20,000 | |
| Retained profits | | 15,000 |
| **Total** | | **35,000** |

Notice how the profit from the P&L statement ends up in the capital section of the balance sheet. As this is the profit from the first year of operations, it is also the retained profit at the end of the year.

If in the next year the company made a profit of €10,000, the retained profit for 2006 would be calculated as follows:

| | |
|---|---|
| Retained profit from 2005 | €15,000 |
| Add profit for 2006 | €10,000 |
| Retained profit for 2006 | €25,000 |

## SAQ 5

1. These interested parties will be eager to know a number of things about a business, but the essential areas of concern are as follows.

    (a) **The banker** will want to know if there is enough cash to pay for current liabilities such as creditors or bank loans.

    (b) **The shareholder** will want to know if there is enough profits to pay a dividend.

    (c) **The trade unionist** will want to know if sales and profits have grown to allow a pay raise to employees.

    (d) **The Revenue Commissioner** will want to ensure that profits are taxed correctly and paid to the government.

## SAQ 6

1. Directors are responsible not only for the internal control system of a company, but also the preparation of the financial statements that rely on good controls for credibility. This task is tested and reviewed by an independent auditor who issues an opinion on whether the statements reflect the true and fair view of the state of affairs at the company. This opinion is provided to the shareholders of the company. It has been necessary to create two legal overseers, the ODCE and IAASA, to ensure that laws and accounting rules are complied with. This interrelated structure of controls and oversight functions confirms that accounting and corporate governance are inseparable activities.

# REFERENCES

Committee on the Financial Aspects of Corporate Governance, Cadbury Committee, GEE Publishing 1992.

Companies (Auditing and Accounting) Act 2003, Dublin: The Stationery Office.

Company Law Enforcement Act 2001, Dublin: The Stationery Office.

DiPiazza, S.A. and Eccles, R.G., *Building Public Trust: The Future of Corporate Reporting*, New York: John Wiley & Sons 2002.

Hampton, J., *Modern Financial Theory*, Virginia: Reston Publishing Company Inc. 1982.

Hawkins, D.F., *Corporate Financial Reporting and Analysis*, New York: Irwin/McGraw-Hill 1998.

Heneghan, J. and O'Regan, P., *Accounting*, Limerick: Centre for Project Management, University of Limerick 2000.

Higgs, D., *Review of the Role and Effectiveness of Non-Executive Directors*, London: The Stationery Office 2003.

O'Regan, P., *Introduction to Accounting*, Limerick: The International Equine Institute, University of Limerick 1998.

OECD, *Principles of Corporate Governance*, Paris: OECD 1999.

# 2

# *Accounting Concepts and Regulations*

**C O N T E N T S**

# INTRODUCTION

The credibility and acceptance of any profession by a society is predicated on how well it defines and maintains standards of performance. National and global economies rely on accountants to determine what is good accounting practice so that financial information is seen to be relevant and reliable. The rules and standards used by the accounting profession make up what we refer to as **regulation**. As with all other professions, accountants must also adhere to the laws of the land and therefore we must also be aware of the legislative process, the corporate law that businesses must comply with. Accountants play a major part in assisting businesses in this compliance, and as a result of recent legislation are now themselves coming under direct supervision by the law.

This chapter will examine the principles and concepts on which the standards, i.e. regulations, are built. We will then discuss how accounting policies guide one in applying the principles. This will be preceded by a look at the regulator's role and the emergence of international standards. The role of the legislative process will conclude the discussion.

> ## OBJECTIVES
>
> **When you have finished this chapter, you will be able to:**
> - identify the role of the regulator
> - understand the emergence of international accounting
> - identify the concepts and rules of accounting
> - understand what is meant by compliance and the role of the legislator.

# THE REGULATORY LANDSCAPE

The issuance and maintenance of accounting standards and rules for Britain and Ireland is carried out by the Accounting Standards Board (ASB), which was founded in 1990. It is an independent body with a full-time staff of experts and researchers dedicated to keeping standards up to date and providing guidance on emerging issues to accounting professionals.

## Financial reporting standards

Financial reporting standards (FRSs) are built on concepts or principles that are often referred to as generally accepted accounting principles (GAAP). The first standard launched by the ASB was **FRS 1 Cash Flow Statements** in September 1991. Previous to the FRSs, the standards in place were called statements of standard accounting practice (SSAP), twenty-five of which were issued up to 1990. Since 1990, the ASB has issued almost thirty FRSs and withdrawn or replaced the majority of the twenty-five SSAPs.

FRSs are designed to avoid conflict with the law and are therefore not statutory requirements. However, in a court of law, judges regard FRSs as a key code of practice, and unless a weakness is found in a FRS, courts defer to them in decisions. The ASB is thus recognised as the independent regulator and commands much greater power to enforce its recommendations than its predecessor. It is a strong advocate of international accounting standards.

## ASB announcements

The ASB may issue pronouncements to accompany FRSs, and as each one appears, the board states what authority, scope and application it will have. The FRSs are drafted so that they comply with British and Irish law and with European Union Directives.

## International standards

A long-time goal of the accounting profession worldwide has been the harmonisation of the various accounting codes practised by different countries. With encouragement from the US, Britain, Ireland and the EU generally, a set of international standards has been created. From 1 January 2005, all publicly traded companies throughout the EU must present their financial statements using standards set by the International Accounting Standards Board (IASB). These standards are comprised of international accounting standards (IAS) and the more recently released standards now referred to as international financial reporting standards (IFRS). At the end of 2004, over ninety countries, including the US, had signed up to the international standards. Although it is a strong advocate for the international standards, the US regulator, the Public Company Accounting Oversight Board (PCAOB), will continue to insist on American GAAP presentation by foreign companies listed in its stock exchanges until the former take hold.

## Principles versus rules

One of the debates in accounting today centres on whether accounting standards should be based on principles or on rules. The US approach is to create rules, the logic being that with enough rules, loopholes can be reduced or even eliminated. This may explain why there are in excess of 150 standards to comply with in the US. In the UK and Ireland, the ASB uses a principles approach that avails of long-established concepts and is regarded as best suited to the use of professional judgment. There are approximately forty standards (FRSs and SSAPs) maintained by the ASB. A criticism of the rules approach is that accountants are reduced to compliance by ticking off boxes (Jopson 2005). Those criticising the other approach note that a principle may be stated briefly but accompanied by a large number of interpretations. Of relevance to us here is that the international standards are principles based, a fact that has not prevented the US's PCAOB from encouraging their use.

Further discussion on the topic is beyond the scope of this book, but suffice it to say that the principles versus rules debate will continue. The substance of the principles or concepts will be the focus of our studies in the next section.

## Implications for Ireland

Two points regarding the IASs have significance for Irish business:

- The theory and approach of the FRSs used in the UK and Ireland also form the basis for the international standards.
- The model of accounting used in Ireland (and in our studies) is the Anglo-American model.

These are positive developments for the career of the Irish accountant and for inward and outward investment in Ireland. Although the EU is endeavouring to create international standards for non-publicly traded companies, the FRSs will continue to be in use, primarily because the majority of companies in Ireland are small and medium-sized enterprises (SMEs).

Having reviewed the role of the regulator, we can now proceed to the underlying principles and theory of accounting.

### *Self-Assessment Question 1*

1. Why should Irish and UK accountants feel comfortable with the emergence of international accounting standards?

## ACCOUNTING CONCEPTS

In Chapter 1 we completed an income statement and balance sheet, and although very elementary, we can nevertheless make three observations at this stage:

- accounting measures transactions in money
- agreement is reached among people as to the monetary value of a transaction
- there is a consistency in the preparation of financial statements, e.g. in layout, the yearly time interval and the intent to communicate.

These are obvious characteristics, but accounting does not tell us everything about a business (O'Regan 1998). For instance, accounting does not tell us whether the managers of a business are good or bad. Nor does it tell us whether a new EU Directive will add significant expense in the future. If a company's latest P&L shows a profit, do we assume it is healthy and that it will still be around tomorrow?

In addition to these observations, we must understand that most of the numbers shown on a financial statement are an aggregate of many individual transactions. Can we rely on such aggregates? Estimates are also contained in some of the accounts. For instance, the debtor figure in the balance sheet is a net number, having been reduced by an estimate of what is considered to be bad debt and thus may never be collected. We will discuss this phenomenon in Chapter 4, but for now we should ask what the rationale behind making such an estimate is. Can we rely on it and is it consistent with the previous year?

## Conceptual basics

Creating regulations and guidance for the accounting professions in Ireland and the UK is approached in several ways (O'Regan, 1998):

- agree on underlying assumptions, then develop accounting practices that are consistent with those assumptions
- develop standards that are in compliance with the law.

These assumptions (concepts) and resulting rules have evolved over years of practice and are regarded as the underlying or fundamental ideas of accounting. Taking note of the law minimises any conflict between corporate law and accounting standards (Wood and Sangster 2002). This is critical because much of the law is in response to EU Directives, an important catalyst for updating standards.

Most commentators agree that the following four concepts are fundamental to accounting:

- prudence
- matching
- going concern
- consistency.

## Prudence

The prudence rule is a response to uncertainty and where a conservative stance is required. Regarded as practical wisdom by the ancient Romans, prudence is defined as 'careful conduct to avoid undesirable consequences' (Random House 1966). Uncertainty is as pervasive in business as it is in life. The prudence rule injects a note of caution where, in the absence of measurable facts, estimates are required. Business managers, for instance, generally tend to be overoptimistic when making predictions, e.g. about future sales or anticipated costs. They may be reluctant to acknowledge that slow-moving inventory is the result of obsolescence or perhaps a customer with an overdue debt may have to be written off. Certainly, where loss is probable rather than possible, prudence requires that these losses be accounted for. Where there is doubt, accountants should advise managers to lean toward overstating losses and understating profits.

## Matching

This rule, often referred to as the **accruals concept**, states that revenues and expenses are recognised as they are earned or incurred, rather than when money is received or paid. The intent here is to have revenues and profits of a period match with the expenses incurred in earning them.

As we will see later, cash received in a period could be for payment for services performed in the previous period or even for services to be performed in the following period. The question to be answered is: when was the sale realised, as distinct from when it was paid?

Later we will distinguish between the **accrual basis** and the **cash basis** of accounting, a distinction greatly assisted by the matching principle. For now we can say that when a business has provided a service in a period and is not paid for it until the next period, then the business must accrue an amount for that sale. Similarly, if a business has paid for a service in advance, the business must recognise that one asset, cash, has been translated into another asset, a prepayment. And what about the business that has been paid in advance for a service by a customer? It must recognise that it has a liability until it fulfils that service. This accounting for accruals and prepayments (see Chapter 5) is the essence of the matching principle.

## Going concern

To a large extent, the going concern concept overcomes the limitations resulting from the historical nature of the financial statements. Regardless of how good and timely the financial statements are, the information is dated. The going concern concept states that the business will continue operating for the foreseeable future and that the values of the assets are appropriately accounted for in the accounts. Unless the company states to the contrary, users of the financial statements assume that the company is not under an imminent financial threat. If the business was being wound up, then the assets would need to be valued at their market value.

## Consistency

Users of financial statements need to be able to compare businesses based on performance and financial position. They must also be able to compare a company's performance over a number of periods. The consistency rule requires that there should be consistent treatment of similar events within each accounting period and from one period to the next. For instance, if a new business depreciates its equipment using the straight line method in the first year, then it should continue with the same method in subsequent years (depreciation is discussed in depth in Chapter 5).

Can a business change its methods of accounting? Yes, but only in exceptional cases (beyond the scope of this book). Where there is a change in an accounting method, the effect of this change has to be calculated and specified as an effect of a change in accounting principle in the financial report.

In recent years, with the advent of the service and knowledge economy, **consistency** has to be applied a little more cautiously. We will look more closely at this issue when we discuss FRS 18 later in the chapter. For now, the rule does provide confidence to users of accounting statements when comparing present and previous sets of accounts.

### Self-Assessment Question 2

1.  Identify the appropriate concept suggested by each of the following statements.
    (a) The profit and loss account and balance sheet assume no intention or necessity to liquidate.
    (b) Accounting for similar events within each accounting period and from one period to the next.
    (c) Revenue and profits disclosed in the income statement are matched with associated costs and expenses.
    (d) A business must accept that inherent in any debtor balance is the risk that some customers will not or cannot pay what they owe.

## FURTHER OVERRIDING CONCEPTS

In addition to the four concepts already listed above, there are a number of implicit concepts that are generally accepted and that have been assimilated into accounting practice:

- materiality
- separate valuation
- entity
- dual aspect
- monetary measurement
- historic cost
- realisation
- objectivity.

### Materiality

An error in the accounts may or may not have a significant impact on the financial statements. What constitutes a big or small error or when a result is 'significant' depends on the circumstance. A €1,000 error in the cash account of a multinational is certainly immaterial, unlike that of a local retailer, where such an error would materially affect the reported position. The essence of the test is whether the financial statements will show the true and fair picture. If it continues to be true, then the error is not material. Clearly, judgment is required by the accountant to make the determination.

Materiality will feature later when we study the audit process. For now, where errors are deemed to be material, they must be corrected. If an item is considered to be immaterial, then how it is accounted for is not of any great consequence, as its effect on the financial picture is insignificant.

### Separate valuation

This concept requires that reciprocal purchasing and selling between two businesses must be valued separately in the accounts. There should be no setting off of balances to determine net balance. Where a business is both a debtor and a creditor to the same business, the balances must be separately valued.

### Entity

A business has its own identity and existence distinct from the owners. Whether it is a profit or a non-profit organisation, only the financial matters relating to that entity can be included, and not those of the owners or others. Establishing the dividing line between private dealings and the transactions of the business is imperative for the accountant, as he or she is interested only in the business.

### Dual aspect

This is the basis for the accounting equation that has been previously discussed. The concept states that there are two aspects to accounting for financial information, one represented by the assets of the business and the other by the claims against those assets. The following equation captures this:

$$\text{assets} - \text{liabilities} = \text{capital}$$

### Monetary measurement

Only those transactions and events that can be measured in monetary terms can be recorded in the accounts. Without this monetary unit, we could not achieve any meaningful comparisons of value or measurement. By being able to convert value into a monetary unit, objectivity becomes more evident in business dealings.

## Historic cost

The historic cost concept values a transaction at its original cost and is recorded in the books as such. In this way we can regard this concept as an extension of the monetary measurement rule. Although events such as inflation may affect costs, subsequent changes in prices or value are usually ignored.

## Realisation

This concept allows a business to realise a transaction when a value can be placed on it and when we are reasonably certain that resources will be transferred. This means that if there is a sale in November but the business does not get paid for it until December, we can recognise the sale in November. Title to the product must have passed to the customer or the service must have been performed. The sale has been realised.

## Objectivity

Objectivity is a requirement for business owners if agreement on value is to be attained. Accountants who prepare one set of financial statements for different users are pursuing an objective course. Clearly, this has been achieved for the most part by using historic costs and maintaining the consistency rule. Where there is doubt about assets or threats to performance and these are resolved through the prudence rule, then objectivity is further underlined.

Those rules are the foundation of accounting. Since its inception in 1990, the Accounting Standards Board (ASB) has been proactive in providing insights on the use of these concepts and rules. One of its most important efforts has been the gradual publication of the Statement of Principles, from which the qualitative characteristics of financial statements (see below) have been taken. Its publication of FRS 18 Accounting Policies in December 2000 provides useful insight for an economy or companies in transition from manufacturing to service or knowledge based. We will discuss FRS 18 in the next section.

### Self-Assessment Question 3

1. State which accounting rule is referred to in each of the following.
    (a) Should we concern ourselves with the number of paper clips used in the last month?
    (b) The sole trader paid for his annual holiday out of his business account.
    (c) The receipt of a loan by the business was processed with one entry to the cash account and one to the liability account.
    (d) Goods purchased and taken into stock in December were not paid for until January.

# QUALITATIVE CHARACTERISTICS OF FINANCIAL STATEMENTS

Users of financial statements require the following characteristics to pertain to the statements if they are to have confidence in them:

- relevance
- reliability
- comparability
- understandability.

Once we have described these, we will re-examine them within the context of one of the most important standards issued by the ASB, **FRS 18 Accounting Policies** (December 2000). Its international equivalent was issued by IASB over two standards, **IAS 1 Presentation of Financial Statements** and **IAS 8 Net Profit or Loss for the Period, Fundamental Errors and Changes in Accounting Policies**. Both essentially capture all the key points in FRS 18.

## Relevance

When information can influence decision makers by helping them to evaluate events, be it by confirming or altering evaluations, then we can state that that information has relevance. Relevant information will assist in making predictions. What should be included as information may often depend on the accountant's judgment, but certainly it must be material and be of help to the user.

## Reliability

Information that is free from material error and deliberate bias is regarded as being reliable and can be depended upon by the users. It also implies that information has been faithfully represented in an effort to avoid misleading the user.

Relevance and reliability are greatly enhanced when information is deemed neutral and is complete. Neutral information is free from bias and does not attempt to influence the making of a decision. In regard to completeness, an omission that is material will cause financial statements to be unreliable.

## Comparability

We have already referred to comparability in the context of the consistency rule. Users must be able to compare different businesses or compare a number of years' statements for the one business. This is essential to evaluating financial positions and trends.

## Understandability

This requires that financial statement information be readily understandable to the user. That may require an understanding of how information is gathered, processed and reported, and it may also depend on the ability of the user. Because users can acquire advice independently to understand the information, omission of complex issues cannot be justified.

## Accounting policies: A graphical presentation

**FRS 18 Accounting Policies** provides a sophisticated yet articulate guide for accountants in marshalling the various concepts discussed above. As economies moved from manufacturing, whereby the accounting of buying and selling was straightforward, to an economy dominated by services and knowledge-based business, it has become more challenging to know when exactly a sale has taken place or indeed the expenses associated with that sale. The need for estimating increases and a firm grasp of the realisation principle becomes important. The challenge is to ensure that the statements reflect the true and fair view.

FRS 18 suggests that the **going concern** and **accruals (matching)** concepts have a 'pervasive role' in processing and eventually presenting information (ASB 2000). What determines useful information, as an adaptation of Black's graphic (2003) shows, are the qualities of relevance, reliability, comparability and understandability:

- These four qualities become the objectives to be pursued in reaching the true and fair view.
- Prudence is seen as a driving force in achieving reliability.
- Consistency should be subservient to comparability.

This last point implies that accounting for something in the same old way may not be appropriate when the economic activity of a business is changing.

---

### Self-Assessment Questions 4

1. What are the key determinants of useful information? Explain why they are referred to as such.

2. Why do you think FRS 18 refers to the going concern principle as having a 'pervasive role'?

FIGURE 2.1: QUALITATIVE CHARACTERISTICS OF FINANCIAL INFORMATION (ADAPTED FROM BLACK 2003)

| Determinants of Useful Information | | | |
|---|---|---|---|
| Relevance | Reliability | Comparability | Understandability |
| • Predictive value<br>• Confirmation value | • Prudence<br>• Neutral<br>• Complete | • Consistency<br>• Disclosure | • Versatility<br>• Classification |

# LEGISLATION

The recent legislation enacted in Ireland is having a major, if not a dramatic, impact on Irish companies and the accounting profession. Responding to Ireland's own scandals (DIRT[1], Ansbacher, National Irish Bank, etc.), the Companies Acts 2001 and 2003 are additions to the relevant body of corporate law commencing in 1963. In the words of barrister Mark O'Connell, the term 'corporate law enforcement' was a favourite oxymoron circulating among lawyers and businesspeople in Ireland (2003). This appears to be changing.

## Company Law Enforcement Act 2001

The 2001 Act established the **Office of Director of Corporate Enforcement (ODCE)**, whose remit under Section 12 of the Act is as follows:
- Investigate cases of suspected offences.
- Enforce company law by either prosecution of summary offences or by referring cases to the Director of Public Prosecution where there is a suspicion that an indictable offence has been committed.
- Supervise the activities of liquidators and receivers.
- Investigate companies, including insolvent companies.
- Encourage compliance with the Companies Acts.

---

[1] DIRT (Deposit Interest Retention Tax) refers to an inquiry carried out by an Irish government committee from 1997 to December 1999 into the creation of bogus non-resident accounts at the country's main banks that facilitated evasion of this tax.

- Extra duties assigned by the Minister of Enterprise, Trade and Employment, where appropriate.

The Act was in response to the realisation that compliance to company law was minimal in Ireland. The phenomenon of the **'Phoenix' syndrome** in Ireland, whereby directors of insolvent companies 'walk away', leaving behind unpaid debts, and then proceed to set up new but similar businesses later, was putting Ireland's corporate reputation at risk.

Company directors must pay particular attention to this legislation, as the ODCE can restrict and disqualify directors. What are the implications for the accountant? The accountant auditing a company who detects fraud or any one of 128 offences must report the finding to the ODCE.

## Companies (Auditing and Accounting) Act 2003

The Act established the **Irish Auditing and Accounting Supervisory Authority (IAASA)**, a fourteen-person board that will supervise all of the accountancy bodies in Ireland. With only four accountants on the board, it effectively means that the Irish accountant has lost his or her independence and will have to meet formalised structures of accountability that are bound to change the face of the profession in Ireland. The Act also requires directors of companies to complete a compliance statement declaring that they have met their relevant obligations (Section 42). At the time of writing, this requirement is under review.

Under Section 8 of the Act, the IAASA is authorised to:
- supervise regulation of accountancy bodies and monitor their members
- promote adherence to high standards
- monitor whether the accounts of qualifying companies adhere to corporate law.

It is generally regarded that both Acts will greatly enhance corporate governance in Ireland.

### *Self-Assessment Questions 5*

1. What parties or players will be impacted by the recent legislation in Ireland?

2. How will the legislation enhance corporate governance?

## CHAPTER REVIEW

While there are many mechanisms that must be understood in preparing financial statements, it is the accounting concepts or principles that are fundamental to the profession in presenting reliable financial information. The use of the concepts as guidance is carried out in two ways. First, there is acceptance of the underlying assumptions, four of which are the foundation to accounting practice: prudence, matching, consistency and going concern. Second, accounting practices are developed that are consistent with these assumptions. Additional concepts, such as materiality, entity, historic cost and realisation, provide the practical steps in support of the four mentioned above. Financial statements are considered to be useful when they are relevant, reliable, comparable and understandable. These qualities are articulated by FRS 18 as addressing the needs of a knowledge-based or services economy.

The legislative environment in Ireland has been significantly impacted with the passing into law of the Companies Acts 2001 and 2003. The ODCE and IAASA, created by each of the Acts, respectively, are expected to improve corporate governance in Ireland. Directors and auditors will be held accountable by the ODCE. IAASA will also monitor the accounting bodies and their members.

# SELF-ASSESSMENT QUESTION ANSWERS

## SAQ 1

1. Firstly, the basis for IASs comes from the UK and Irish FRS. Secondly, the model of accounting for the UK and Ireland is the Anglo-American model, which facilitates doing business with US firms. Irish accountants can choose to pursue opportunities with American companies and accounting firms.

## SAQ 2

1. (a) Going concern
   (b) Consistency
   (c) Accruals
   (d) Prudence

## SAQ 3

1. (a) Materiality
   (b) Entity
   (c) Dual aspect
   (d) Realisation

## SAQ 4

1. The determinants are relevance, reliability, comparability and understandability. They are so-called because in pursuing them, companies will succeed in reporting the true and fair view.
2. One way of interpreting the pervasiveness of the going concern concept is that regardless of how accurate the financial statements are, if a company is going out of business, then this fact and its implications takes precedence over everything being

reported.

Virtually every business uses the accrual basis of accounting, whereby transactions are accounted for when they take place, as distinct from when the money changes hands.

## SAQ 5

1. Directors of companies and auditors will be impacted by the 2001 and 2003 Acts. The 2001 Act created the ODCE, which is empowered to restrict or disqualify directors convicted of non-compliance with corporate law. It also has the power to proceed against auditors who facilitate such non-compliance. The 2003 Act created a supervisory authority, the IAASA, to oversee accounting bodies and if need be to charge accountants with wrongdoing. It will also monitor companies in how they apply accounting standards.

2. Directors are responsible for overseeing controls and the reporting process in their companies. Accountants, as independent auditors, review such processes and issue an opinion on them to the shareholders. With the ODCE and IAASA as essentially the 'new sheriff in town', we can expect greater compliance to company law and accounting standards.

## REFERENCES

Accounting Standards Board, *FRS 18 Accounting Policies*, London: ASB 2000.

Black, G., *Students' Guide to Accounting and Financial Reporting Standards*, Harlow: Financial Times Prentice Hall 2003, p. 32.

Companies (Auditing and Accounting) Act 2003, Dublin: The Stationery Office.

Company Law Enforcement Act 2001, Dublin: The Stationery Office.

Jopson, B., 'Reality is set to intrude on principles', *Financial Times*, 28 July 2005.

O'Connell, M., *Who'd Want to Be a Company Director? A Guide to the Enforcement of Irish Company Law*, Dublin: First Law 2003.

O'Regan, P., *Introduction to Accounting*, Limerick: The International Equine Institute, University of Limerick 1998.

*Random House Dictionary of the English Language*, New York: Random House 1966.

Wood, F. and Sangster, A., *Business Accountancy 1*, 9th ed., Harlow: Financial Times Prentice Hall 2002.

# 3

# *The Accounting Information System*

**C O N T E N T S**

# INTRODUCTION

The system of collecting and processing transactions and communicating the result as financial information to interested parties is known as the **accounting information system**. We have already described accounting as having its own environment, catering for various users and producing reports on a regular basis. The accounting system will vary from one business to the next, depending on the nature and size of the business, the volume of the transactions and the demands made on it by management. Having said that, the system's components and method of processing are essentially the same in all accounting systems (Heneghan and O'Regan 2000). We will now explore these elements, commencing with the basic transaction and ending with the preparation of the financial statements.

Accountants often refer to the financial statements as final accounts, and we see both terms used interchangeably.

The following are the elements that make up the system that processes financial data for accounting purposes:

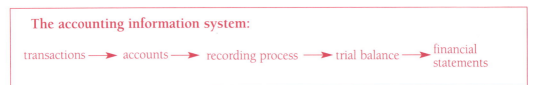

The accounting information system:

transactions ⟶ accounts ⟶ recording process ⟶ trial balance ⟶ financial statements

We will examine each of these elements in this chapter:

## OBJECTIVES

**When you have finished this chapter, you will be able to:**

- understand that financial information is processed in an accounting information system
- identify the basic steps in the recording process
- understand double entry bookkeeping
- understand the books of original entry and their role in the recording process
- explain the purpose of a trial balance.

# THE TRANSACTION

Earlier we suggested that the recording of a transaction in accounting is triggered by certain economic events. To determine what constitutes such an event, we ask the question: has the financial position (assets, liabilities and shareholders' equity) of the firm changed?

Buying a truck, paying the rent or selling products all constitute economic events and are referred to as accounting transactions. They are recorded in the accounting system. Other events, such as answering the phone, locking the safe or hiring employees, do not affect the assets, liabilities and shareholders' equity and are ignored. Let's examine the decision process used to decide whether or not to record economic events.

## Analysis of transactions

Transactions are analysed to identify their economic impact on the basic formula of accounting:

$$assets = liabilities + shareholders' \ equity$$

If the equation is to remain in balance, any transaction will have to have a twin or double-sided effect on the equation. For example, if an asset increases, there must be a corresponding
- decrease in another asset **or**
- increase in a liability **or**
- increase in shareholders' equity.

Let's look at a few examples.

A group of people start off a business by creating a limited company and collectively putting €50,000 into it. Two things have happened:
- cash has increased by €50,000
- the business owes the shareholders €50,000.

Place these transactions in the accounting equation to create the following presentation:

$$A \ = L + E$$
$$€50,000 = 0 + €50,000$$

The accounting equation continues to be true.

If the company then decides to acquire a loan for €30,000 to buy a truck, agreeing to repay within one year (very unlikely), we will see again that two things happen:
- liabilities have increased by €30,000
- assets in the form of a truck have increased by €30,000.

The presentation of the equation is now as follows:

| A | = | L | + | E |
|---|---|---|---|---|
| €50,000 = | | 0 | + | €50,000 |
| +30,000 = | | +30,000 | | |
| €80,000 | | €30,000 | | €50,000 |

Again, the accounting equation remains true.

Even with this small number of transactions, we can create a balance sheet.

| Balance sheet as at \<date\> | € | € |
|---|---|---|
| **Fixed assets:** | | |
| Truck | | 30,000 |
| | | |
| **Current assets:** | | |
| Cash | 50,000 | |
| | | |
| **Current liabilities** | (30,000) | |
| | | 20,000 |
| | | 50,000 |
| | | |
| **Financed by:** | | |
| Capital | | 50,000 |

The actual recording of the transactions is called the **bookkeeping** stage and is the initial step required to get the event into the accounting system.

## Self-Assessment Question 1

1. Are the following events recorded in the accounts? Explain your answer in each case.
   (a)  A major shareholder dies.
   (b)  Supplies are purchased on account, i.e. on credit.
   (c)  An employee is fired.
   (d)  The company pays a cash dividend to its shareholders.

## Transactions over a period of time

To confirm the core role of the accounting equation in the accounting system right from the transaction through to the financial statements, let's analyse and process the following eleven transactions over a 30-day period. This time period is chosen because most companies, big and small, prepare financial statements at least on a monthly basis.

### EXAMPLE

The following events took place during the first month of business for Maple Graphics.

1. Maple Graphics starts business at the beginning of the month with €2,000 in cash.
2. The company buys a computer (slightly used) for €1,000 and some furniture for €800.
3. Supplies such as paper, toner, staplers, etc. are purchased for €500 on credit.
4. The company completes its first assignment and gets paid €650.
5. Maple pays its creditor €500.
6. Additional supplies for €1,000 are purchased on credit.
7. Maple completes another assignment and charges €1,200. Payment is expected in thirty days.
8. The debtor pays €500 a few days after receiving Maple's invoice.
9. Maple pays €100 wages for some part-time help.
10. Maple negotiates a forty-five-day credit period with its main creditor.
11. An inventory count at month's end indicates an ending balance of €600.

**Event 1:** This is an accounting transaction because there is an increase in both assets and owners' equity.

| | Assets | = | Liabilities + Owners' equity |
|---|---|---|---|
| | Cash | = | Capital |
| Event 1 | +2,000 | = | +2,000 Issued shares |

**Event 2:** The company buys its first assets and pays out cash in the transactions. While there has been a decrease in cash, the corresponding action is an increase in assets of furniture and computer equipment. You will notice that the right side remains unchanged.

| | Assets | | | = | Liabilities | + Owners' equity |
|---|---|---|---|---|---|---|
| | Cash | Furniture | Computer | = | | Capital |
| Old balance | 2,000 | | | | | 2,000 |
| Event 2 | −1,800 | +800 | +1,000 | | | |
| New balance | 200 | 800 | 1,000 | | | 2,000 |

The total of assets continues to be €2,000, equal to the total on the right side of the equation.

**Event 3:** Supplies are bought on credit. This transaction increases assets but creates an obligation on the company to pay for the supplies sometime in the future. As a result, this event is also an increase in liability.

| | Assets | | | | = Liabilities | + Owners' equity |
|---|---|---|---|---|---|---|
| | Cash | Furniture | Computer | Supplies | = Creditors | Capital |
| Old balance | 200 | 800 | 1,000 | 0 | 0 | 2,000 |
| Event 3 | | | | +500 | = +500 | |
| New balance | 200 | 800 | 1,000 | 500 | = 500 | 2,000 |

Again, if we add up both sides, the assets total is €2,500 and is equal to the €2,500 total for the liabilities and shareholders' equity.

**Event 4:** The company performs its first job and generates its first sale, or revenue. It also gets paid on completing the job. While all sales ultimately go to shareholders' equity, the accounting system will contain a separate account called Sales so that this information can be readily accessible. For now we will place the amount on the right side of the equation under Capital.

| | Assets | | | | = Liabilities | + Owners' equity |
|---|---|---|---|---|---|---|
| | Cash | Furniture | Computer | Supplies | = Creditors | Capital |
| Old balance | 200 | 800 | 1,000 | 500 | 500 | 2,000 |
| Event 4 | +650 | | | | = | +650  Sales |
| New balance | 850 | 800 | 1,000 | 500 | = 500 | 2,650 |

**Event 5:** Maple decides to repay part of its obligation to the creditor, and in doing so, it reduces both its assets and its liabilities.

| | Assets | | | | = Liabilities | + Owners' equity |
|---|---|---|---|---|---|---|
| | Cash | Furniture | Computer | Supplies | = Creditors | Capital |
| Old balance | 850 | 800 | 1,000 | 500 | 500 | 2,650 |
| Event 5 | −500 | | | | = −500 | |
| New balance | 350 | 800 | 1,000 | 500 | = 0 | 2,650 |

The total on each side is €2,650, thus maintaining the equation.

**Event 6:** The company acquires additional supplies and again makes a credit purchase.

| | Assets | | | | = Liabilities | + Owners' equity |
|---|---|---|---|---|---|---|
| | Cash | Furniture | Computer | Supplies | = Creditors | Capital |
| Old balance | 350 | 800 | 1,000 | 500 | 0 | 2,650 |
| Event 6 | | | | +1,000 | = +1,000 | |
| New balance | 350 | 800 | 1,000 | 1,500 | = 1,000 | 2,650 |

Do both sides balance? Yes, at €3,650 on each side.

**Event 7:** Maple achieves another sale, but this time agrees to be paid at a later date. By allowing this, the company now has a claim against its customer and will record this claim as an asset. We call such an asset a debtor.

| | Assets | | | | | = Liabilities | + Owners' equity |
|---|---|---|---|---|---|---|---|
| | Cash | Furniture | Computer | Supplies | Debtor | = Creditors | Capital |
| Old balance | 350 | 800 | 1,000 | 1,500 | 0 | 1,000 | 2,650 |
| Event 7 | | | | | +1,200 | = | +1,200 Sales |
| New balance | 350 | 800 | 1,000 | 1,500 | 1,200 | = 1,000 | 3,850 |

Observe now that both sides continue to be in balance and also that the asset total has grown from €3,650 to €4,850.

**Event 8:** The cash of the company is increased again as Maple receives a payment from its debtor. There will be no movement on the right side of the equation.

| | Assets | | | | | = Liabilities | + Owners' equity |
|---|---|---|---|---|---|---|---|
| | Cash | Furniture | Computer | Supplies | Debtor | = Creditors | Capital |
| Old balance | 350 | 800 | 1,000 | 1,500 | 1,200 | 1,000 | 3,850 |
| Event 8 | +500 | | | | −500 | = | +1,200 |
| New balance | 850 | 800 | 1,000 | 1,500 | 700 | = 1,000 | 3,850 |

Two accounts on the asset side have changed, but the overall total is still the same.

**Event 9:** The company pays wages for part-time help. This is an expense item which will reduce cash and also reduce shareholders' equity. As all expenses ultimately go against shareholders' equity, the capital account will reflect this reduction.

| | Assets | | | | | = | Liabilities | + Owners' equity | |
|---|---|---|---|---|---|---|---|---|---|
| | Cash | Furniture | Computer | Supplies | Debtor | = | Creditors | Capital | |
| Old balance | 850 | 800 | 1,000 | 1,500 | 700 | | 1,000 | 3,850 | |
| Event 9 | −100 | | | | | = | | −100 | Wages |
| New balance | 750 | 800 | 1,000 | 1,500 | 700 | = | 1,000 | 3,750 | |

**Event 10:** The company has negotiated new credit terms with a creditor. There is no effect on the assets, liabilities or shareholders' equity and consequently this is not an accounting transaction.

**Event 11:** Maple has chosen the end of the month to calculate the amount of supplies used. Because of the nature of office supplies, it makes good sense to take an inventory at regular intervals. Subtracting the ending balance found by the inventory (€600) from the total amount purchased (€1,500) leads you to recognise €900 as the supplies expense, the amount used during the period in question.

| | Assets | | | | | = | Liabilities | + Owners' equity | |
|---|---|---|---|---|---|---|---|---|---|
| | Cash | Furniture | Computer | Supplies | Debtor | = | Creditors | Capital | |
| Old balance | 750 | 800 | 1,000 | 1,500 | 700 | | 1,000 | 3,750 | |
| Event 11 | | | | −900 | | = | | −900 | Supplies expense |
| New balance | 750 | 800 | 1,000 | 600 | 700 | = | 1,000 | 2,850 | |

As the financial statements will make clear, there is a distinction between the asset called Supplies and the expense called Supplies.

## Self-Assessment Questions 2

1. What are the effects on the accounting equation if a business performs services for cash?
2. Determine the effect on assets, liabilities and shareholders' equity of the following events:
   (a)  Issued shares to investors in exchange for cash.
   (b)  Received cash by way of a loan from a bank.

## Summary of transactions

The transactions of Maple Graphics are summarised below and confirm the constancy of the accounting equation. Remember that Event 10 is not included, as we established that it did not constitute an accounting transaction.

It is important to observe four key facts from the completion of this exercise.

1. Each transaction is analysed to determine if it has an effect on assets, liabilities and shareholders' equity.
2. The accounting equation is maintained.
3. Sales increase and expenses decrease the shareholders' equity, respectively.
4. We can complete a set of financial statements from this system.

| Event | Assets | | | | | = | Liabilities | + Owners' equity | |
|-------|--------|-----------|----------|----------|--------|---|-------------|---------|---|
|       | Cash   | Furniture | Computer | Supplies | Debtor | = | Creditors   | Capital | |
| 1     | 2,000  |           |          |          |        |   |             | 2,000   | Issued shares |
| 2     | −1,800 | 800       | 1,000    |          |        | = |             |         | |
| 3     |        |           |          | 500      |        | = | 500         |         | |
| 4     | 650    |           |          |          |        | = |             | 650     | Sales |
| 5     | −500   |           |          |          |        | = | −500        |         | |
| 6     |        |           | 1,000    |          |        | = | 1,000       |         | |
| 7     |        |           |          |          | 1,200  | = |             | 1,200   | Sales |
| 8     | 500    |           |          |          | −500   | = |             |         | |
| 9     | −100   |           |          |          |        | = |             | −100    | Wages |
| 11    |        |           |          | −900     |        | = |             | −900    | Supplies expense |
|       | 750    | 800       | 1,000    | 600      | 700    | = | 1,000       | 2,850   | |

Total assets                                     3,850 = Total L and E  ⟶  3,850

The summary above is essentially a balance sheet, complete with month-end balances, and provides us with the financial position of the business at that date.

Now, with a little 'tweaking', we can complete the income statement and the balance sheet in the standard form shown in Chapter 1.

**Maple Graphics**

**Income statement for the month ended 31 January 2005**

|  | € | € |
|---|---|---|
| Sales (650 + 1,200) |  | 1,850 |
| **Less expenses:** |  |  |
| Wages | 100 |  |
| Supplies expense | 900 |  |
| Total expenses |  | 1,000 |
| Operating profit |  | 850 |

**Maple Graphics**

**Balance Sheet as at 31 January 2005**

|  | € |  |
|---|---|---|
| **Fixed assets:** |  |  |
| Furniture | 800 |  |
| Computer | 1,000 |  |
|  |  | 1,800 |
| **Current assets:** |  |  |
| Debtors | 700 |  |
| Supplies | 600 |  |
| Cash | 750 |  |
|  | 2,050 |  |
| Less current liabilities: |  |  |
| Creditors | 1,000 |  |
| Net current assets |  | 1,050 |
| Total assets |  | 2,850 |
| **Financed by:** |  |  |
| Capital |  | 2,000 |
| Retained profit 1 Jan | 0 |  |
| Add operating profit | 850 |  |
| Retained profit 31 Jan |  | 850 |
| Total |  | 2,850 |

The two statements as distinct from the summary provide us with greater insights. We can see that Maple generated a profit. We can also note that its current assets exceed its current liabilities. Both observations are good signs for the company. You will also note how sales and expenses were netted out first before resulting profit was transferred to the owners' equity.

## Self-Assessment Question 3

1. Summarise the effects of each of these transactions on the accounting equation.
   (a) Payment of €500,000 by cheque for a warehouse.
   (b) Payment of €5,000 cash to a creditor.
   (c) A credit sale of €2,000 (where the goods sold originally cost €1,500).
   (d) Receipt of €1,000 from a debtor.

# THE ACCOUNT

In the last section we learned one way to keep accounts. The balance sheet we completed after each transaction showed how:
- each transaction was recorded twice
- the accounting equation always balanced.

Drawing up a balance sheet at the end of each day with only one transaction is manageable, but what if there were thousands of transactions? How efficient would the business be if thousands of balance sheets had to be completed daily?

## Double entry bookkeeping

A solution that solves this problem is **double entry bookkeeping**, a common technique used to record transactions. It is the bookkeeping part of accounting. In place for over 500 years, it continues to be the basis of an accounting information system today. The system uses **accounts**, which are individual accounting records capturing increases and decreases in a specific asset, liability or shareholders' equity item. A business may have separate accounts, such as:
- cash
- account receivable (debtors)
- equipment
- loan payable
- sales
- wages expense
- telephone expense, and so on.

You saw how we created these in the previous section.

In its simplest form, an account has three parts:

- title of the account
- left, or **debit**, side
- right, or **credit**, side.

It will look like this:

| Title of account | |
| --- | --- |
| Left, or debit, side | Right, or credit, side |
| Debit balance | Credit balance |

This layout is often referred to as a T-account.

Before we look more closely at the debits and credits concept, we must first understand where the account fits in.

## General ledger accounts

The **general ledger (G/L)** contains all of the T-accounts in the accounting information system. These accounts are distinguished by one of essentially five different account types within the G/L, most of which you will recognise:

- **Assets**: Equipment, debtors, cash.
- **Liabilities:** Bank loans, creditors.
- **Expenses:** Wages, rent, insurance, purchases.
- **Sales:** Sales (often called revenues), discounts received, interest earned.
- **Capital or equity:** Common stock (shares) issued, profits retained.

Because transactions are captured in the accounts by double entry, the general ledger can be balanced regularly (it must balance!), and these ending balances (month-end or year-end) will allow us to create the financial statements.

It is a mechanical process, efficient and practical, and many people are gainfully employed in maintaining general ledger systems. When the law states that proper accounts must be kept, companies address the requirement by keeping the G/L up to date.

## Debits and credits

The terms '**debit**' and '**credit**' apply to the left and right sides, respectively, and are used repeatedly in the recording of entries to accounts. For instance, when we are entering an amount in the left side of an account, we say that we are **debiting the account**. Similarly, entering an amount on the right side is referred to as **crediting the account**.

A **T-account** will have a **debit balance** when the total of the debit amounts exceed the total of credit amounts. Conversely, an account will have a **credit balance** when the credit amounts exceed the debits.

Let's refer to the summary we completed for Maple Graphics, and looking just at the cash account, compare that now with the double entry approach.

| Tabular summary | Account form | |
|---|---|---|
| Cash | Cash | |
| €2,000 | (Debits)   2,000 | 1,800  (Credits) |
| −1,800 | 650 | 500 |
| 650 | 500 | 100 |
| −500 | | |
| 500 | Balance b/d   750 | |
| −100 | (Debit) | |
| €750 | | |

*Where one side exceeds the other, we 'bring down' the net balance and hence the description Balance b/d.*

## Double entry procedures

The basic rules for double entry bookkeeping are:

- Step 1: Calculate or determine the amounts involved. This is usually obvious.
- Step 2: Choose the two ledger accounts involved. Practice makes this easy.
- Step 3: Decide which account to debit and which to credit using the following rules:
  - **debit** for increases in assets or expenses or for decreases in liabilities or revenues
  - **credit** for increases in liabilities or revenues or for decreases in assets or expenses.

Normally, assets and expenses will have debit balances, whereas liabilities, revenues and capital accounts will have credit balances.

A trial balance lists all the accounts, whereby the debit balances should equal the credit balances.

To put into practice what you have learned about double entry bookkeeping and the accounts involved, go through the exercise in Self-Assessment Question 5 below of balancing off the accounts at the end of the year and transferring the balances to a **trial balance**. A trial balance is merely a list of the account balances at the end of the accounting period that are placed in either a debit or credit column. If the total of the debit balances agrees with the credit balances total, then the books are said to be balanced. The layout of the trial balance looks like this:

| Trial Balance | | |
|---|---|---|
| as at 31 Dec 2005 | | |
| Account title | Debit balances | Credit balances |
| Cash | xxx | |
| Debtors | xxx | |
| Creditors | | xxx |
| Capital | | xxx |
| etc. | | |
| | | |
| | | |
| | | |
| Total | yyy | yyy |

We will return to the trial balance in Chapter 4 as we complete the accounting cycle by preparing the financial statements. For now, this exercise should consolidate your understanding of the double entry system.

## Self-Assessment Question 5

1. The following transactions relate to Frisbee Company for the month ended 31 December 2005.

| Dec 1 | Commenced business with €10,000 cash |
| Dec 3 | Bought goods on credit for €13,000 |
| Dec 5 | Sold goods on credit for €7,000 |
| Dec 8 | Returned goods to suppliers €3,000 |
| Dec 11 | Bought additional goods on credit for €7,000 |
| Dec 15 | Sold more goods on credit for €5,000 |
| Dec 20 | Paid out office expenses in cash for €5,000 |

Dec 23    Received cash from debtor customers totalling €10,000

Dec 28    Paid €14,000 to creditors

You are required to:

(a)  Enter the above transactions in ledger accounts.

(b)  Balance the accounts as at 31 December 2005.

(c)  Bring down the balances as at 1 January 2006.

(d)  List the debit and credit balances in separate debit and credit columns (the trial balance) as at 31 December 2005. Do both totals agree?

*If the totals do agree, you will have completed your first trial balance successfully.*

## THE RECORDING PROCESS

We have kept the recording process simple up to now by referring to the following sequence:

Recording transactions to the accounts ——→ Trial balance ——→ Final accounts

The nuts and bolts of this process, however, is a far more sophisticated world of procedures, controls and computer systems of varying complexities that culminate in the reporting of the financial statements. The legal obligation to maintain an adequate system of accounts that 'correctly record and explain the transactions of the company' (Companies Act 2001) emphasises the **corporate governance** issue. This section attempts to give you some sense of these mechanics and an awareness of the potential for errors and fraud.

Before proceeding, you may ask: why all the mechanics when computer software does so much of the work? The strength of the accounting system is reflected in the fact that software packages have essentially replicated the manual system. Processing and posting to accounts is certainly faster, but some procedures, such as balancing a day's transactions before posting them to the general accounts, makes for sound controls. There are less people needed to run the system, yet key duties must be segregated to minimise errors and potential for fraud.

Most businesses have such a huge number of transactions every year that it would be very difficult to record them directly into the accounts (O'Regan 1998). This problem is resolved by the use of a bookkeeping system involving **day books**, **journals** and **ledgers**, collectively known as the **books of original entry (BOE)**. The recording process uses them in the following steps:

*Generally, the preparation of accounts to the degree of detail that involves day books does not come up in exams. It is usually pursued in a case study or project. Day books are discussed here to illustrate their use, and it is the understanding of their use that is often the subject of exams.*

1.  Analyse each transaction in terms of its effects on the accounts.
2.  Enter the transaction information into a day book.
3.  Transfer the day book information to the journal.
4.  Transfer the journal entries to the accounts.

Before we examine the BOE in depth, keep in mind that the actual sequence of events begins with a source document, such as a sales slip, a bill or a cheque, which is then **analysed** before being **recorded** in the BOE.

## The day books

The day books are used to compile lists of similar transactions. They are totalled periodically, and these totals form the basis for entries into the **nominal ledgers** (a term used to describe the T-accounts that make up the general ledger). In this way, a business such as a retailer with thousands of cash transactions daily can efficiently handle its workload.

A business can open day books for any type of common transaction. Examples are:
- sales day book: contains lists of credit sales
- sales returns day book: contains lists of credit sales returned
- purchases day book: contains lists of credit purchases
- purchases returns day book: contains lists of credit purchases returned
- petty cash book: contains lists of sundry cash payments
- cash receipts book: contains lists of cash receipts
- cheque payments book: contains lists of cheque payments.

The following example will demonstrate how the day books are used. Big Ideas Co. had these sales transactions (all credit sales) for June:

| | |
|---|---|
| June 1 | Sold goods to ROM Co. for €10,000 |
| June 2 | Sold goods to COD Co. for €20,000 |
| June 10 | Sold goods to ZAG Co. for €30,000 |
| June 12 | Sold goods to ROM Co. for €20,000 |
| June 15 | Sold goods to BAM Co. for €50,000 |
| June 19 | Sold goods to BAM Co. for €10,000 |
| June 25 | Sold goods to COD Co. for €30,000 |
| June 28 | Sold goods to ROM Co. for €10,000 |
| June 30 | Sold goods to ROM Co. for €20,000 |

The sales day book will look like this:

| Sales day book | | | |
|----------------|----------|-----------|--------|
| **Date** | **Customer** | **Reference** | **Amount** |
| June 1 | ROM Co. | | 10,000 |
| June 2 | COD Co. | | 20,000 |
| June 10 | ZAG Co. | | 30,000 |
| June 12 | ROM Co. | | 20,000 |
| June 15 | BAM Co. | | 50,000 |
| June 19 | BAM Co. | | 10,000 |
| June 25 | COD Co. | | 30,000 |
| June 28 | ROM Co. | | 10,000 |
| June 30 | ROM Co. | | 20,000 |
| | | | 200,000 |

Instead of making nine individual entries in the nominal ledger, Big Ideas Co. makes only *one* entry at the end of the month. The total of €200,000 in the **sales day book** for June is then processed with this double entry:

| | | | |
|---|---|---|---|
| Dr | Total debtors account | €200,000 | |
| Cr | Sales account | €200,000 | |

We will use these helpful abbreviations:
Dr = Debit
Cr = Credit

The two totals must agree, an important CONTROL check before proceeding.

The accounts in the nominal ledger will look like this:

| Total debtors account | | | | | |
|---|---|---|---|---|---|
| June | | € | June | | € |
| 30 | Sales | 200,000 | | | |

| Sales account | | | | | |
|---|---|---|---|---|---|
| | | € | June | | € |
| | | | 30 | Debtors | 200,000 |

Whether this double entry is done at the end of the day or the week, you can see that a large business with a huge volume of transactions will find this system very useful.

Otherwise, the debtor account and sales account, for instance, would become very cluttered and hinder searching for errors or finding a particular transaction.

## Personal ledgers and total (control) accounts

The day books have certainly solved one problem, but unfortunately they have created another. Had we not availed of the day books with the example just above, the nine transactions would have been recorded individually with a double entry similar to the following:

| Dr | Debtor ROM account | €10,000 |
|----|--------------------|---------|
| Cr | Sales account | €10,000 |

In this way, each debtor would have its own account. Unfortunately, under the day book system there are no individual accounts in the nominal ledger. Instead there is only one **total debtors account**, also called the **debtors control account**. All transactions relating to debtors for a day or a month (depending on the number of transactions) are totalled and recorded in the control account as a single amount. There will be no information about individual debtors even though they will need to be billed.

*The personal ledgers are not part of the main double entry system and are not needed to produce the final accounts.*

The problem is solved by introducing another set of books, which operate in parallel to the main bookkeeping system. These books are called the **personal ledgers** and they contain the accounts of *each* individual debtor and creditor. The trick is to have the total of the individual balances in the personal ledger agree with the balance in the control account in the nominal ledger. To understand how they fit into the accounting information system, note the following.

- The **day book** provides the basic information to construct the nominal ledger and the personal ledgers.
- The **personal ledgers** are made up of the individual debtors (the result of sales) ledger and creditors (the result of purchases) ledger and are updated from the day book.
- The **nominal ledger** and **personal ledgers** run in parallel. While the individual balances in the personal ledger are updated with single transactions, the control account in the nominal ledger is updated with a summary total of a day's or month's activity.

Assuming accurate accounting, the total of the balances in the personal ledger should agree with the control account in the nominal ledger. This is an important CONTROL check at this point.

## Posting

You will notice a little peculiarity with the T-account. When we want to balance it, we use the phrase Balance c/d above the total line, and when we bring down that balance we show it below the total line as Balance b/d.

The procedure of transferring entries from the day books to the nominal ledger is called **posting**. As the following example will show, the double entry system is continued throughout.

Let's look again at our original nine entries and see what the debtors ledger of Big Ideas Co. looks like. It has at least four individual debtors, each with its own account. The information in each account came from the **sales day book.**

### ROM account

| June | | € | June | | |
|---|---|---|---|---|---|
| 1 | Sales | 10,000 | | | |
| 12 | Sales | 20,000 | | | |
| 28 | Sales | 10,000 | | | |
| 30 | sales | 20,000 | 30 | Balance c/d | 60,000 |
| | | 60,000 | | | 60,000 |
| July 1 | Balance b/d | 60,000 | | | |

### COD account

| June | | € | June | | |
|---|---|---|---|---|---|
| 2 | Sales | 20,000 | | | |
| 25 | Sales | 30,000 | 30 | Balance c/d | 50,000 |
| | | 50,000 | | | 50,000 |
| July 1 | Balance b/d | 50,000 | | | |

### ZAG account

| June | | € | June | | |
|---|---|---|---|---|---|
| 10 | Sales | 30,000 | | | |
| | | 30,000 | 30 | Balance c/d | 30,000 |
| | | | | | 30,000 |
| July 1 | Balance b/d | 30,000 | | | |

| BAM account | | | | | | |
|---|---|---|---|---|---|---|
| June | | € | June | | | |
| 15 | Sales | 50,000 | | | | |
| 19 | Sales | 10,000 | 30 | Balance c/d | | 60,000 |
| | | 60,000 | | | | 60,000 |
| July 1 | Balance b/d | 60,000 | | | | |

The total of the debit balances in the debtors ledger is €200,000 and is equal to the single debit entry made to the nominal ledger that we showed earlier and repeated below. Big Ideas Co. chose to post this at the end of the month.

| Dr | Total debtors (control) account | €200,000 |
|---|---|---|
| Cr | Sales account | €200,000 |

## General journal

The **general journal (GJ)** is a day book used to keep a list of certain double entries. Included will be the entries to the control accounts shown above and any corrections or adjustments. The format will normally look like this:

| Date | Accounts | Folio | Debit € | Credit € |
|---|---|---|---|---|
| | | | | |
| | | | | |
| | | | | |
| | | | | |
| | | | | |
| | | | | |

A very useful feature of the general journal is that it contains (or at least it should) a reason for the double entry. Let's say that the purchase of a conveyor belt on 10 June for €20,000 was posted in the nominal ledger to the vehicles account instead:

| Dr | Vehicles account | €20,000 |
|---|---|---|
| Cr | Cash account | €20,000 |

Later, on 30 June, the error is discovered. The adjusting entry to remove it from the vehicle account and place it in the equipment account is as follows:

| | | |
|----|----|----|
| Dr | Equipment account | €20,000 |
| Cr | Vehicle account | €20,000 |

The amount is now shown in the correct account. Because this is an adjusting entry, it is shown separately in the general journal with a short explanation attached, as follows:

| Date | Accounts | Folio | Debit € | Credit € |
|------|----------|-------|---------|----------|
| June 30 | Equipment account | | 20,000 | |
| | Vehicle account | | | 20,000 |
| | (incorrect posting of 10 June rectified) | | | |

Please note that the general journal only **records** the double entry. The G/L is the source of information for the double entry to be **posted** to the accounts in the nominal ledger.

## Purchases day book

Some day book systems include a large amount of detail and analysis. For example, the purchases day book lists not just purchases for resale, but also other expenses.

At the end of July, the Big Ideas Co. purchases day book, which records all the purchases and expenses acquired on credit, looks like this:

| Date | Supplier | Ref | Total | Purchases | Heat | Repairs | Phone | Sundry |
|------|----------|-----|-------|-----------|------|---------|-------|--------|
| 5 | Eircom | | 988 | | | | 988 | |
| 8 | Smyth | | 10,000 | 10,000 | | | | |
| 12 | ESB | | 5,632 | | 5,632 | | | |
| 15 | QuikRepair | | 1,098 | | 1,098 | | | |
| 22 | Windows Clear | | 470 | | | | | 470 |
| 25 | Chadwicks | | 9,180 | 9,180 | | | | |
| 26 | Murphy | | 10,031 | 10,031 | | | | |
| 28 | QuickRepair | | 509 | | | 509 | | |
| | Total | | 37,908 | 29,211 | 6,730 | 509 | 988 | 470 |

As well as recording the total amount of the transaction as a normal day book would, the purchases day book includes an analysis of the types of purchases. In other words, instead of posting the total, €37,908, to one account in the nominal ledger, Big Ideas Co. will post the sub-totals to the accounts shown in the analysis. The double entry will be as follows:

| | | | | |
|---|---|---|---|---|
| Dr | Purchases account | €29,211 | |
| Dr | Heat account | €6,730 | |
| Dr | Repairs account | €509 | |
| Dr | Phone account | €988 | |
| Dr | Sundry account | €470 | |
| Cr | Creditors control account | | €37,908 |
| | Total debits and credits | €37,908 | €37,908 |

Do not be confused by the fact that there are more than two accounts involved here. This still qualifies as a double entry, since the total debits, €37,908, equals the total credits, €37,908. Technically, the term 'double entry' refers to the amounts of money, not necessarily the number of accounts involved.

## Petty cash book

This is a day book used to record various minor cash payments by a business. Again, it lists the various payments made and analyses them under different categories.

| Date | Details | Folio | Total | Petrol | Repairs | Sundry |
|---|---|---|---|---|---|---|
| 2 | Tea and coffee | | 27 | | | 27 |
| 5 | Petrol | | 38 | 38 | | |
| 6 | Motor repairs | | 77 | | 77 | |
| 12 | Tea and coffee | | 18 | | | 18 |
| 18 | Petrol | | 21 | 21 | | |
| 18 | Petrol | | 29 | 29 | | |
| 24 | Toiletries | | 4 | | | 4 |
| 31 | Repairs to gutter | | 25 | | 25 | |
| | Total | | 239 | 88 | 102 | 49 |

To recap, then, the **day books** serve two purposes:

- They help to streamline the recording process by ensuring that the nominal ledger is used to record only total entries.
- They provide useful analyses of the various transactions of the business.

## Self-Assessment Question 6

1. If the books are balanced, does that mean they are accurate? Explain your reasoning.

## THE CORPORATE GOVERNANCE ISSUE

In some entities, particularly start-ups or entrepreneurially driven businesses, the attention to accounting detail may be less than satisfactory. There is no doubt that keeping track of transactions can be arduous, and referring to the function as 'back-office work' may not help with morale. However, there are a variety of computer software packages that makes the job much easier and allows the bookkeeping to be more involved with front-office activity. Clearly, the law fully expects that systems be kept up to date, and that is a priority for the accountant.

### The legal obligation

The legal obligation of companies to maintain accurate books is stipulated in the Companies Act 1990 (Hogan *et al.* 2002) that every company must 'correctly record and explain the transactions of the company' (Section 202). Based upon 2003 legislation, directors must also prepare a compliance statement confirming that 'the company has internal financial and other procedures in place' (Section 42) and that they have reviewed the effectiveness of these procedures. This means that the recording process is at the core of the accounting information system.

### Internal control system (ICS)

The more accurate name for the accounting system is the internal control system (ICS) and it is usually set up by an accountant in the company. Directors, however, are legally responsible for it. As this chapter implies, the ICS is a world unto itself, involving rules, controls, computers, machines and people. As we will see later in Chapter 11, it features in legislation on both sides of the Atlantic. American CEOs and CFOs must personally sign off on the ICS in addition to the financial statements. Auditors are required to examine and test it before issuing an opinion on the financial statements. In light of recent scandals, the one-time back office is now very much to the forefront.

# CHAPTER REVIEW

In this chapter we identified the elements of the accounting information system to allow us to understand how transactions are captured and processed to give the user a picture of the business at the end of a period. The elements are transactions, accounts, the recording process, the trial balance and the financial statements.

The discussion of the accounts introduced the concept of the double entry system, whereby any transaction is processed into the accounts by a combination of equal debit and credit amounts to separate accounts. At the end of a period, balances from these accounts are taken and placed into a trial balance, which contains two columns, one for debit balances and one for credit balances. If we have been processing our double entries properly, the total of the debit balances should equal the total of the credit balances.

In general, assets and expenses will have debit balances, while liabilities, capital and revenue accounts will have credit balances. Once the trial balance is in order, we are then in a position to prepare the financial statements, namely the income statement and the balance sheet.

We also discussed how the system dealt with the number of transactions that could overwhelm a business if day books were not used. Essentially, the day books will group together similar transactions such as sales or cash transactions; at the end of a day's business, one total will go to the sales account or the cash account instead of hundreds of individual transactions.

It is interesting to note that whether we are talking about a large multinational or a small local business, the same accounting information system is used. Certainly, the number of transactions is greater for the multinational, but the steps taken to complete those statements and each entity's concern for what the statements tell us are the same. The system is specifically referred to as the internal control system (ICS) and it allows directors to fulfil their legal obligation of keeping proper books. This is a core requirement of good corporate governance.

Once these mechanics are understood, we will be in a position to integrate the more conceptual ideas that accounting practice avails of.

# SELF-ASSESSMENT QUESTION ANSWERS

## SAQ 1

1. (a) The shareholder dies but there is no impact on the financial statements, so it is not a transaction.

   (b) Supplies purchased on credit means that the asset Supplies has increased and so too has the liability Creditor. A transaction has taken place and the balance sheet has been affected.

   (c) The firing of an employee is not a transaction, so nothing is recorded. Assuming that the employee is not replaced, wages may be lower in subsequent periods.

   (d) Cash has left the company, so the dividend paid must be recorded. A transaction has taken place.

## SAQ 2

1. The assets increase by virtue of an increase to Cash. Because Sales have increased and they ultimately go to shareholders' equity, the right side of the equation will also increase.

2. (a) The asset cash increases, as does the shareholders' equity.

   (b) The asset cash increases, and because this was facilitated by way of a loan, the liabilities will also increase.

## SAQ 3

1. (a) Payment of €500,000 by cheque for a warehouse: increase in fixed asset €500,000; decrease in bank €500,000.

   (b) Payment of €5,000 cash to a creditor: decrease in cash €5,000; decrease in creditor €5,000.

   (c) A credit sale of €2,000 (goods sold originally cost €1,500): increase in debtor €2,000; decrease in stock €1,500; increase in capital €500 (a little profit).

   (d) Receipt of €1,000 from a debtor: increase in cash €1,000; decrease in debtor €1,000.

## SAQ 4

1. Debit and credit refer to the left side and right side, respectively, of a T-account.

2. When revenues are generated, the revenue account is credited (the right side increases). When expenses are incurred, the expense accounts are debited (the left side increases).

3. The normal balance for asset is debit; liability is credit; shareholders' equity is credit.

4. The statement is partially true: if we **debit** an asset we are increasing it. If we are **crediting** it, then we are decreasing the asset. With a liability, a debit is a decrease, whereas a credit increases the liability.

## SAQ 5

1. The accounts of Frisbee Co.:

### Cash account

| 2005 | | € | 2005 | | |
|------|------|--------|--------|------|--------|
| Dec 1 | Capital | 10,000 | Dec 20 | Office expenses | 5,000 |
| Dec 23 | Debtors | 10,000 | Dec 28 | Creditors | 14,000 |
| | | | Dec 31 | Balance c/d | 1,000 |
| | | 20,000 | | | 20,000 |
| 2006 | | | | | |
| Jan 1 | Balance b/d | 1,000 | | | |

### Capital account

| 2005 | | | 2005 | | |
|------|------|------|--------|------|--------|
| | | | Dec 1 | Cash | 10,000 |
| | | | Dec 31 | | 10,000 |
| 2006 | | | Jan 1 | Balance b/d | 10,000 |

### Purchases account

| 2005 | | | 2005 | | |
|------|------|--------|--------|------|--------|
| Dec 3 | Creditors | 13,000 | | | |
| Dec 11 | Creditors | 7,000 | Dec 31 | Balance c/d | 20,000 |
| | | 20,000 | | | 20,000 |
| 2006 | | | | | |
| Jan 1 | Balance c/d | 20,000 | | | |

### Creditors account

| 2005 | | | 2005 | | |
|------|------|--------|--------|------|--------|
| Dec 8 | Purchases ret'd | 3,000 | Dec 3 | Purchases | 13,000 |
| Dec 28 | Cash | 14,000 | Dec 11 | Purchases | 7,000 |
| Dec 31 | Balance c/d | 3,000 | | | |
| | | 20,000 | | | 20,000 |
| 2006 | | | | | |
| | | | Jan 1 | Balance b/d | 3,000 |

## Sales account

| 2005 | | | | | | |
|------|------------|--------|--------|--------|------------|--------|
| | | | Dec 5 | Debtors | 7,000 |
| Dec 31 | Balance c/d | 12,000 | Dec 15 | Debtors | 5,000 |
| | | 12,000 | | | 12,000 |
| 2006 | | | | | | |
| | | | Jan 1 | Balance b/d | 12,000 |

## Debtors account

| 2005 | | | | | | |
|------|------------|--------|--------|------------|--------|
| Dec 5 | Sales | 7,000 | Dec 23 | Cash | 10,000 |
| Dec 15 | Sales | 5,000 | Dec 31 | Balance c/d | 2,000 |
| | | 12,000 | | | 12,000 |
| 2006 | | | | | | |
| Jan 1 | Balance b/d | 2,000 | | | |

## Purchases returned account

| 2005 | | | | | | |
|------|------------|-------|--------|----------|-------|
| Dec 31 | Balance c/d | 3,000 | Dec 8 | Creditors | 3,000 |
| 2006 | | | | | | |
| | | | Jan 1 | Balance b/d | 3,000 |

## Office expenses account

| 2005 | | | | | | |
|------|------------|-------|--------|------------|-------|
| Dec 20 | Cash | 5,000 | Dec 31 | Balance c/d | 5,000 |
| 2006 | | | | | | |
| Jan 1 | Balance b/d | 5,000 | | | |

Ordinarily, the sales, purchases, purchases returned and office expenses accounts will have ZERO balances on 1 January. However, getting to that step is left for Chapter 4 and the above accounts will suffice for now.

**Frisbee Co.**
**Trial Balance as at 31 December 2005**

|  | € Debit | € Credit |
|---|---|---|
| Cash | 1,000 | |
| Capital | | 10,000 |
| Purchases | 20,000 | |
| Creditors | | 3,000 |
| Sales | | 12,000 |
| Debtors | 2,000 | |
| Purchases returned | | 3,000 |
| Office expenses | 5,000 | |
| | 28,000 | 28,000 |

**SAQ 6**

1. The books may be balanced, i.e. the total debits equal the total of the credits. Potential for error arises when the amount debited and credited is incorrect, e.g. posting €10,000 debit and credit instead of €1,000. There is also the chance of posting to the wrong accounts. Good controls such as segregating duties or supervising end-of-day posting and training usually minimise errors.

# REFERENCES

Companies (Auditing and Accounting) Act 2003, Dublin: The Stationery Office.

Company Law Enforcement Act 2001, Dublin: The Stationery Office.

Heneghan, J. and O'Regan, P., *Accounting*, Limerick: Centre for Project Management, University of Limerick 2000.

Hogan, D., Bowen-Walsh, J. and O'Neill, B., *The Combined Companies Acts*, Dublin: Gill & Macmillan 2002.

O'Regan, P., *Introduction to Accounting*, Limerick: The International Equine Institute, University of Limerick 1998.

# 4

# The Closing Process: From Trial Balance to Financial Statements

**C O N T E N T S**

# INTRODUCTION

As previously discussed, the accounting cycle winds its way toward the trial balance, an orderly listing of the account balances, and is usually completed at month's end and almost certainly at the year-end. It is a juncture at which accountants make adjustments to the accounts such as missed transactions, end-of-period estimations or correcting errors. It is an important time because this is when we establish that the books are balanced and that preparation of the financial statements can then proceed. The layout of the financial statements is dictated by IAS 1 Presentation of Financial Statements. From now on this will prompt you toward greater preciseness in completing the statements. This chapter will give you of a sense of the dynamic of accounting as you are introduced to some new accounts.

From a corporate governance perspective, we will be introduced to the key issue of disclosure as it relates to sales and purchases and will also ensure that the balances in the trial balance are consistent with the financial statements. As we will discuss later, the independent auditor pays close attention to this final step.

## OBJECTIVES

**When you have finished this chapter, you will be able to:**
- understand the purpose of the trial balance
- understand the limitations of the trial balance
- avail of new accounts resulting from a business's buying and selling activities
- apply the key requirements of IAS 1 in completing the income statement and balance sheet
- determine the corporate governance concerns.

# CONTRA ACCOUNTS

In the day-to-day running of a business, it sometimes happens that an item sold or purchased is returned for a variety of reasons. Negotiation and compromise also feature in business activity, resulting in the offer and pursuit of discounts. These result in transactions and accordingly must be posted to accounts in the general ledger called contra accounts. Contra is the Latin for 'against', an appropriate term as the account is presented in the financial statements as going against another account.

There are other accounts that also must entertain the possibility of adjustment before the account balances are finalised at a period end. Among the debtors, for instance, will be a number (hopefully a small number) of customers unable to pay. This reality must be captured in the accounts by estimating what this expense might be. This will result in a contra account that is presented as reducing the debtor balance. Another contra account is needed to reflect the loss in value in equipment and other fixed assets due to wear and tear. We call this contra account **depreciation**.

## Selling activity

When a business sells a product or service, two additional transactions may arise: (i) goods may be returned and (ii) a discount may have to be offered to close the sale.

### SALES RETURNED

This is the account used when goods sold are returned or where a service customer is not satisfied with the service and requests a refund. Goods that are returned may have been defective, and most companies reimburse the customer in this situation. Two accounts are impacted, namely the **cash account** and the **sales returned account**. We credit (decrease) the cash and debit (increase) the sales returned accounts, as follows.

| | | |
|---|---|---|
| Dr | Sales returned | 300 |
| Cr | Cash | 300 |

The sales returns account is a **debit** balance and is presented in the income statement as netted against the sales amount. This is why it is referred to as a **contra account**. If the €300 above represented the only returns out of €100,000 in sales, then the income statement presentation will look like this:

| Big Company | |
|---|---|
| **Income statement** | |
| Sales | €100,000 |
| Less sales returned | 300 |
| Net sales | €99,700 |

### DISCOUNTS ALLOWED

This arises when the business gives a discount to its customer. Discounts are used in special circumstances, such as a first-time customer, clearing out stock or perhaps to satisfy a disgruntled client. Regardless of the reason, it is an expense to the business and must be recognised as such. An item on sale for €3,000 is eventually sold after the seller agrees to sell it at a 10 per cent discount. Three accounts are impacted here.

   **Sales** account is credited (increased) by €3,000 and is balanced with amounts debited (increased) to the **cash** and **discounts allowed** accounts, as follows:

| | | |
|---|---|---|
| Dr | Cash | 2,700 |
| Dr | Discounts allowed | 300 |
| Cr | Sales | 3,000 |

*Ultimately all expenses 'go against' sales.* As with all expense accounts, the balance in discounts allowed is a debit balance. Strictly speaking, this account is not a contra account but is included here to give you a fuller sense of the sales dynamic.

## Purchasing activity

Businesses may also have a need to return goods to suppliers, and as a result two accounts may arise to capture the transaction: (i) purchase returns and (ii) discounts received.

### PURCHASE RETURNS

A business may find that materials are defective and is forced to return them. If the supplier agrees to reimburse its client, the client will record the transaction as follows:

| Dr | Cash | 2,000 |
|----|------|-------|
| Cr | Purchase returns | 2,000 |

Because the cash is increased, it is debited. The purchase returns is a credit balance and is presented against the purchases (debit balance) to calculate cost of goods sold (COGS). This is why purchase returns is called a contra account. The COGS is presented in the income statement and is calculated as follows:

| Cost of goods sold: | |
|---|---|
| Beginning Stock 1 Jan | €5000 |
| Purchases for the year | 100,000 |
| **Less purchase returns** | **−2,000** |
| Available stock | 103,000 |
| Less ending stock 31 Dec | −6,000 |
| COGS | €97,000 |

The COGS figure is usually presented without the calculation shown here, with the latter consigned to the notes accompanying the financial statements.

### DISCOUNTS RECEIVED

Suppliers who are anxious to win new business or perhaps to make amends to a dissatisfied client may offer a **discount** to the client. The business that receives the discount is required to present it immediately after gross profit, as it essentially reduces the **cost of goods sold**. It is credited (increased) and thus has a credit balance. A business in receipt of a 20 per cent discount on purchases of €100,000 processes the transaction as follows:

| Dr | Purchases | 100,000 |
|----|-----------|---------|
| Cr | Cash | 80,000 |
| Cr | Discounts received | 20,000 |

Although this involved three accounts, the total of the credits equals the debit amount. The discounts received account is not strictly a contra account, but its inclusion here adds to understanding the purchasing picture.

## Disclosure

Adequate disclosure is a key concern of corporate governance. It may seem easier to simply reduce the sales and purchases accounts directly when items are returned. However, such actions may hide a problem with quality or with dissatisfied customers. For instance, if a company's sales returned was 15 per cent of total sales, that number would generally be considered as high. In fact, it would throw doubt over the remaining 85 per cent. Not to disclose such a situation would probably mislead existing shareholders and potential investors.

An egregious example of how this was abused concerns the US telecom company WorldCom. The company discovered that it had overcharged customers during the late 1990s, and although it reimbursed its customers, it processed the reimbursement as an expense instead of reducing the sales figure.

---

### Self-Assessment Question 1

1. Where will the following accounts be found in the financial statements? Decide whether the balance in each is debit or credit.
   (a) Discount received
   (b) Discount allowed
   (c) Sales returned
   (d) Purchase returns

---

## THE TRIAL BALANCE

A trial balance is a statement that lists ledger account balances, with debit balances grouped separately from credit balances. It is usually prepared at the end of a month's activity and certainly at the end of the financial year. If the double entries have been entered correctly, then the resulting debit balances at the end, when totalled, should agree with the total of the ending credit balances. The primary purpose, then, of the trial balance is to prove the mathematical equality of the debits and credits after posting. Once you have prepared the trial balance, you can make adjustments prior to issuing a final trial balance and then proceed to preparing the balance sheet and income statement.

## Preparation

A trial balance is prepared by:

- listing the account titles and their balances
- totalling the debit and credit columns
- verifying that both totals agree.

It is a major event in the accounting cycle. Once it is finalised, a business is essentially declaring that its books (the general ledger) are balanced. The independent auditor will determine if the trial balance does in fact reflect *all* of the counts in the general ledger. Further, the auditor will examine the adjustments and determine if they are justified. As we will discuss later, the auditor will trace the trial balance amounts into financial statements.

A trial balance will look like this:

**The Celtic Construction Company**
**Trial Balance 31 December 2005**

| Account title | Debit balances | Credit balances |
|---|---|---|
| Stock 1 Jan 2005 | 2,000 | |
| Cash | 10,100 | |
| Office supplies | 1,500 | |
| Vehicle | 13,000 | |
| Office equipment | 7,000 | |
| Notes payable | | 8,000 |
| Common stock | | 5,000 |
| Sales | | 59,800 |
| Sales returned | 5,000 | |
| Discounts received | | 3,000 |
| Purchases | 30,000 | |
| Purchases returned | | 1,000 |
| Salaries expense | 4,300 | |
| Rent expense | 2,400 | |
| Discounts allowed | 1,500 | |
| | 76,800 | 76,800 |

A characteristic of the trial balance in Irish accounting is that the stock balance is that at the beginning of the year. In the next section we will demonstrate how this is adjusted.

## Limitations of a trial balance

A trial balance does not prove that all transactions have been recorded and that the amounts entered into the ledger accounts are in fact correct. Numerous errors may exist even though the trial balance columns agree. For example, the trial balance may balance even when:

- a transaction is not journalised
- a correct journal entry is not posted
- a journal entry is posted twice
- incorrect accounts are used in journalising or posting
- offsetting errors are made in recording the amount of the transactions.

In other words, as long as equal debits and credits are posted, even to the wrong account or in the wrong amount, the total debits will equal the total credits. But despite its limitations, the trial balance is a useful device for finding errors.

### Self-Assessment Questions 2

1. Can we assume that the financial statements are fine when the trial balance is balanced?
2. Explain how an error may never be found in the trial balance.
3. What are the limitations of the trial balance?

## THE FINAL ACCOUNTS: THE FINANCIAL STATEMENTS

You have now learned how to write up ledger accounts and to prepare a trial balance. You were also introduced earlier to the final accounts for a business, i.e. the balance sheet and the income statement. How do we now progress from the trial balance to the financial statements?

In commencing this process, let's consider how some accounts in the general ledger are regarded as temporary while others are permanent. It may seem strange to describe an account as 'temporary' or 'permanent', but it is appropriate when examining the end of the accounting cycle. In Chapter 1 we distinguished between the income statement and the balance sheet, whereby the former tracked financial performance **over a time period** while the latter provides the financial position **at a point in time** which is the end of the performance period. It is this distinction that divides the accounts into temporary and permanent status.

## Temporary accounts

We consider the revenue and expense accounts as temporary because if they are to capture performance they must:

- be at *zero* balance on day one of the period
- increase over the following month or year
- provide an *ending* balance on the last day of the period and then
- be reduced to *zero* balance so that the performance in the *next* period can be tracked.

This reducing process is referred to as **closing out the accounts** and is done mechanically by the double entry system, those matching debits and credits that we have already explored. The ending balances are closed out and transferred to the **profit and loss T-account** to determine whether the business made a profit or loss. If the revenue exceeds the expenses, then there is a profit.

Using The Celtic Construction Company example, we identify what the ending balances of the temporary accounts are and proceed to close them out as follows:

| | | |
|---|---|---:|
| Dr | Sales | 59,800 |
| Cr | Profit and loss | 59,800 |

And the expenses:

| | | |
|---|---|---:|
| Dr | Profit and loss | 38,200 |
| Cr | Purchases | 30,000 |
| Cr | Salaries expense | 4,300 |
| Cr | Rent expense | 2,400 |
| Cr | Discounts allowed | 1,500 |

The total of the expenses credited is €38,200. Both the sales account and the expense accounts are now at *zero* balance. Incidentally, the purchases returned, sales returned and discounts received are also closed out to zero.

In some systems (usually the US), this profit (or loss) is then transferred to the retained earnings account, which would then make the P&L account a temporary account too. In the UK and Ireland, the P&L account is usually a permanent account to which the revenue and expense accounts are closed, and the resulting ending balance will have increased or decreased from the beginning of the period. The P&L account will then be shown in the balance sheet in the capital section.

## Permanent accounts

The balance sheet accounts of assets, liabilities and capital are called permanent accounts in the sense that their balances at the end of the period continue into the next period; the 31 December figure becomes the 1 January figure.

From the above it can be deduced that the P&L account is the connection between the income statement and the balance sheet.

## Stock

We have previously discussed stock, which as an asset is located in the balance sheet. However, because it is needed in the calculation of cost of goods sold (COGS), it is often shown in the income statement. This presents us with two questions to answer:
- Why is an asset shown in the income statement?
- Why does the trial balance show the stock balance as that from the beginning of the period?

As shown earlier, the stock shown in the income statement is part of a calculation to determine the COGS, a key expense item, as follows:

| Cost of goods sold: | |
| --- | --- |
| Opening stock 1 Jan | xxx |
| Add: Purchases | xxx |
| Less returns | xxx |
| Less closing stock 31 Dec | (xxx) |
| COGS | xxx |

Therefore, its inclusion is to demonstrate the COGS calculation.

The second question deals with the way ending stock was calculated. In pre-computer days, an inventory was taken after the close of business on the last day of the period. We then fall back upon the double entry system to calculate the COGS and replace the beginning stock with the ending balance. To incorporate the correct amount of stock in the two final statements, it will be useful to understand the mechanics surrounding the movements in stock. We can grasp that:
- stock must be acquired, then
- used up through resale or manufacture
- followed by replenishments, so that
- by the end of the period, a balance remains.

As our goal is to match the cost of sales in a period against the sales for that period, we can convert those steps into the presentation used in the income statement.

Let's use these numbers: beginning stock €2,000; purchases €30,000; purchase returns €1,000; and ending stock €3,000. We can calculate the COGS as follows:

| Cost of goods sold: | |
|---|---|
| Opening stock 1 Jan | 2,000 |
| Add: Purchases | 30,000 |
| Less returns | (1,000) |
| Less: Closing stock 31 Dec | (3,000) |
| COGS | 28,000 |

This is the income statement presentation, but how do we get ending stock into the system? Keep in mind that the purchases account and the purchase returns used above have already been closed out to the P&L account. We fall back on the double entry system again.

The following entry reduces the stock account to *zero* balance:

| Dr | P&L | 2,000 |
|---|---|---|
| Cr | Stock | 2,000 |

Whereas the next entry adjusts the stock account to its correct balance, the ending balance:

| Dr | Stock | 3,000 |
|---|---|---|
| Cr | P&L | 3,000 |

By accounting for stock in this way, the ending stock balance is correct and the P&L account has all it needs to determine a profit or loss. Let's assume that the sales figure was €50,000 for the year, then the P&L account will look like this:

| P&L account | | | | | |
|---|---|---|---|---|---|
| **December** | | | **December** | | |
| 31 | Purchases | 30,000 | 31 | Sales | 50,000 |
| 31 | Stock (begin) | 2,000 | 31 | Purchase returns | 1,000 |
| 31 | **Balance c/d** | **22,000** | 31 | Stock (end) | 3,000 |
| | | 54,000 | | | 54,000 |
| | | | | **Balance b/d** | **22,000** |

€22,000 is the gross profit.

Using the following self-assessment question, we can place the mechanic just discussed within the income statement.

## Self-Assessment Question 3

1. Downtown Company has been trading for a number of years. At the beginning of the year the company had stock totalling €20,000. During the year it purchased €500,000 in stock and there were no returns. At the end of the year stock remaining was calculated to be €30,000. If sales were €600,000, calculate the gross profit.

## Preparing final accounts

Now that you have learned how to handle stock, you can prepare a set of final accounts.

The trial balance contains the ending account balances at the end of the period, and you must decide which final account or statement all these items should go to. Sometimes you will find items listed after the trial balance totals. These items, which are called **post-trial balance adjustments**, are items that have only come to light after the ledger accounts have been closed and the trial balance prepared. In other words, no entry has been made in the accounts for them; nevertheless, they must be incorporated.

There are two rules for preparing final accounts.

1. Every item in the trial balance must be placed in **either** the income statement **or** the balance sheet.
2. Sales and expenses are placed in the income statement. Assets, liabilities and capital accounts are placed in the balance sheet.

The principal post-trial balance items (accruals, prepayments, depreciation and bad debts) will be covered in Chapter 5; for now the only post-trial balance adjustment that we will encounter is closing stock. Present ending stock as a:

- deduction from purchases in the income statement
- current asset in the balance sheet.

With these basic rules, you are now ready to prepare a final set of accounts.

### EXAMPLE: GREEN ACRES COMPANY

Here is the trial balance for Green Acres Company, a gardening implements retailer, which has just finished its first year of business.

**Green Acres Company**
**Trial Balance 31 December 2005**

|  | Dr | Cr |
|---|---|---|
|  | € |  |
| Stock, 1 Jan 2005 | 10,000 |  |
| Cash | 40,000 |  |
| Delivery van | 30,000 |  |
| Forklift truck | 10,000 |  |
| Capital |  | 70,000 |
| Purchase of implements | 100,000 |  |
| Sale of implements |  | 175,000 |
| Rent | 15,000 |  |
| Wages | 45,000 |  |
| Creditors |  | 15,000 |
| Debtors | 6,000 |  |
| Discounts received |  | 4,000 |
| Discounts allowed | 2,000 |  |
| Sales returns | 6,000 |  |
| **Total** | **264,000** | **264,000** |

Closing stock is €30,000.

You must now place each one of the above amounts in either the income statement or the balance sheet. Remember that the closing stock is placed twice, once in the COGS in the income statement and in the current assets section of the balance sheet.

**Green Acres Company**
**Income statement for the year ended 31 December 2005**

| Sales |  | 175,000 |
|---|---|---|
| Less: Sales returns |  | 6,000 |
|  |  | 169,000 |
|  |  |  |
| Opening stock | 10,000 |  |
| Add: Purchases | 100,000 |  |
| Less: Closing stock | −30,000 |  |
| Cost of sales |  | 80,000 |
| Gross profit |  | 89,000 |
|  |  |  |
| Add: Sundry income: Discounts received |  | 4,000 |

Less expenses:

| | | |
|---|---|---|
| Rent | 15,000 | |
| Wages | 45,000 | |
| Discounts allowed | 2,000 | |
| | | 62,000 |
| Net profit | | 31,000 |

**Green Acres Company**
**Balance Sheet as at 31 December 2005**

Fixed assets:

| | | |
|---|---|---|
| Delivery van | | 30,000 |
| Forklift truck | | 10,000 |
| | | 40,000 |
| Current assets: | | |
| Closing stock | 30,000 | |
| Debtors | 6,000 | |
| Cash | 40,000 | |
| | 76,000 | |
| Less: Current liabilities: | | |
| Creditors | −15,000 | |
| Net current assets | | 61,000 |
| | | 101,000 |
| | | |
| Capital and reserves: | | |
| Balance at 1 Jan 2005 | | 70,000 |
| Net profit | | 31,000 |
| | | 101,000 |

Notice how returns are subtracted from sales to give a net sales figure. Closing stock has now been shown twice, once in the income statement and once in the balance sheet.

## Self-Assessment Question 4

1. Differentiate between the terms 'P&L statement' and 'P&L account'. In your response, include the role that each has in the accounting process.

# PRESENTATION AND READABILITY

Presentation of the financial statement is important and was alluded to when discussing the accounting concept of **understandability** in Chapter 2. Not only are we concerned about the order of accounts (fixed assets followed by current assets), but we must also understand what distinguishes a fixed asset from a current asset. Much of accounting regulation today is hugely influenced by guidance provided by the EU. This guidance, referred to as a Directive, reflects the EU effort to further harmonisation among various accounting systems within the EU. The EU Fourth Directive in particular impacted the rules of accounting and the presentation of financial statements (O'Regan 2001).

## EU Fourth Directive and IAS 1

This directive was adopted in 1978, and the presentation of statements that it recommended became the basis for IAS 1 in its revised format, the latest revision having taken place in 2003. Accordingly, IAS 1 requires that the financial statements must be distinguished from other information that forms part of an annual report. Amounts and accounts by type must be clearly described and presented in an order that adds to the understanding of the financial picture. We will now look at the suggested layout for both the balance sheet and the income statement.

## Balance sheet content and layout

The balance sheet should present separate classifications for:
- current and non-current assets
- current and non-current liabilities.

General practice has been to present assets and liabilities in order of their liquidity, with cash presented last. While IAS 1 does not specify whether cash should start or end this spectrum of liquidity, European practice commences with fixed assets and makes its way down toward cash. The standard also specifies what items should appear on the balance sheet:
- property, plant and equipment
- investment property
- intangible assets
- financial assets
- investments in other entities
- biological assets
- inventories (stock)
- trade receivables (debtors)
- cash and cash equivalents (see Chapter 8)

- trade payables (creditors)
- provisions
- financial liabilities (loans)
- tax liabilities
- minority interest (see Chapter 7)
- issued capital and reserves.

The Fourth Directive provided two formats on how the information should be presented: the **horizontal** format and the **vertical.** The latter format is presented in Figure 4.1. At this juncture in our studies we are not too concerned with all of the items listed there, as it is provided to give you some exposure to the variety of accounts that companies use and report on.

FIGURE 4.1: EU FOURTH DIRECTIVE VERTICAL BALANCE SHEET FORMAT

**A. Called-up share capital not paid**

**B. Formation expenses**

**C. Fixed assets**

I *Intangible assets*

    1. Cost of research and development

    2. Concessions, patents, trademarks and similar rights and assets

    3. Goodwill

    4. Payments on account

II *Tangible assets*

    1. Land and buildings

    2. Plant and machinery

    3. Fixtures, fittings, tools and equipment

    4. Payments on account and assets in course of construction

III *Financial assets*

    1. Shares in group undertakings

    2. Loans to group undertakings

    3. Participating interests

    4. Loans to undertakings in which the company has a participating interest

    5. Investments held in fixed assets

    6. Other loans

    7. Own shares

**D. Current assets**

I *Stocks*

    1. Raw materials and consumables

    2. Work in progress

    3. Finished goods and goods for resale

    4. Payments on account

II *Debtors*

    1. Trade debtors

    2. Amounts owed by group undertakings

    3. Amounts owed by undertakings in which the company has a participating interest

    4. Other debtors

    5. Called-up share capital not paid

    6. Prepayments and accrued income

III *Investments*

    1. Shares in group undertakings

    2. Own shares

    3. Other investments

IV *Cash at bank and in hand*

**E. Prepayments and accrued income**

**F. Creditors: amounts falling due within one year**

    1. Debenture loans

    2. Bank loans and overdrafts

    3. Payments received on account

    4. Trade creditors

    5. Bills of exchange payable

    6. Amounts owed to group undertakings

    7. Amounts owed to undertakings in which the company has a participating interest

    8. Other creditors, including taxation and social security

    9. Accruals and deferred income

**G. Net current assets/liabilities**

**H. Total assets less current liabilities**

**I. Creditors: amounts falling due after one year**

    1. Debenture loans

    2. Bank loans and overdrafts

    3. Payments received on account

    4. Trade creditors

    5. Bills of exchange payable

    6. Amounts owed to group undertakings

    7. Amounts owed to undertakings in which the company has a participating interest

    8. Other creditors, including taxation and social security

    9. Accruals and deferred income

## J. Provisions
    1. Pensions and similar obligations
    2. Taxation, including deferred taxation
    3. Other provisions
## K. Accruals and deferred income
## L. Capital and reserves
I *Called-up share capital*

II *Share premium account*

III *Revaluation reserve*

IV *Other reserves*
    1. Legal reserve
    2. Reserve for own shares
    3. Reserves provided for by the articles of association
    4. Other reserves
V *Profit or loss brought forward*

VI *Profit or loss for the financial year*

In Figures 4.1 and 4.2 you will notice the term 'undertakings'. An undertaking (also called a subsidiary) is a company that is controlled by another (see Chapter 7).

### Current versus non-current

IAS 1 suggests how this distinction should be made. For an asset to be considered current, it should satisfy any one of the following criteria (Alfredson *et al.* 2005):

- it is expected to be realised in, or is intended for sale or consumption in, the entity's normal operating cycle;
- it is held primarily for the purpose of being traded;
- it is expected to be realised within twelve months after the balance sheet date; or
- it is cash or cash equivalent (see Chapter 8 on cash flow statement) unless it is restricted from being exchanged or used to settle a liability for at least twelve months after the balance sheet date.

All other assets should be classified as non-current.

In regard to liabilities, a liability is current when it satisfies any one of the following:

- it is expected to be settled in the entity's normal operating cycle;
- it is held primarily for the purpose of being traded;
- it is due to be settled within twelve months after the balance sheet date; or
- the entity does not have an unconditional right to defer settlement of the liability for at least twelve months after the balance sheet date.

All other liabilities should be classified as non-current.

## Income statement content and layout

The
terms
revenue,
sales
and
turnover
all mean
the
same
thing.

IAS 1 stipulates a number of items to be disclosed on the income statement. These items include:

- revenues
- finance costs
- share of the after-tax profits and losses of associates and joint ventures
- pre-tax gain or loss on disposal of assets and/or liabilities of discontinued operations
- tax expense
- profit or loss
- minority interest
- net profit or loss.

Taking its cue from Britain and Ireland's **FRS 3 Reporting Financial Performance** (1993), IAS 1 also abolished extraordinary items (see Chapter 6) from the income statement.

The Fourth Directive suggested a number of layouts for the statement. In addition to a horizontal and vertical layout, it also suggested that expenses be listed either by the:

- **nature of the expense**: purchases, wages, advertising; or by the
- **function they serve**: distribution, administration.

Figure 4.2 provides the vertical layout by function. The income statements that we have completed to date have essentially followed the former by listing each expense item. We will continue to use this approach throughout the remainder of the book.

FIGURE 4.2: EU FOURTH DIRECTIVE VERTICAL INCOME STATEMENT FORMAT

1  Turnover
2  Cost of sales
3  Gross profit (or loss)
4  Distribution costs
5  Administrative expenses
6  Other operating income
7  Income from shares in group undertakings
8  Income from participating interests
9  Income from other fixed asset investments
10 Other interest receivable and similar income
11 Amounts written off per value adjustments
12 Interest payable and similar charges
13 Tax on profit or loss on ordinary activities
14 Profit or loss on ordinary activities after tax

15 Extraordinary income
16 Extraordinary charges
17 Extraordinary profit or loss
18 Tax on extraordinary profit or loss
19 Other taxes not shown under the above items
20 Profit or loss for the financial year

In addition to the layouts for both balance sheet and income statement, IAS 1 also requires notes to accompany the statements and disclose such things as number of shares issued, par value of the stock, write downs to stock, disposal of property, plant and equipment, discontinued operations and legal settlements (O'Regan 2001). The accompanying notes appear in discussions later in Chapter 6 and again in Chapter 12.

### Connection between statements

Seeing the connection between the financial statements is a major step forward and takes you beyond the bookkeeping function. You will have noticed how the profit for the year is added to the P&L account at the beginning of the year to come up with the ending balance in the P&L account in the balance sheet. On US balance sheets the P&L account is called the **retained earnings**. The next self-assessment question will allow you to apply this understanding.

### Self-Assessment Question 5

1. In the early 1990s, when IBM was going through a difficult trading period, its new CEO, Louis Gerstner, made dramatic cuts to the workforce. The response was an immediate increase to the company's share price.
   (a) Why do you think the share price rose?
   (b) Can you explain the impact of the cuts on IBM's financial statements?

Before proceeding to the final self-assessment question, it should be pointed out that the trial balance is the last output from the general ledger but *not* the final event in the reporting process. The ending account balances in the trial balance are placed in the financial statements so that the financial picture can be more readily understood. This final act of re-presenting the trial balance in the form of the income statement and balance sheet is closely monitored by external auditors. A threat to good **governance** arises if management reports a financial picture at variance with the trial balance. We return to this corporate governance issue later in the auditing process in Chapter 12.

## Self-Assessment Question 6

1. The trial balance of IT Wave Ltd at 31 December 2005 is presented below. Complete the income statement and the balance sheet at 31 December 2005 in accordance with the EU Fourth Directive format (vertical). The expenses should be listed individually (nature of expense format).

|  | Debit | Credit |
|---|---|---|
|  | € | € |
| Sales |  | 310,000 |
| Purchases | 160,000 |  |
| Discounts received |  | 10,000 |
| Wages | 30,000 |  |
| Rent | 5,000 |  |
| Administration | 15,000 |  |
| Marketing expenses | 18,000 |  |
| Sales returned | 5,000 |  |
| Share capital |  | 100,000 |
| Cash | 25,000 |  |
| Stock 1 Jan 2005 | 63,000 |  |
| Trade creditors |  | 83,000 |
| Electricity payable (liability) |  | 7,000 |
| Trade debtors | 85,000 |  |
| Property and equipment | 100,000 |  |
| Vehicle | 30,000 |  |
| Patents and copyrights* | 140,000 |  |
| Discounts allowed | 5,000 |  |
| Purchase returns |  | 6,000 |
| 10-year loan |  | 60,000 |
| P&L account 1 Jan 2005 |  | 105,000 |
|  | 681,000 | 681,000 |

*Intangible assets

Additional information: Ending stock was €75,000.

# CHAPTER REVIEW

This chapter identified the elements of the accounting information system to allow us to understand how transactions are captured and processed to give the user a picture of the business at the end of a period. The elements are transactions, accounts, the recording process, the trial balance and the financial statements.

The discussion of the accounts introduced the concept of the double entry system, whereby any transaction is processed into the accounts by a combination of equal debit and credit amounts to separate accounts. At the end of a period, balances from these accounts are taken and placed into a trial balance, which contains two columns, one for debit balances and one for credit balances. If we have been processing our double entries properly, the total of the debit balances should equal the total of the credit balances.

In general, assets and expenses will have debit balances, while liabilities, capital and revenue accounts will have credit balances. Once the trial balance is in order, we are then in a position to prepare the financial statements, namely the trading, profit and loss account and the balance sheet. So that we can complete the trading, profit and loss account correctly, we must be told the ending stock balance; the trial balance will show the stock balance as of the beginning of the period. This ending balance becomes the beginning balance in the next period.

As a result of EU Directives, the layout of the income statement and balance sheet has emphasised disclosure and readability. The EU Fourth Directive in particular has been the key influence on both FRS 3 and IAS 1. IAS 1 provides guidance on what distinguishes current from non-current assets and liabilities. In the income statement it suggests that expenses be listed by either the nature of the expense or by the function it serves. Clutter in the statements is avoided by providing accompanying notes where important disclosures can be made.

# SELF-ASSESSMENT QUESTION ANSWERS

### SAQ 1

1.  (a) Discount received is located in the income statement immediately after the gross margin. Credit balance.
    (b) Discount allowed is located among the operating expenses in the income statement. Debit balance.
    (c) Sales returned is found immediately after sales in the income statement. Debit balance.
    (d) Purchase returns is shown in the COGS calculation in the income statement. Credit balance.

## SAQ 2

1.  Even though the books are balanced, as evidenced by the trial balance, the fact remains that those ending numbers are transferred into the income statement and balance sheet and only the review by the independent auditor confirms that last step to be correct.
2.  A trial balance may be in balance despite having missed a transaction or incorrect accounts were debited and credited.
3.  Similar to the above, transactions may be missed entirely or the wrong accounts were used. The next step to the financial statements will compound the problem.

## SAQ 3

1.

| Sales | €600,000 |
|---|---|
| Cost of goods sold: | |
| Opening stock | 20,000 |
| Add: Purchases | 500,000 |
| Less: Closing stock | (30,000) |
| Cost of sales | 490,000 |
| Gross profit | €110,000 |

## SAQ 4

1.  The **P&L statement** is also referred to as the **income statement** and is one of the major financial statements required for reporting purposes. It discloses the sales and expenses for the financial period, thereby determining whether the business made a profit or a loss. Because the information in the statement comes from the individual sales and expense accounts that make up the general ledger, the P&L statement is a presentation device for users to read.

    The **P&L account** is a T-account and is therefore part of the general ledger. It is a device that facilitates the closing out of sales accounts and expense accounts. It has a balance at the beginning of the year, and when the sales and expenses are transferred to it at the end of the year, the resulting profit or loss will produce a new balance at year-end. This balance will show up in the capital section of the balance sheet.

## SAQ 5

1.  Investors interpreted Louis Gerstner's decision as stopping the haemorrhaging of cash out of the company. By controlling costs he bought IBM some time so that the company could think and work its way back to increasing revenues.
2.  Cutting staff meant reducing expenses, and assuming all other things being equal, the cuts would have increased profits. This means that the P&L account or the retained earnings in the capital section of the balance sheet would increase. The corresponding increase in the assets would take place in the cash as a result of the cash savings.

## SAQ 6

**IT Wave Ltd**
**Income statement for the year ended 31 December 2005**

|  |  | € |
|---|---:|---:|
| Sales |  | 310,000 |
| Less sales returned |  | 5,000 |
| Net sales |  | 305,000 |
|  |  |  |
| COGS: |  |  |
| Beginning stock | 63,000 |  |
| Add purchases | 160,000 |  |
| Less purchase returns | 6,000 |  |
|  | 217,000 |  |
| Less ending stock | 75,000 |  |
| COGS: |  | 142,000 |
| Gross profit |  | 163,000 |
| Add discounts received |  | 10,000 |
|  |  | 173,000 |
|  |  |  |
| Operating expenses: |  |  |
| Wages | 30,000 |  |
| Rent | 5,000 |  |
| Administration | 15,000 |  |
| Marketing | 18,000 |  |
| Discounts allowed | 5,000 |  |
|  |  | 73,000 |
| Operating profit |  | 100,000 |
| Add P&L account 1 Jan 2005 |  | 105,000 |
| Ending P&L account 31 Dec 2005 |  | 205,000 |

**IT Wave Ltd**

**Balance Sheet as at 31 December 2005**

|  |  |  | € |
|---|---|---|---:|
| **Fixed assets:** | | | |
| Intangible assets: | | | |
| Patents and copyrights | | | 140,000 |
| | | | |
| Tangible assets: | | | |
| Plant and equipment | | | 100,000 |
| Vehicle | | | 30,000 |
| | | | 270,000 |
| | | | |
| **Current assets:** | | | |
| Stock | | 75,000 | |
| Trade debtors | | 85,000 | |
| Cash | | 25,000 | |
| | | 185,000 | |
| Less current liabilities: | | | |
| Trade creditors | | 83,000 | |
| Electricity payable | | 7,000 | |
| | | 90,000 | |
| Net current assets | | | 95,000 |
| Total assets | | | 365,000 |
| Long-term loan | | | 60,000 |
| | | | **305,000** |
| | | | |
| **Capital and reserves:** | | | |
| Share capital | | | 100,000 |
| P&L account 31 Dec 2005 | | | 205,000 |
| | | | **305,000** |

A slightly different presentation also makes for acceptable practice:

| | |
|---|---|
| **Total assets** | **365,000** |
| **Financed by:** | |
| Capital and reserves: | |
| Share capital | 100,000 |
| P&L account 31 Dec 2005 | 205,000 |
| | 305,000 |
| Long-term loan | 60,000 |
| | 365,000 |

# REFERENCES

Accounting Standards Board, *FRS 3 Reporting Financial Performance*, London: ASB 1992 (revised).

Alfredson, L., Picker, R., Pacter, P. and Radford, J., *Applying International Accounting Standards*, Milton, Australia: John Wiley & Sons 2005.

Heneghan, J. and O'Regan, P., *Accounting*, Limerick: Centre for Project Management, University of Limerick 2000.

International Accounting Standards Board, *IAS 1 Presentation of Financial Statements*, London: IASB 2003 (revised).

O'Regan, P., *Introduction to Accounting*, Limerick: The International Equine Institute, University of Limerick 1998.

O'Regan, P., *Financial Information Analysis*, Chichester: John Wiley & Sons 2001.

# 5

# *Accrual Accounting: Principles and Application*

C
O
N
T
E
N
T
S

# INTRODUCTION

Grasping the accrual basis of accounting is a defining moment in the study of accounting in that it separates the accounting professional from the bookkeeper. Its proper use is also one of the major corporate governance challenges for businesses today. Up to now we have discussed accounting for the most part in cash terms – the **cash basis of accounting** – but how do we deal with a situation where cash is not immediately involved? You have already got a hint of this when in discussing trade debtors we recognised that a quantifiable transaction had taken place, even though no money had exchanged hands. Similarly, for a trade creditor we recognised that a purchase of goods on credit at an agreed amount was a transaction. Although no money was exchanged at the time of the transaction in either case, we still recognised it by accruing it. This is the **accrual basis of accounting:** transactions that are quantifiable and that affect the financial statements are recorded in the period in which they occur rather than when the cash is paid or received. It allows us to overcome a timing issue: goods sold near the end of 2005 but not paid for until the next year must be accounted for as revenue in 2005 (Heneghan and O'Regan 2000).

**Trade debtors** are those who owe a business for goods or services bought from the business on credit.

Applying the accrual concept requires judgment, a fundamental attribute of the accounting professional. The concept is described as having a 'pervasive role' in analysing transactions (ASB 2000). While some transactions, such as a sale or a purchase, produce documents to prompt recording, there are situations when an event takes place before the documentation arrives or when there is no documentation at all. For instance, the ESB bill arrives every two months, but if we prepare a monthly income statement we cannot ignore that electricity has been used and must therefore recognise one month's expense. Another example of a problem tackled by accrual accounting arises when a customer pays for a product or service in advance of delivery; clearly the business has an obligation (a liability) until the product or service is delivered. Understanding the accrual concept arms us in responding to these situations.

Because the accrual concept demands sound judgment on the part of the accounting professional, the concept is at the heart of the corporate governance challenge. At what point has a transaction taken place, or been *realised,* and when should it be *recognised*?

We will study the situations requiring the accrual basis and apply the mechanics of the double entry system to capture the adjustments. It will become apparent that the concept provides ample opportunities for abuse, and rereading the section on realisation and recognition principles in Chapter 2 (pp. 22–31) is recommended at this point.

# THE ACCRUALS CONCEPT: AN OVERVIEW

The **accrual concept** (often referred to as **matching principle**) is one of the fundamental concepts of accounting. As discussed in Chapter 2, we understand the concept to mean that income and expenses should be matched together and dealt with in the income statement for the period to which they relate, regardless of the period in which the cash was received or paid. So we have matching in two ways:
- **Matching by time:** Recognising the expense in the period in which it occurs.
- **Matching of revenues and expenses**: Matching the expense to the revenue to which it relates.

This theory confirms for us that adjusting entries will be required if we are to have a correct set of financial statements. You will recall from Chapter 2 that on completing a trial balance, we then have the basis for creating the financial statements. We also examined one adjustment to the trial balance (relating to stock) to come up with an adjusted trial balance.

In this chapter we look at additional adjustments: the adjusting entries are classified as either **accruals** or **prepayments**. The topics of **depreciation** and **bad debts**, which are themselves accrual items, are treated in separate sections on account of their complexity.

## Realisation versus recognition

The terms 'realisation' and 'recognition' are not the same. For a sale or expense amount to be recognised, the transaction must be judged to have taken place, or realised. One commentator discerns the transaction to be a '**critical event**' that is **measurable** (Revsine *et al.* 2005). When these conditions are in place, the sale or expense has been realised at that point and we proceed to recognise it in the accounts.

**Self-Assessment Questions 1**

1. What is the difference between the cash basis of accounting and the accrual basis of accounting?
2. If a business sold a product in March but did not get paid until April, which month's profit and loss account will show the sale?

## ACCRUALS

There are two types of accruals:

- **Accrued revenues:** Revenues earned but not recorded and awaiting receipt of payment.
- **Accrued expenses:** Expenses incurred but not recorded nor paid for.

### Accrued revenues

These revenues may accrue with the passing of time, as in the case of interest earned, or they may result from services that were performed but not yet billed. They will require an adjusting entry to increase the debtor account and also to increase the revenue account.

Cosmos Company had not billed a client for €1,000 in research services carried out in March. This will require an adjusting entry for 31 March as follow

| March 31 | Dr | Debtors | 1,000 | |
|----------|-----|-----------------|-------|-------|
|          | Cr  | Service revenue |       | 1,000 |

Failure to make these adjustments will cause the assets and the capital section in the balance sheet and revenues and net income in the P&L statement to be understated.

*Why the capital section in the balance sheet? Remember that the net profit belongs to the owners of the business and is therefore added to the capital section.*

### Accrued expenses

These are expenses not yet paid for nor recorded at the end of the period. Examples of these expenses are interest, taxes, rent and salaries. They represent obligations on the part of the company requiring adjustments to the liabilities in the balance sheet, and to expenses in the P&L statement, at the end of the period.

Let's take a closer look at these typical examples:

- **Accrued salaries:** End of the month is on Wednesday, but payday is not until Friday. If payday is a weekly event covering the period from Monday to Friday, an adjustment must be made for salary expense incurred up to Wednesday.

  For example, the weekly payroll at Morris Ltd is €15,000. By the end of Wednesday, three days of salary expense will have been incurred and must be accrued as follows:

| March 31 | Dr | Salary expense | 9,000 | |
|----------|----|----------------|-------|-----|
| | Cr | Salary payable | | 9,000 |

Notice that we have accrued not only the expense but also the liability called **salary payable**.

- **Accrued interest**: A €100,000 loan with an interest rate of 12 per cent per annum is due for total repayment within nine months. As each month goes by, interest is accruing on the loan at €1,000 per month (100,000 × 12 per cent divided by 12 months = €1,000). The adjustment required is as follows:

| March 31 | Dr | Interest expense | 1,000 | |
|----------|----|------------------|-------|-----|
| | Cr | Interest payable | | 1,000 |

These adjusting entries will prevent liabilities in the balance sheet and expenses in the P&L from being understated. Accountants need systems to remind them to accrue for these items, and as we will discuss in Chapter 12, the independent auditor will pay close attention to these end-of-month transactions.

## Self-Assessment Question 2

1. Carla Computer Graphics is closing its books for the year ended 30 June.
   - On 30 June, the company owes salaries of €5,000, payment due on 1 July.
   - Carla has a loan of €60,000 with a rate of 10 per cent per annum.
   - Unrecorded revenue in June totalled €2,100.
     Prepare the adjusting entries for 30 June.

## The implications for corporate governance

The potential for error or manipulation through the letter versus the spirit of the law is present when applying the accrual concept. This is because the use of judgment is considerable. Failing to capture expenses, either mistakenly through bad controls or through deliberate intent, will overstate profits (Hawkins 1998). Accordingly, it is not only reported numbers that are scrutinised, but also the extent of judgment used.

# PREPAYMENTS

There are two categories of prepayments, both of which require adjusting entries:

- **Prepaid expenses:** Expenses paid in advance and recorded as an asset until the expense is realised.
- **Unearned revenues:** Cash received in advance and recorded as a liability until revenue is earned.

## Prepaid expenses

These arise when payments for expenses are made in advance and will therefore benefit more than one accounting period. We can only expense them, however, when the expense has taken place. At the time that we make the payment we have merely taken cash out of the asset (cash) and transferred into another asset called **prepaid**. Examples of prepayments are insurance, rent and supplies. When payment is made, the double entry transaction is as follow

| January 1 | Prepaid rent | 12,000 | |
| | Cash | | 12,000 |
| *(One year's rent paid in advance)* | | | |

Keep in mind that the company has not yet had the benefit of the rent and the transaction is really a reduction in one asset (cash) and the creation of a new one (prepaid rent). As the months go by, the prepaid expense will expire and the business will then be entitled to recognise the expense on a monthly basis, as follows:

| | | **Debit** | **Credit** |
| --- | --- | --- | --- |
| February 28 | Rent expense | 1,000 | |
| | Prepaid rent | | 1,000 |
| *(Rent expense for February)* | | | |

As the expense is **realised**, the above entry **recognises** it. Eventually, the asset **prepaid rent** gets reduced, and by 30 June the balance in the account will stand at €6,000, having been reduced by six months of the expense of €1,000 per month.

This adjustment prevents assets from being overstated and expenses from being understated.

## Unearned revenues

These result from customers paying in advance for a product or service, and until the company delivers, it must regard these advance payments as liabilities.

Let's assume that on 1 May a company is paid €2,400 in advance for providing landscaping services to a client over the next twelve months. This original transaction is captured with the following double entry:

|  |  | Debit | Credit |
|---|---|---|---|
| May 1 | Cash | 2,400 | |
| | Unearned revenue | | 2,400 |
| (*Landscape services paid in advance*) | | | |

Over the next twelve months the liability account (**unearned revenue**) will be reduced, as the landscape company will then be entitled to recognise revenue. So, after one month this recognition is captured with this entry:

|  |  | Debit | Credit |
|---|---|---|---|
| May 31 | Unearned revenue | 200 | |
| | Revenue | | 200 |
| (*One month's revenue*) | | | |

By making this adjustment, revenue and income will not be understated and liabilities will not be overstated.

## Self-Assessment Question 3

1. Rockport Construction has the following items in its trial balance as at 30 June.

| | Debit | Credit |
|---|---|---|
| Prepaid insurance | 3,600 | |
| Office supplies | 2,800 | |
| Unearned revenue | | 8,200 |

Prepare the adjusting entries for June if analysis shows that:
(a) Insurance runs at €100 per month.
(b) Supplies were counted at the end of June and totalled €800.
(c) Half of the unearned revenue was earned in June.

## Summary of the four relationships

| Type of adjustment | Accounts before adjustments | Adjusting entry |
|---|---|---|
| Prepaid expenses | Assets overstated. Expenses understated. | Debit expenses. Credit assets. |
| Unearned revenues | Liabilities overstated. Revenues understated. | Debit liabilities. Credit revenues. |
| Accrued revenues | Assets understated. Revenues understated. | Debit assets. Credit revenues. |
| Accrued expenses | Expenses understated. Liabilities understated. | Debit expenses. Credit liabilities. |

## The implications for corporate governance

In service businesses or those entities with significant revenue from maintenance agreements, there is the potential to inadvertently or otherwise treat payments in advance as revenues in the period of payment. This will perpetuate two errors. Firstly, profits will be overstated, and secondly, the obligation (a liability) to the customer is ignored. The abuse of this aspect of the accrual concept has figured prominently in many of the more noted scandals, such as Enron, Cable & Wireless and WorldCom.

Consider revenue recognition at Enron. The company generated its revenues by signing contracts that provided revenues over several years into the future (BBC 2002). When the accrual concept is applied against a five-year contract, the accountant must determine the rate of the revenue stream when deciding on the amount to be recognised in a period. Is it an equal amount every year, or is a greater portion earned in the earlier years? Enron simply took the total revenue stream from a multiyear contract and recognised it in the first year. As it sought to continue meeting analysts' expectations, it declared in one instance that it had built a pipeline (never built) in the jungles of South America and proceeded to recognise a twenty-year revenue stream in its first year of operation. This fraud, of course, is not the fault of the accrual concept. The concept was abused, a potential that should have been addressed by the independent auditor.

## DEPRECIATION

As we stated earlier in this chapter, depreciation is an accrual item. It is one of those expenses that is not prompted by a document such as an invoice or a receipt, therefore the accountant must remember to capture it at the end of each period.

A review of the assets owned by companies will indicate assets such as equipment, vehicles and buildings as having useful lives of several years. These items provide a benefit over a number of years and are therefore recorded as assets rather than as expenses. Over time, however, these assets lose their value through wear and tear and this loss, referred to as **depreciation**, must be recorded as an expense.

## Allocation of the expense

What is the accounting rationale for recording depreciation? How can loss in value be proven unless the asset is sold? How do we reflect the whole process in the financial statements? We will see that certain assumptions can be made that logically reflect the physical deterioration and thus allow us to capture depreciation as an expense.

From an accounting perspective, the key characteristic of depreciation is that it is an allocation concept (O'Regan 1998), not a valuation concept. We depreciate an asset to allocate its cost to the future periods of its use. No attempt is made to reflect the actual change in the value of the asset.

In this way we are satisfying the matching principle: a portion of the asset's cost is reported as an expense during each period of the asset's useful life.

## Calculation of the expense

Some essential information is required to calculate the depreciation expense:
- original cost of the asset
- useful life of the asset
- scrap or disposal value.

Of the three elements, the original cost is the only item that the accountant is sure of. The other items are estimates based on past experience.

EXAMPLE

Earth Movers Ltd purchases a new truck for €100,000 on 1 January 2005 and determines that it will have a life of ten years. It also determines that the truck will have a disposal value of €10,000 at the end of that time.

We will calculate the depreciation expense for the first two years and provide the resulting journal entries. We will also show the financial statement presentation for the end of each year.

We are going to assume that the loss in value is consistent over the ten years. The depreciation method in this case is called the **straight line** method. We are also going to assume that Earth Movers Ltd will dispose of the truck for €10,000.

Firstly, let's show the entries to purchase the truck.

| 2005 | | Debit | Credit |
|---|---|---|---|
| Jan 1 | Truck | 100,000 | |
| | Cash | | 100,000 |
| (Purchase of a truck with cash) | | | |

After one year we calculate the depreciation expense using the straight line method, as follows:

$$\frac{\text{cost of asset} - \text{disposal value}}{\text{life of asset in years}} = \frac{\text{€}100,000 - \text{€}10,000}{10} = \text{€}9,000 \text{ depreciation expense}$$

Notice that the disposal amount is subtracted first from the cost before determining the annual expense.

The double entry to capture the depreciation expense will be at the end of its first year:

| 2005 | | Debit | Credit |
|---|---|---|---|
| Dec 31 | Depreciation expense | 9,000 | |
| | Accumulated depreciation | | 9,000 |
| (Depreciation expense on truck) | | | |

Eventually the depreciation expense amount will be transferred to the P&L account and will be listed among the expenses in the P&L financial statement. The **accumulated depreciation** account, as the name suggests, will accumulate the depreciation expense and will continue to exist as long as the asset exists. Its place among the accounts is better understood when we indicate it in the financial statement presentation. But firstly, let's look at the T-account itself.

| Accumulated depreciation account | | | |
|---|---|---|---|
| **December 2005** | | **December 2005** | |
| Balance c/d | 9,000 | Dec 31  P&L a/c | 9,000 |
| | | Balance b/d | 9,000 |

From there we go to the financial statement presentation at the end of the first year, which in the case of assets is the balance sheet as at 31 December 2005.

| (Extract) as at 31 December 2005 | | | |
|---|---|---|---|
| Fixed asset | Cost | Accumulated depreciation | Net book value (NBV) |
| Truck | 100,000 | 9,000 | 91,000 |

The accumulated depreciation is a credit balance and it reduces the original cost of the truck. It is another example of a **contra account**.

## Self-Assessment Questions 4

1.  What does it mean that depreciation is an allocation concept rather than a valuation concept?
2.  Distinguish between **depreciation expense** and **accumulated depreciation.**

In the second year (2006), we capture the expense again as follows:

| 2006 | | Debit | Credit |
|---|---|---|---|
| Dec 31 | Depreciation expense | 9,000 | |
| | Accumulated depreciation | | 9,000 |
| (Depreciation expense on truck) | | | |

This is exactly what happened in the previous year. The balance in the accumulated depreciation account, however, has grown as follows:

| Accumulated depreciation account | | | | | |
|---|---|---|---|---|---|
| 2006 | | € | 2006 | | € |
| | | | Jan 1 | Balance b/d | 9,000 |
| | Balance c/d | 18,000 | Dec 31 | P&L a/c | 9,000 |
| | | | | | |
| | | | | Balance b/d | 18,000 |

This will further reduce the NBV for the truck in the balance sheet:

| (Extract) as at 31 December 2006 | | | |
|---|---|---|---|
| Fixed asset | Cost | Accumulated depreciation | Net book value (NBV) |
| Truck | 100,000 | 18,000 | 82,000 |

This presentation is very illuminating, as it gives some idea of the age of assets and whether they need to be replaced.

## Original cost, book value and market value

Some clarifying comments may be appropriate at this time. The **original,** or **historical, cost** is entered into the accounts as demanded by the **historical cost principle** and it must be shown in the balance sheet when calculating the net book value (NBV).

The **book value,** or net book value, is defined as the historical cost less the accumulated depreciation. The book value is often referred to as the **carrying value**. The NBV will always be shown on the balance sheet.

The **market value** is in most cases an educated guess as to the real value of an asset. When the asset is sold, then its market value will be known. Because depreciation is an **allocation** concept and not a value concept, the market value in general is not an issue for an existing asset.

## Self-Assessment Question 5

1. An asset is purchased for €20,000 with an estimated useful life of five years with zero scrap value. Depreciation is by the straight line method. What is the NBV of the asset at the end of year two?

## Disposal of an asset

Fixed assets are not bought with the intention of reselling them. However, the time will come when they are regarded as no longer useful and they will have to be disposed of.

This is the juncture at which **market value** materialises and is compared with the NBV at the time of disposal. If the proceeds from the sale exceed the NBV, then a profit or gain has been made. The opposite situation will result in a loss.

As we will see, a number of issues arise that must be dealt with. For instance, an asset has been removed from the plant and therefore it must be removed from the books. How is this processed? Cash may have been received and a loss may have resulted. How is this captured in the books?

## USE OF A DISPOSAL ACCOUNT

A **disposal account** is opened when an asset is sold. It conveniently pulls together three key numbers:

- the (original) cost of the asset
- the accumulated depreciation to date
- the proceeds from the sale.

As the following example shows, the remaining balance will be a profit or loss and will be transferred to the P&L to close out the disposal account.

### EXAMPLE

A printing press purchased for €10,000 and with accumulated depreciation to date of €8,000 was sold for €3,000 on 1 July 2005.

We will provide all the journal entries used to process this transaction correctly and show the movement in the relevant accounts.

| 2005 | | Debit | Credit |
|---|---|---|---|
| Juy 1 | Cash | 3,000 | |
| | Disposal account | | 3,000 |
| (Proceeds from sale of asset) | | | |
| | Disposal acccount | 10,000 | |
| | Asset: Printing press | | 10,000 |
| (Asset removed at original cost) | | | |
| | Accumulated depreciation | 8,000 | |
| | Disposal account | | 8,000 |
| (Close out accumulated depreciation on sold asset) | | | |

Was there a gain or a loss in this transaction? Before we examine the mechanics of the disposal account, let's understand intuitively what is going on.

What was the NBV of the asset?

| | |
|---|---|
| Cost | 10,000 |
| Less accumulated depreciation | 8,000 |
| NBV | 2,000 |

Now, how much did the company receive for the machine?

| | |
|---|---|
| Cash received | 3,000 |
| **Gain on disposal** | **1,000** |

In other words, at date of disposal the **market value** of the printing press exceeded its **net book value**. This gain is captured with the following entry:

| 2005 | | Debit | Credit |
|---|---|---|---|
| July 1 | Disposal account | 1,000 | |
| | P&L account | | 1,000 |
| *(Closing out the disposal account)* | | | |

Notice how this entry closes out the disposal account and transfers the gain to the P&L account. The gain will be disclosed in the income statement, usually after the gross profit.

We can now look at all of the movements in the **disposal account** and readily see how a disposal is processed in the accounts:

| | | Disposal account | | | | |
|---|---|---|---|---|---|---|
| **2005** | | € | **2005** | | | € |
| July 1 | Asset a/c | 10,000 | July 1 | Cash a/c | | 3,000 |
| July 1 | P&L a/c | 1,000 | July 1 | Accum deprec | | 8,000 |
| | | 11,000 | | | | 11,000 |

Before the final entry was made, the right side exceeded the left side (therefore a gain), thus triggering recognition of the gain in the P&L account. Had it been disposed of at a loss, the amount would be a credit in the disposal account and debited to the P&L account. Loss on disposal is presented among the operating expenses in the income statement.

## Self-Assessment Questions 6

1. What are the three accounts that feature in the disposal account to determine whether an asset was sold for a gain or a loss?
2. Calculate a gain or loss in this situation: a truck costing €100,000 was sold after three years for €25,000. When it was purchased, it was deemed to have a useful life of five years and zero scrap value.
3. Explain how a gain or loss comes to be disclosed in the income statement (P&L statement).

## BAD DEBTS

The final post-trial balance adjustment concerns bad debts, a possibility faced by all businesses that sell on credit. Good management usually minimises write-offs but rarely eliminates them.

### An overview

In any business there is always the risk of debtors not being able to pay for goods that were sold on credit. Even long-time customers may suddenly go through a bad patch that strains a relationship going back many years. The issue brings management skill in two areas into focus:

- extending credit
- estimating a realistic level of doubtful accounts.

Although we are mostly concerned with the second area, good credit control demands an analytical eye when extending credit and maintaining a regular review of payment history so that problems can be spotted on a timely basis. Management must produce the rationale for determining the doubtful debt inherent in any debtor balance. This sheds light on the decision-making process concerning debtors (Heneghan and O'Regan 2000):

- What are the criteria for issuing credit?
- Does management examine outstanding debtors regularly?
- When does management regard a debt as doubtful?
- Does management have a good estimate of what is inherently doubtful in its debtor portfolio?

We will distinguish between:

- dealing with specific debtors that are bad debts
- determining what is doubtful in the total portfolio of debtors.

## Specific bad debt

Debts that cannot be collected are called **bad debts**. They may result from bankruptcy or from fraud. Regardless of the reason, they are accounted for by:
- removing the debtor from the accounts
- indicating the lost amount in the income statement by means of the bad debt expense account.

The journal entry is as follows:
- DR bad debts expense account
- CR debtors account.

Management may be very reluctant to write off a debtor, hoping against hope that the customer will come good. But if the probability is that the account is lost, the **prudence concept** will insist on recognising the loss.

## Provision for doubtful debts

We have discussed the situation where an individual debtor is deemed to be bad, forcing the business to write it off. Does this complete our consideration of doubtful accounts? Do we assume that once a bad debtor is written off, the remaining debtors are fine?

Let's consider for a moment the whole area of **risk**. Most businesses have to extend credit to attract customers if they want their businesses to grow. They will also require credit to be extended to them. Successful businesses, which have a significant number of debtors, pay close attention to their asset so that if a debtor has a problem repaying, the business will know about it at the earliest possible moment. The fact remains that there is risk in extending credit: businesses can minimise it but never eliminate it.

How, then, do we account for this risk? A business may identify debtors who are having trouble repaying or at least are slow in making payments. There is always the possibility of those accounts going bad, while not yet a probability. In addition to this consideration, we must accept that inherent in any portfolio of debtors is a weakness and that over a number of years, experience will show that a number of accounts eventually go bad. The **prudence concept** requires that management make a **best-faith estimate** of what this weakness is and set up (or set aside) a **provision for doubtful debts**. This effort calls for sound judgment on the part of the accountant together with a conservative view of things.

### Self-Assessment Question 7

1. Explain why there is a need to estimate a provision for doubtful debt even though individual bad debt customers cannot be identified for certain.

## Establishing the debt provision

Let's examine a trading company that has completed its first year of business and has amassed a €500,000 debtor balance by year-end. Even if individual doubtful debtors are not apparent, common sense and experience will conclude that some accounts are destined to be doubtful. The loss may not assert itself within the year of business, but it may arise in the next year. By availing of the prudence principle, the company makes a conservative and educated guess as to the size of loss. It then adheres to the matching principle by setting up the provision at the end of this first year of business.

Management determines that 3 per cent of the portfolio is doubtful – that's €15,000 (3 per cent × €500,000). Even though it is in its first year of business, information on other comparable businesses in the same business sector is usually available. This qualifies as an acceptable rationale for making the estimate.

The transaction is captured with the following double entry:

| 2005 | | Debit | Credit |
|------|------|-------|--------|
| Dec 31 | Bad debt expense | 15,000 | |
| | Provision for doubtful debts | | 15,000 |
| *(Creation of provision for DD)* | | | |

We discuss the factors that prompt the change in the account balance later in this section.

This account (**provision for doubtful debts**) has set aside an amount to cover future losses. Therefore, the account will exist for as long as the business has debtors, although the balance in the provision may change.

The relevant accounts will look like this when the above entries are made:

### Debtors account

| 2005 | | € | 2005 | | € |
|------|------|------|------|------|------|
| Dec 31 | Sales | 500,000 | | | |

### Bad debt expense account

| 2005 | | € | 2005 | | € |
|------|------|------|------|------|------|
| Dec 31 | Provision for DD | 15,000 | | | |

### Provision for doubtful debts account

| 2005 | | € | 2005 | | € |
|------|---|---|------|---|---|
|  |  |  | Dec 31 | Bad debt exp | 15,000 |

Once these accounts are balanced (closed out) at the end of the year, they look like this:

### Debtors account

| 2005 | | € | 2005 | | € |
|------|---|---|------|---|---|
| Dec 31 | Sales | 500,000 | Dec 31 | Balance c/d | 500,000 |
|  |  | 500,000 |  |  | 500,000 |
| 2006 |  |  |  |  |  |
| Jan 1 | Balance b/d | 500,000 |  |  |  |

### Bad debts account

| 2005 | | € | 2005 | | € |
|------|---|---|------|---|---|
| Dec 31 | Provision for DD | 15,000 | Dec 31 | P&L account | 15,000 |

Like all expenses, the bad debt expense account is closed out to the P&L account with a credit entry and will commence on 1 January 2006 with a zero balance. It is disclosed among the operating expenses in the income statement for the year ended 31 December 2005.

### Provision for doubtful debts account

| 2005 | | € | 2005 | | € |
|------|---|---|------|---|---|
| Dec 31 | Balance c/d | 15,000 | Dec 31 | Bad debt a/c | 15,000 |
|  |  | 15,000 |  |  | 15,000 |
|  |  |  | 2006 |  |  |
|  |  |  | Jan 1 | Balance b/d | 15,000 |

Notice that the balance in the provision is a credit balance. As we explained earlier, the **provision for doubtful debts** will exist as long as the business has debtors and therefore it is logical that the balance (credit balance) be presented as a deduction from debtors (debit balance) in the balance sheet. Because of this presentation, the provision is one more example of a **contra account**.

The presentation in the balance sheet will look like this:

---

**Extract from the balance sheet as on 31 December 2005**

Current assets

| | | |
|---|---|---|
| Stock | | 60,000 |
| Debtors | 500,000 | |
| Less: Provision for doubtful debts | 15,000 | |
| Net book value of debtors | | 485,000 |
| Cash at bank | | 100,000 |

---

## A change in the provision balance

What happens when management decides in the next year to increase the provision to 4 per cent of the debtor balance at the end of the year? The balance on the debtors account is €400,000, and at 4 per cent the bad debt level is anticipated at €16,000 (4 per cent × €400,000). Because a provision already exists for €15,000, management only needs to increase it by €1,000.

The double entry for this is as follows:

---

| 2006 | | Debit | Credit |
|---|---|---|---|
| Dec 31 | Bad debt expense | 1,000 | |
| | Provision for doubtful debts | | 1,000 |
| *(Increase in the provision for DD)* | | | |

---

How will the various accounts look as a result? The movements in the debtors account are added to explain how the balance might have gone to €400,000. It would appear that there were credit sales of €900,000 in 2006 and cash paid by debtors totalling €1 million over the same period.

---

**Debtors account**

| 2006 | | € | 2006 | | € |
|---|---|---|---|---|---|
| Jan 1 | Balance c/d | 500,000 | Dec 31 | Cash | 1,000,000 |
| Dec 31 | Sales | 900,000 | Dec 31 | Balance c/d | 400,000 |
| | | 1,400,000 | | | 1,400,000 |
| **2007** | | | | | |
| Jan 1 | Balance b/d | 400,000 | | | |

---

### Bad debts account

| 2006 | | € | 2006 | | € |
|------|---|---|------|---|---|
| Dec 31 | Provision for DD | 1,000 | Dec 31 | P&L account | 1,000 |

### Provision for doubtful debts account

| 2006 | | € | 2006 | | € |
|------|---|---|------|---|---|
| Dec 31 | Balance c/d | 16,000 | Jan 1 | Balance b/d | 15,000 |
| | | 16,000 | Dec 31 | Bad debt a/c | 1,000 |
| | | | | | 16,000 |
| | | | 2007 | | |
| | | | Jan 1 | Balance b/d | 16,000 |

The balance sheet extract will look like this for 31 December 2006:

| | | |
|---|---|---|
| Current assets | | |
| Stock | | 51,000 |
| Debtors | 400,000 | |
| Less: Provision for doubtful debts | 16,000 | |
| Net book value of debtors | | 384,000 |
| Cash at bank | | 80,000 |

What would happen if the provision for doubtful debts needed to be reduced? Very simply, the business would:

- **debit** provision for doubtful debts accounts
- **credit** bad debts expense account.

## Combining a change in the provision and a bad debt write-off

When there is a write-off, how does it affect the provision for doubtful debts? How do the accounts look when all the double entries have been made? You may have noticed already that the **bad debt expense account** has been affected twice, albeit in two separate situations. Let's use the above details for the year 2006 and add the event of a debtor balance of €2,000 being written off on 15 October.

As we stated earlier, a write-off is accounted for as follows:

| 2006 | | Debit | Credit |
|---|---|---|---|
| Oct 15 | Bad debt expense | 2,000 | |
| | Debtors | | 2,000 |
| *(Write off of debtor account)* | | | |

By 31 December, the debtor balance has been reduced to €398,000 (400,000 – 2,000). The provision will change slightly as the 4 per cent is calculated on the €398,000 to provide a provision of €15,920. As the balance in the account is €15,000, the increase will be €920 and is captured with this double entry:

| 2006 | | Debit | Credit |
|---|---|---|---|
| Dec 31 | Bad debt expense | 920 | |
| | Provision for doubtful debts | | 920 |
| *(Increase in the provision for DD)* | | | |

The bad debt expense account now has two entries in the debit side that were entered prior to the closing entry to the P&L:

**Bad debt expense account**

| 2006 | | € | 2006 | | |
|---|---|---|---|---|---|
| Oct 15 | Debtors | 2,000 | | | |
| Dec 31 | Provision for DD | 920 | Dec 31 | P&L account | 2,920 |
| | | 2,920 | | | 2,920 |

This may seem unusual to have the write-off and the increase in the provision aggregated in the expense account. However, in keeping with the prudence concept, the bad debt expense account has captured an actual write-off *and* the likelihood of write-offs inherent in the *remaining* debtor balance.

## Self-Assessment Question 8

1. World Set Communication Ltd is a young company that started operating in 2001. By 2003 a new accounting firm helped World Set to gets its accounting system in order.

   In regard to doubtful accounts, the accountant firm recommended that the provision for 2003 should be 5 per cent of debtors. In 2004 the provision remained at the same rate. However, in 2005 the company felt it could reduce it to 3 per cent of debtors.

   The debtor balances for each are as follows:
   - 2003: €500,000
   - 2004: €600,000
   - 2005: €700,000.

Show the provision for doubtful debts account and complete an extract from the company's balance sheet for each of the three years mentioned.

## Summary of adjustments

Bad and doubtful debts are usually presented as post-trial balance adjustments.

1. **Write off bad debt**. The double entry adjustment:
   - shows the bad debt as an expense in the P&L
   - deducts the amount of bad debt from debtors.

2. **Creating provision for doubtful accounts (first time)**. Calculate the amount of the provision by applying the percentage to the debtor balance. The double entry adjustment:
   - increases bad debt expense in the P&L
   - creates the provision, which is presented as a deduction from the debtors balance in the balance sheet.

3. **Increase or decrease the existing provision**. Firstly, calculate the amount of the provision. Compare this number with the existing provision amount, and if the latter is lower, increase the provision. The double adjustment:
   - increases bad debt expense account in the P&L
   - increases the existing provision, which in turn is presented as a deduction from debtors in the balance sheet.

This is the type of question that you are expected to answer in an examination setting. Because there is the need to process the information efficiently in order to complete the requirements on time, organise your rough work (called **workings** in accounting) to assist with this. For instance, when calculating the depreciation expense for the P&L, see whether you can also anticipate the accumulated depreciation for the balance sheet. The solution to the question attempts to demonstrate this technique.

## Self-Assessment Question 9

Carmen Cars Company has the following trial balance as of 31 December 2005. You are required to prepare a profit and loss account and a balance sheet for the year ended 31 December 2005.

|  | Debit € | Credit € |
|---|---|---|
| Share capital |  | 10,840 |
| Debtors | 6,530 |  |
| Creditors |  | 5,210 |
| Sales |  | 71,230 |
| Purchases | 29,760 |  |
| Stock 1 Jan 2005 | 4,340 |  |
| Rental | 800 |  |
| Heat and light | 2,650 |  |
| Wages | 8,250 |  |
| Bad debt expense | 230 |  |
| Provision for bad debt |  | 280 |
| General expenses | 2,340 |  |
| Motor expenses | 3,240 |  |
| Premises at cost | 30,000 |  |
| Fixtures | 8,000 |  |
| Vehicles | 12,000 |  |
| Accumulated depreciation: 1 Jan 2005 |  |  |
| Premises |  | 2,400 |
| Fixtures |  | 1,600 |
| Vehicles |  | 5,400 |
| Cash | 820 |  |
| Loan |  | 12,000 |
|  | 108,960 | 108,960 |

The following information was omitted from the trial balance:
● Stock as at 31 December 2005 was €4,870.
● Light and heat due €120 and general expenses due €80, at year end.
● Depreciation for the year as follows:
    (a) Premises: 2 per cent on cost.
    (b) Fixtures: 10 per cent on cost.
    (c) Vehicles: calculated to be €1,320.
● Bad debt written off for €130 and provision for bad debt to be at 5 per cent of remaining debtors.
● Loan interest due of €600.

## CHAPTER REVIEW

At this point we begin to make the distinction between **when a transaction takes place** and **when money changes hands** relating to that transaction. We have considered expenses up to now as taking place when we pay for them. This is the cash basis of accounting. However, using the accrual basis of accounting, a business that buys goods in March but agrees to pay for them in the following month must recognise that purchase as a transaction in the March books.

The **accrual concept** (often referred to as the **matching concept**) is the fundamental principle guiding us in analysing these types of transactions. The requirement for professional judgment is crucial as good corporate governance relies on the accrual basis to be applied as accurately as possible. This matching is reflected in two ways. Firstly, expenses are recognised over the period in which they occur. Secondly, expenses are matched with the revenue incurred in the pursuit of those revenues. Thus we find that if we pay one year's rent in advance and we prepare monthly statements, we will have to adjust the expense to one-twelfth for each month.

These adjustments are divided into **accruals** and **prepayments**. Accruals called **accrued revenues** entail revenues earned but not yet paid to the business; **accrued expenses** are accruals that describe expenses incurred but not yet paid for by the business. Prepayments, too, are of two types: **prepaid expenses** are those that have been paid for in advance by the business, whereas **unearned revenues** arise when customers pay in advance for services or products. Until the business fulfils its obligation, an unearned revenue is a liability of the business. The prepaid expense is an asset until the expense is incurred.

Having established the rationale for the accrual basis of accounting, we are able to extend this thinking to two concerns of most businesses: **depreciation** and **bad debts**. We saw that as equipment is used, it incurs wear and tear; logically we can allocate this in each period as an expense to the income statement (P&L). The bad debts expense recognises that in all credit sales, there is a risk that a business will not get paid for such sales. The write-off of a bad debt takes place several months after the initial sale, yet the accrual concept demands that we make an estimate of this inherent risk at the end of every period and call it a **provision for doubtful debts**. The first estimate is processed as an expense (bad debt expense). Changes to the provision in subsequent periods will be debited or credited to the expense account. Good governance is achieved when profit is not overstated or liabilities understated. The accrual basis strives to present the truest view.

# SELF-ASSESSMENT QUESTION ANSWERS

## SAQ 1

1. In the cash basis of accounting, revenues and expenses are recognised at the point when cash from revenues is received and cash is paid out for expenses. The accrual basis of accounting, on the other hand, recognises revenues and expenses when they are earned and incurred, respectively.

2. Under the cash basis of accounting, the sale is recorded in April. With the accrual basis of accounting, the sale is recorded in March.

## SAQ 2

1. Adjusting entries for Carla Computer Graphics on 30 June:

|  | Debit | Credit |
|---|---|---|
| 1. Salary expense | 5,000 | |
| Salary payable | | 5,000 |
| | | |
| 2. Interest expense | 6,000 | |
| Interest payable | | 6,000 |
| | | |
| 3. Accounts receivable (debtors) | 2,100 | |
| Sales | | 2,100 |

## SAQ 3

Adjusting entries for Rockport Construction Co. on 30 June 2005:

|  | Debit | Credit |
|---|---|---|
| 1. Insurance expense | 100 | |
| Prepaid insurance | | 100 |
| | | |
| 2. Office supplies expense* | 2,000 | |
| Office supplies | | 2,000 |
| | | |
| 3. Unearned revenue** | 4,100 | |
| Sales | | 4,100 |

\*   If supplies balance was €2,800 in the asset account and the actual was calculated to be €800, then we must assume that €2,000 (2,800 − 800) was used up.

\*\* The liability account has been reduced by €4,100 as the business fulfilled 50 per cent of its obligation to customers who paid in advance (8,200 ÷ 2 = 4,100).

## SAQ 4

1. To capture the wear and tear in a physical asset that has a useful life of several years and expense it in a logical way requires us to estimate what this depreciation might be and allocate it to each of the years of useful life.

2. Depreciation expense captures the loss in value of a fixed asset in each year of the asset's existence. Like all expenses, it goes to the income statement. The account will have a zero balance at the beginning of each period. The accumulated depreciation account, on the other hand, accumulates the expense over the life of the asset and at the balance sheet date is presented as a contra account against the historical cost of the asset. The accumulated account will exist as long as there are fixed assets on the books.

## SAQ 5

1. $\dfrac{20,000 - 0 \text{ disposal value}}{5 \text{ years useful life}} = 4,000 \text{ depreciation yearly}$

After two years, accumulated depreciation grows to €8,000.

| Year 2 | | |
|---|---|---|
| | Cost | 20,000 |
| | Less accumulated depreciation | 8,000 |
| | NBV | 12,000 |

## SAQ 6

1. Cash, asset and accumulated depreciation accounts feature in double entries to the disposal account.

2. Yearly depreciation: €100,000 ÷ 5 years = 20,000
   Accumulated depreciation at disposal: €60,000

**NBV and gain/loss calculation:**

| | |
|---|---|
| Cost | €100,000 |
| Less accum dep | 60,000 |
| NBV | 40,000 |
| Proceeds | 25,000 |
| LOSS | €15,000 |

3. Depending on whether the debit or credit side in the disposal account has a greater balance, the lesser side will have a balance carried down to balance it out. This is the amount that will go to the P&L.

## SAQ 7

1. Inherent in any debtor balance is the risk that some customers will be unable to repay. A company will not be able to state with certainty who is going to go bad or when it will happen to a customer. Experience shows that when you sell on credit, a certain percentage will 'go south' and only close attention by management minimises the damage to the business. This percentage may fluctuate from one year to the next based on management's assessment of the risk, a risk that is always there.

## SAQ 8

You were asked to show the **provision for doubtful debts account** and to complete an extract from the balance sheet for the years 2003, 2004 and 2005.

**2003:** 500,000 × 5% = 25,000 = provision for doubtful debt

The double entry to process this is:

| 2003 | | Debit | Credit |
|---|---|---|---|
| Dec 31 | Bad debt expense | 25,000 | |
| | Provision for doubtful debts | | 25,000 |
| *(Create the provision for DD)* | | | |

| Balance sheet extract 2003 | |
|---|---|
| Debtors | 500,000 |
| Less: Provision for DD | 25,000 |
| | 475,000 |

**2004:**
600,000 × 5% = 30,000 = provision for doubtful debt

But the provision account has a balance of €25,000, therefore it must be increased by €5,000. The following double entry caters for that:

| 2004 | | Debit | Credit |
|---|---|---|---|
| Dec 31 | Bad debt expense | 5,000 | |
| | Provision for doubtful debts | | 5,000 |
| *(Increase in the provision for DD)* | | | |

The T-account for the **provision** will look like this:

| Provision for doubtful debts account | | | | | | |
|---|---|---|---|---|---|---|
| **2004** | | € | **2004** | | | € |
| Dec 31 | Balance c/d | 30,000 | Jan 1 | Balance b/d | | 25,000 |
| | | | Dec 31 | Bad debt exp | | 5,000 |
| | | | **2005** | | | |
| | | | Jan 1 | Balance b/d | | 30,000 |

**Balance sheet extract 2004**

| | |
|---|---|
| Debtors | 600,000 |
| Less: Provision for DD | 30,000 |
| | 570,000 |

**2005:** 700,000 × 3% = 21,000 = provision for doubtful debt

The new provision has been calculated at €21,000 and is less than the provision account that has a balance of €30,000. The account must therefore be decreased by €9,000 by means of the following double entry:

| **2005** | | **Debit** | **Credit** |
|---|---|---|---|
| Dec 31 | Provision for doubtful debts | 9,000 | |
| | Bad debt expense | | 9,000 |
| *(Decrease in the provision for DD)* | | | |

The **provision** account will look like this:

| Provision for doubtful debts account | | | | | |
|---|---|---|---|---|---|
| **2005** | | € | **2005** | | € |
| Dec 31 | Balance bad debt exp | 9,000 | Jan 1 | Balance b/d | 30,000 |
| Dec 31 | Balance c/d | 21,000 | | | 0 |
| | | 30,000 | | | 30,000 |
| | | | **2006** | | |
| | | | Jan 1 | Balance b/d | 21,000 |

**Balance sheet extract 2005**

| Debtors | 700,000 |
|---|---|
| Less provision for DD | 21,000 |
| | 679,000 |

## SAQ 9

As stated earlier, workings assist the preparer to complete the statements on a timely basis. Accountants maintain well-organised work papers as part of their work to support their conclusions. The use of the W annotation in the statements here, however, is only for the student's benefit and would not ordinarily appear in financial statements.

**Carmen Cars Ltd**

**Profit and loss account for the year ended 31 December 2005**

| | | € |
|---|---|---|
| Sales | | 71,230 |
| Opening stock | 4,340 | |
| Add: Purchases | 29,760 | |
| | 34,100 | |
| Less: Closing stock | 4,870 | |
| Cost of goods sold | | 29,230 |
| Gross profit | | 42,000 |
| | | |
| Less: Operating expenses: | | |
| Rental | 800 | |
| Heat and light **W1** | 2,770 | |
| General expenses **W1** | 2,420 | |
| Motor expenses | 3,240 | |
| Wages | 8,250 | |
| Bad debt expense **W3** | 400 | |
| Depreciation: | | |
| Premises **W2** | 600 | |
| Fixtures **W2** | 800 | |
| Vehicles **W2** | 1,320 | |
| Loan interest **W1** | 600 | |
| | | 21,200 |
| **Net profit** | | **20,800** |

Carmen Car Ltd

Balance sheet as at 31 December 2005

| | Cost | Accumulated depreciation (W2) | Net book value |
|---|---|---|---|
| **Fixed assets:** | | | |
| Premises | 30,000 | 3,000 | 27,000 |
| Fixtures | 8,000 | 2,400 | 5,600 |
| Vehicles | 12,000 | 6,720 | 5,280 |
| | 50,000 | 12,120 | 37,880 |
| | | | |
| **Current assets:** | | | |
| Stock | | 4,870 | |
| Debtors | 6,400 | | |
| Less provision for DD (W3) | 320 | 6,080 | |
| Cash | | 820 | |
| | | 11,770 | |
| **Current liabilities:** | | | |
| Creditors | 5,210 | | |
| Accruals (W1) | 800 | 6,010 | 5,760 |
| Net assets | | | 43,640 |
| | | | |
| **Financed by:** | | | |
| **Capital:** | | | |
| Share capital | | 10,840 | |
| Add net profit | | 20,800 | 31,640 |
| **Long-term liabilities:** | | | |
| Loan | | | 12,000 |
| Total capital and LT debt | | | 43,640 |

## Workings

### W1: The accruals adjustments:

| | | |
|---|---|---|
| Debit heat/light | 120 | |
| Debit gen expenses | 80 | |
| Debit interest expense | 600 | |
| Credit accruals | | 800 |

Heat/light:  2,650 + 120 = 2,770

Gen exp:  2,340 +  80 = 2,420

Remember: To increase an expense you debit the expense account. To increase a liability you credit the liability account (in this case it is the liability called accruals or accrued expenses).

**W2: Depreciation:**

| | 1<br>Cost | 2<br>Rate | 3<br>Expense | 4<br>Begin<br>accum | 5<br>End<br>accum | 6<br>NBV |
|---|---|---|---|---|---|---|
| Premises | 30,000 | @2 per cent | = 600 | 2,400 | 3,000 | 27,000 |
| Fixtures | 8,000 | @10 per cent | = 800 | 1,600 | 2,400 | 5,600 |
| Vehicles | 12,000 | n/a | = 1,320 | 5,400 | 6,720 | 5,280 |

**W3: Bad debt expense and provision:**

| | |
|---|---|
| Bad debt expense debit balance | 230 |
| Add write-off | 130 |
| Change in provision (ADD) see below | 40 |
| Total bad debt expense | 400 |

**Calculation of provision:**

| | |
|---|---|
| Debtors | 6,530 |
| Less write-off | 130 |
| End debtors | 6,400 |
| Provision | @ 5 per cent = 320; compare to beginning balance of 280 |

Must increase provision by 40 as follows:

| | Debit | Credit |
|---|---|---|
| Bad debt expense | 40 | |
| Provision for DD | | 40 |

# REFERENCES

Accounting Standards Board, *FRS 18 Accounting Policies*, London: ASB 2000.

BBC Television, *The Enron Story*, 4 April 2002.

Hawkins, D.F., *Corporate Financial Reporting and Analysis*, New York: Irwin/McGraw-Hill 1998.

Heneghan, J. and O'Regan, P., *Accounting*, Limerick: Centre for Project Management, University of Limerick 2000.

O'Regan, P., *Introduction to Accounting*, Limerick: The International Equine Institute, University of Limerick 1998.

Revsine, L., Collins, D. and Johnson, W., *Financial Reporting and Analysis*, Upper Saddle River, NJ: Pearson Education 2005.

# 6

# *Limited Companies*

**C
O
N
T
E
N
T
S**

# INTRODUCTION

Up to now we have been using the corporate or limited company form when referring to business entities. In doing so, we have completed the financial statements in somewhat simplistic terms. For instance, we have referred to the capital section of the balance sheet as **capital** or **shareholders funds** without mentioning the types of shares found there. We must go beyond this because a company is an independent legal entity, usually set up to pursue business activities (O'Connell 2003). It has certain powers that allows it to enter contracts, it can sue and it can be sued. In this chapter we will highlight the key characteristics of the limited company and also make reference to another entity type, the **sole trader**, to which the corporate form is compared.

The corporate form in Ireland is subject to a vast amount of law, referred to collectively as **the Companies Acts 1963 to 2003**. That the latest Acts, 2001 and 2003, have an enforcement character reflects the importance of understanding the obligations in running a company today. The Director of Corporate Enforcement makes the point that individuals who avail of the benefits and privileges of incorporation should be aware of the duties and responding duties that come with it (ODCE 2002). The accountant, particularly the financial controller, will carry a significant portion of that responsibility by setting up and maintaining proper accounts. Equally, the independent auditor is now obliged to report to the ODCE what he or she believes to be an indictable offence under the Companies Acts (Companies Act 2001, Section 8). The **corporate governance** issue should therefore be very clear to the accounting profession – to account for companies requires an understanding of their structure, their responsibilities and a penchant on the accountant's part for achieving the true and fair view in financial reporting.

> ### OBJECTIVES
>
> **When you have finished this chapter, you will be able to:**
> - understand how a limited company differs from other entities
> - complete the capital section of the company's balance sheet
> - understand appropriations and reserves
> - complete the income statement (P&L) and the balance sheet of a limited company.

# THE CORPORATE FORM

There are various types of companies. **Public limited companies (plc)** are usually large entities whose shares are quoted on the stock exchange; they may have thousands of shareholders. But the vast majority of companies are **private limited companies (Ltd)**, which may be large or small. Their shares are not traded on the stock exchange and they may not have more than fifty shareholders. The shares are usually confined to family members or friends. An advantage of this form is that in certain circumstances, it may not need to have its accounts audited.

Companies can also be classified by purpose. For instance, Dell Computers and Independent Newspapers are organised to pursue profits. The Society of St Vincent de Paul, on the other hand, is organised as a non-profit entity.

## Characteristics of a limited company

There are essentially three characteristics that distinguish the limited company from other business forms:

- It is owned by more than one individual; these individuals are called **shareholders**. If the company fails, the shareholders' losses are limited (hence the name **limited company**). They are not responsible for company debt.
- It is a separate legal entity, i.e. the company instead of the owners can be sued and can sue others.
- It is managed by directors, who need not be shareholders, and who are appointed at the annual general meeting (AGM).

## Public and private limited companies

As you learned above, companies can be either public or private. However, there are also public and private companies that are not limited. Without going into this too deeply, an unlimited company has many disadvantages, but the benefits, which include easier distribution of capital to shareholders, also include less mandatory disclosures to the Companies Registration Office (CRO), discussed below.

**Public limited companies (plc)** are usually large entities whose shares are quoted on the stock exchange. They are required to have 'public limited companies', or 'plc', after their names. Described as limited by shares, the minimum share capital required at present to start the company is €38,100 in Ireland.

In **private limited companies (Ltd)**, shares are not traded on the stock exchange. Most are small or medium-sized family businesses that sell shares to a small circle of family or friends. Transferring these shares, however, is restricted. While it can have two but no more than fifty shareholders, there are circumstances when one shareholder is allowed. This type of entity may also be exempt from filing company information to the Companies Registration Office, again under certain circumstances. As stated above, it may also be exempt from having its accounts audited (ODCE 2002).

*The vast majority of companies are private limited companies.*

### Self-Assessment Question 1

1. What are the characteristics that distinguish a limited company as an entity?

## Why are companies formed?

In answering this question, comparisons with the **sole trader** form readily come to mind. When considering incorporation, a look at some of the restraints on a sole trader business is reasonable. It must be stated, however, that the **sole trader** has been a key contributor to the domestic economy, an incubator, if you will, for the substantial entrepreneurial spirit that emerged in Ireland during the 1990s (Heneghan and O'Regan 2000). Therefore, one form or another is usually dictated by a number of factors, including size, type of business activity and the need to grow.

As you've seen, a company is a legal entity, separate from its owners. That limits the possibility of claims against the assets of its owners and places an onus on creditors to be careful when doing business with companies.

### Limited liability

On the last point above regarding growth, it is generally agreed that as a small business grows, the personal risk to the owner increases, which is a major drawback to developing a business. The emergence of **limited liability** limited the personal liability to owners. It also focused on the entity concept that separates the private affairs of owners from their public or business affairs. While the legal demands of setting up a company and maintaining compliance seem onerous, this is to be expected if investors are to be encouraged to invest. The privilege of limiting liability should more than compensate.

What are the restraints on a sole trader?

Just in case there is some confusion on the tax issue relating to the sole trader, it must be understood that sole traders are taxed when they present their personal tax returns. The drawings from the business represent income in the personal tax return of the sole trader.

- A sole trader is personally responsible for the debts of the business, so creditors can pursue the personal assets of the sole trader.
- A sole trader is limited in resources, particularly capital, and may also be limited in skills such as management and marketing. This lack of expertise may prevent the business from growing.
- The business is dependent on the sole trader.

A limited company, in contrast, can expand the number of owners to acquire additional funding or to acquire new skills. It generally has greater access to banks. Owners of the business can change without having any effect on the business.

Below is a further comparison between the two forms.

## Sole trader vs. limited company

|  | Sole trader | Limited company |
|---|---|---|
| Statutory regulation required? | None | Companies Acts |
| Who owns the business? | Sole trader | Shareholders |
| Who manages the business? | Sole trader | Board of directors appointed by shareholders |
| Is business a separate legal entity? | No | Yes |
| Does business change when owners change? | Yes | No |
| Is taxation an expense of the business? | No | Yes |
| How do owners extract profits from the business? | Drawings | Dividends |
| Is the business quoted on the stock exchange? | No | Yes (if a plc) |

## Self-Assessment Question 2

1. How does a sole trader differ from a limited company in regard to ownership?

# CAPITAL AND ITS FORMATION

We have stated that a publicly traded company can have thousands and even hundreds of thousands of shareholders. Those shareholders can include individuals and pension funds, so that today a wide variety of stakeholders have an interest in company performance. It is sobering to note that the value of the stock exchanges in the US prior to 2001 exceeded $15 trillion, but by early 2002 was reduced to just over $8 trillion. Many of these shares were invested in by Irish fund managers. Most countries place stringent demands on limited companies so that the public interest is protected and confidence is maintained. Readable financial statements that are informative and consistent in their preparation are expected to underline this confidence (Cadbury 1992).

## Formation of a company

There must be at least two individuals in any company, and invariably they will avail of the services of a solicitor to form a company according to their specifications. Certain information, as follows, must be submitted to the **Registrar of Companies** (also called the

Companies Registration Office, or CRO), which registers all companies formed in Ireland.

- Company name: The CRO may refuse if the name is already in use or it is offensive.
- A declaration that the company will conduct business in the state.
- Address of its place of business and its registered office.
- Confirmation that at least one director is resident in the state.
- Completion of the **memorandum of association** and **articles of association** (see below).

When this information is forwarded and approved, the CRO will issue a Certificate of Incorporation.

## Constitution of a company

Two documents, the **memorandum of association** and **articles of association,** form the constitution of the company. They are important documents because they encompass the internal rules of the company (ODCE 2002).

The **memorandum of association** defines the relationship between the company and any external parties. It also states the objectives of the company and the type of trade it will pursue. The amount of share capital invested in the company by the shareholders will also be stated, as will the maximum number of shares authorised for issuance and at what share price.

Authorised share capital refers to the maximum number of shares that can be issued by the company.

It contains five compulsory clauses:

1. **Name clause:** Contains the company name.
2. **Objects clause:** Lists the objectives of the company.
3. **Liability clause:** States whether it is a limited or unlimited company.
4. **Capital clause:** Indicates the company's authorised share capital.
5. **Association clause:** Contains a statement by those forming the company that they wish to form a company.

The memorandum becomes valid when it is printed, stamped, signed and witnessed.

The **articles of association** define the rights of shareholders, the rules of operation of the company and the rights and duties of owners and employees of the company. In effect, they govern relations between the company and its owners and among the owners themselves. The standard form for the articles is subdivided into a number of headings, such as:

- directors
- powers and duties of directors
- managing directors
- company secretary meetings
- votes of members.

As with the memorandum of association, the articles of association must be printed, stamped, signed by each of those who signed the memorandum and witnessed. Because companies actively seek capital, investors and lenders can feel comfortable knowing they are dealing with a legitimate entity.

## The *ultra vires* doctrine

The objects clause of the memorandum of association calls for particularly close attention by the prospective owners when drawing up objectives. If a company acts outside those objectives, it is said to be acting **ultra vires** (Latin for acting beyond one's legal powers). Therefore, the other party to a transaction considered *ultra vires* can render the transaction void (Callanan 1999). Even if the object clause is altered at a general meeting of the company and confirmed in court (through which it must be processed), the alteration cannot have a retrospective effect. This also means the *ultra vires* act cannot be ratified subsequently by the general meeting, even though the general meeting agreed to alter the objectives.

## Duties of a company

The law places certain duties on a company, confirming it as a separate legal entity. These principal duties are to:
- maintain proper books of accounts
- prepare annual accounts
- have an annual audit (there are exceptions)
- maintain certain registers and other key documents
- file certain documents with the Registrar of Companies
- hold a general meeting of the company.

These duties have been in place for many years. However, the Companies Act 2001 was required to actively enforce compliance with these duties through the Office of Director of Corporate Enforcement (ODCE). We will study corporate compliance in greater depth in Chapter 10.

## Share capital

Companies finance their operations in many ways. Limited companies raise money mainly by issuing shares. The purchasers of these shares become owners as a result. In line with the entity concept, the company will record the cash it receives from the sale of shares as an increase in cash. The corresponding credit or increase is to the account called **share capital** and is found in the **capital and reserves** section of the balance sheet. The share capital is a debt or liability, a unique liability in that it is owed to the owners (O'Regan 1998). So that the significance of this is understood, let's review the **entity concept** again:

- The entity concept states that the business is a separate entity to its owners and that the accounts must be kept from the perspective of the business, not from the owners' perspective.

We must distinguish between **authorised shares** (the maximum number authorised to be issued, as stated in the capital clause of the memorandum) and **shares issued**. This latter type reflects the number of shares that were actually issued.

### ORDINARY AND PREFERENCE SHARES

There are essentially two types of shares: **ordinary shares** and **preference shares**. Other types have evolved from these basic types.

The characteristics of ordinary shares are that:
- they are the most common type of share
- every company must have them
- ordinary shareholders can vote at company meetings
- ordinary shares may receive dividends, but are not usually entitled to them.

If the company goes into liquidation (goes out of business and its assets are sold off), other shareholder types take precedence over the rights of the ordinary shareholder.

€1 is an arbitrary amount used for this example.

They are listed in the **capital and reserves** section of the balance sheet and are usually described as 'ordinary shares of €1 each'. The €1 value is called the **nominal value** and is included in the capital clause of the memorandum of association. When the shares are sold (issued) for the first time, the **issue price** may or may not be equal to the nominal value.

The characteristics of preference shares are that they:
- are not as common as ordinary shares
- receive dividends before ordinary shareholders
- receive a fixed rate dividend every year (assuming dividends are declared)
- do not have a vote.

5 per cent and €1 are arbitrary figures used for this example.

As with ordinary shares, they are listed in the **capital and reserves** section of the balance sheet and are usually described as '5 per cent preference shares of €1 each'.

The 5 per cent is applied to the amount of issued preference shares when a dividend is declared. The authorised amount in euros and the issued amount will also be stated on the same line. Sometimes preference shares may be described as **cumulative**, whereby if a company cannot pay the dividend, the amount is added to the next declared dividend and the accumulated amount is paid when the company is profitable.

## Debentures and debenture stock

Companies can obtain finance from sources other than issues of shares. **Debentures are loans** made to a company by a bank or individual. They are usually subject to a fixed rate of interest and in most cases are secured against the assets of the business. They are long-term loans and the years during which they must be repaid are normally specified.

They are usually listed in the balance sheet immediately below the capital and reserves section and are described as, for example, '10 per cent debenture loan'. If the loan is €60,000, then the annual interest expense is €6,000.

**Debenture stock** is a cross between share capital and debentures. It is similar to a debenture but allows the person or bank that has given the debenture to take shares in the company at some future date instead of receiving repayment of the debenture.

As with debenture loans, debenture stock is usually listed in the balance sheet immediately below the capital and reserves section. It is usually described as '10 per cent debenture stock'. There is no interest expense.

Many companies place debentures in the asset section of the balance sheet to come up with a net asset figure. This is regarded as the **proprietary view,** making it clear that in owning the assets, the shareholders are considered very much part of the company. Others feel that because a loan is a form of capital, it should be shown immediately below the capital section. By placing the phrase 'financed by' immediately before the capital and debt, we understand intuitively that it is these two items that finance the assets. This is sometimes referred to as the **entity view,** which considers the assets as the driving force of economic performance.

*The examples and questions are presented using the entity view.*

## ACCOUNTING FOR CAPITAL

Let's reiterate how capital is increased in a business. Firstly, the company can issue shares. Secondly, it can earn profits, which, as we have demonstrated, are shown as retained profits in the capital section of the balance sheet. In this section we will learn how these two sources are handled and how they are presented in the income statement (P&L) and the balance sheet. We will commence with the issuance of shares.

## Issuance of shares

Assume two people register a new company with a maximum share capital of 200,000 €1 ordinary shares by investing in 25,000 shares each. In other words, they have put €50,000 into the business. As the **issue price** is the same as the €1 nominal value, the double entry for this transaction is as follows:

| Debit | Cash | 50,000 |
|-------|------|--------|
| Credit | Ordinary share capital | 50,000 |

How many shares should be issued will depend on how much capital the company needs to commence its operations. This company has issued 50,000 shares, but it is authorised to issue an additional 150,000 shares.

While most shares may have a nominal value of €1, there can be other prices.

What would happen if the issue price was different from the nominal price? Let's say that management decides to sell an additional 20,000 shares on the market, which are purchased for €1.50 per share. In this case, the nominal value of €1 has been exceeded by the issue price, and these shares have thus been sold at a **premium**. The €0.50 difference is called the **share premium** and the law requires that the share premium component of any share issue be shown separately to the nominal value component on the balance sheet. In this case, the company received cash of €30,000 (20,000 @ €1.50).

What are the journal entries for the transaction?

| Debit | Cash | 30,000 |
|-------|------|--------|
| Credit | Ordinary share capital | 20,000 |
| Credit | Premium on ordinary share capital | 10,000 |

These were sold in 'the market'; let's look at the implications.

## The market and market value

Once a public limited company has made the initial issue of its shares, further trading in these can take place in the market through the stock exchange. Company shares may be bought and sold among investors, but no record of these transactions will appear on the company's books. The market price, then, is the price that a share can command on the open market. For a public limited company it will be the current stock market price. In the case of a private company, the market price is the amount that a family member or friend would be willing to pay.

## Capital and profit

When a company makes a profit, it must show what it intends to do with it. This is achieved by creating an **appropriation section** immediately below **net profit before taxes** in the income statement.

Why account for appropriations of profit for a company? There are three reasons, all of which underline the distinguishing features of the limited company:

- A company is a separate legal entity and is therefore liable for corporation tax. An appropriation of **taxes** is made for taxes.
- A company has many owners, all of whom are entitled to **dividends.**
- A company can set aside profits for particular future purposes, such as replacement of fixed assets. Profits appropriated in this way are called **reserves**.

Interestingly, the term '**appropriation**' is not included in the income statement; this section is understood to begin at the **profit after taxation** section.

The following example provides a layout of the appropriation section:

| | | | |
|---|---|---|---|
| Net profit before taxation | | | 200,000 |
| Taxation (€200,000 × 40 per cent) | | | (80,000) |
| Profit after taxation | | | 120,000 |
| Dividends: | | | |
| Preference dividends: | Paid | 7,000 | |
| | Proposed | 7,000 | |
| | | 14,000 | |
| Ordinary dividends: | Proposed | 20,000 | (34,000) |
| | | | 86,000 |
| Transfer to: | General reserve | | (15,000) |
| Retained profits for year | | | 71,000 |
| Retained profits from last year | | | 11,000 |
| Retained profits | | | 82,000 |

Before we examine the accounting for profit, let's discuss the concept of reserves.

## Reserves

Once a company deducts tax from its profits, it can pursue two courses of action:
- pay out its profits as cash dividends
- put them in reserve.

**Reserves** are profits put aside for particular purposes. In other words, you do not pay them out as dividends. Cash is kept in the company. After deducting for dividends, a company may decide to **appropriate** some of the profits into reserves. There are three types of reserves:
- **Plant replacement reserve:** When inflation is high, it becomes more and more expensive to replace plant and equipment. A plant replacement reserve contains profits that will be used to replace plant and equipment in the future when they may be more expensive.
- **Stock replacement reserve:** High inflation may also increase the cost of stock. A stock replacement reserve contains profits that will be used to replace stock in the future when it may be more expensive.
- **General reserve:** Sometimes a company may want to put some profits aside for no specific purpose. This is a general reserve.

The double entry for creating or increasing a reserve is:

| | |
|---|---|
| **Dr** | Profit and loss account |
| **Cr** | Reserve account |

The reserve account is located in the **capital and reserves** section of the balance sheet.

The following balance sheet presentation from Irish materials company CRH (2005) gives a glimpse of how the equity section appears. An accompanying note is required to fully understand its equity section. The term '**non-equity**' refers to preference shares.

---

**CRH plc**
**Extract from balance sheet dated 31 December 2004**

| **Capital and reserves** | **(€, millions)** |
|---|---|
| *Called up share capital:* | |
| 24 Equity share capital | **181.0** (note 24) |
| 24 Non-equity share capital | **1.2** |

---

| | | |
|---|---|---|
| *Equity reserves:* | | |
| 25 Share premium account | 2,149.3 | |
| 25 Other reserves | 9.9 | |
| Profit and loss account | 2,876.4 | |
| | | |
| 26 **Shareholders' funds** | 5,217.8 | |
| 27 Minority interests | 82.6 | |
| Total capital employed | 5,300.4 | |

Note 24 explains the called up share capital. 'Called up' simply means the shares that are issued. The note includes income shares. These are shares sold to ordinary shareholders that provided certain tax benefits to the shareholders without any additional voting rights. Other than that explanation, we do not need to delve further.

| | Equity | | Non-equity | |
|---|---|---|---|---|
| **Authorised:** | €m | €m | €m | €m |
| At 1 Jan and 31 Dec | 235.2 | 14.7 | 0.2 | 1.1 |
| Number of shares (000s) | 735,000 | 735,000 | 150 | 872 |
| | | | | |
| **Allotted, called up and fully paid:** | | | | |
| At 1 Jan | 168.7 | 10.6 | 0.1 | 1.1 |
| Add options and other | 1.6 | .01 | – | – |
| At 31 Dec | 170.3 | 10.7 | 0.1 | 1.1 |
| Number of shares (000s) | 532,598 | 532,598 | 50 | 872 |

# ACCOUNTING FOR PROFIT

Now that we understand the appropriations aspect of dealing with profit, let's examine how each appropriation is dealt with.

## Corporation tax

A limited company must pay tax on its net profits. This tax is called **corporation tax** and is calculated as a percentage of net operating profit. Corporation tax is processed similarly as all the other expenses and it is accrued as such at the end of the year, as follows:

| | |
|---|---|
| **Dr** | Corporate tax expense |
| **Cr** | Corporate tax payable |

The corporate tax expense is then closed out to the P&L account to determine the profit remaining for the year. In the reporting presentation, however, it is shown in the income statement as a deduction from **profit before tax**. Because the tax is paid within a few months of the end of the year, the corporate tax payable account is shown in the balance sheet under **creditor due within one year,** the section that houses the current liabilities.

## Dividends

Dividends are profits either paid or payable to shareholders as cash. As previously discussed, **preference shareholders** always get their dividends first (assuming, of course, that a dividend is declared). This dividend is fixed, unlike the ordinary share, whose dividend is at the discretion of management.

With a preference share, the dividend is a percentage of the nominal value of the preference share capital. For example, Big Boss Ltd issued 6,000 €1 7 per cent preference shares. This means that the preference shareholders get a dividend equal to 7 per cent of their nominal value investment (in this case, 6,000 × €1 = €6,000). So every year the company must pay these shareholders €420 (€6,000 @ 7 per cent), assuming, of course, that management declares a dividend.

Ordinary shareholders only get their dividends after the preference shareholders have been paid. They are not entitled to receive a fixed dividend every year, so their dividends vary with profit. If profits are good, ordinary dividends may be high. If profits are not good, then ordinary dividends may be low – or there may be none at all.

Ordinary shares are normally expressed as a dividend per share, for example, 12c per share, or as a percentage of the nominal value investment in the same way as preference shares.

For example, a limited company has an authorised 25c ordinary share capital of €100,000. It issued 10,000 of these shares, i.e. its ordinary issued share capital = €2,500 (10,000 × 25c). It decides to pay a dividend of 8c per share. This means that for every share issued it must pay 8c. The total ordinary dividend = €800 (10,000 × 8c).

### INSTALMENTS

Dividends are normally paid in two instalments, i.e. every six months. The first instalment is paid during the year and is called the **interim dividend**.

The double entry for an interim dividend is:

| | |
|---|---|
| **Dr** | Dividends account |
| **Cr** | Bank account |

The second instalment is called the **final dividend** and is usually proposed close to the end of the financial year. It is normally paid shortly after the year-end, and therefore must be treated as an **accrual**. It is often called a proposed dividend.

The double entry for a proposed dividend is:

| | |
|---|---|
| **Dr** | Dividends |
| **Cr** | Dividend payable account: |

The dividends account will now have an amount made up of two entries and the total is then closed out to the P&L account to determine what profits are retained for the year. The dividend payable account is shown as a liability in the **creditors due within one year** section of the balance sheet.

## Self-Assessment Question 5

1. The following is the capital and reserve section of Catapult plc's balance sheet. The company decides to pay an ordinary dividend of 5c per share. Calculate the total dividend for the year.

| | | Authorised | Issued |
|---|---|---|---|
| Share capital: | €1 ordinary shares | 200,000 | 10,000 |
| | €1 6 per cent preference shares | 40,000 | 6,000 |
| | | 240,000 | 16,000 |

## Retained profits

Once all the appropriations of profit are made in the profit and loss account, you have the **retained profits for the year**. Retained profits from previous years are carried forward and added to the latest year's retained profits to come up with **retained profit**. This is considered a type of reserve and is placed in the **capital and reserves** section of the balance sheet.

Retained profits is sometimes called revenue reserve.

## Self-Assessment Question 6

1. Prepare a profit and loss account (appropriation section) for Lanzlot Ltd using the following information:
   - For the year ended 30 September 2005, the profit before tax was €100,000.
   - During the year, an interim preference dividend of €4,000 was paid.

- There was no interim ordinary dividend. The retained profits at the end of the preceding year (2004) were €44,000.

Decisions taken:

- Open a new plant replacement reserve and transfer €3,000 into it.
- Provide for corporation tax at a rate of 40 per cent.
- Provide for a final preference dividend of €6,000.
- Provide for a total ordinary dividend for the year of €22,000.

## Balance sheet presentation

Once the appropriations are made and understood, a review of the capital and reserves section of the balance sheet demonstrates the connection with the income statement.

**Capital and Reserves:**

|  | Authorised | Issued |
|---|---|---|
| Share capital:  €1 ordinary shares | €200,000 | €10,000 |
| 6 per cent preference shares | 40,000 | 6,000 |
|  | 240,000 | 16,000 |
| Share premium |  | 6,000 |
| Plant replacement reserve |  | 4,000 |
| Stock replacement reserve |  | 2,000 |
| General reserve |  | 4,000 |
| Revenue reserve (retained profit) |  | 10,050 |
|  |  | €42,050 |

Limited companies play a vital part in the running of any economy and are an integral part of the globalisation process prevalent today. On a domestic level, limited companies pursue resources and hire employees at a level that the sole trader is unable to attain. Therefore, accounting must recognise that meaningful disclosure by companies is critical to attracting new investors. This is why reporting on companies and the accounting process cannot be separated. The next section attempts to explore this opinion.

## REPORTING ON THE CORPORATE FORM

Accounting for limited companies tries to provide the most appropriate information that assists shareholders and other users who interact with corporations. As the next chapter demonstrates, companies are always changing. They may move into new markets, acquire other companies or even sell companies that are not considered profitable or a strategic fit.

The reporting process needs to somehow explain or make evident how such changes impact performance.

## FRS 3: Reporting Financial Reporting

This standard was issued in October 1992 and amended in June 1993 to disclose through better presentation where exactly many of the income statement numbers came from. Companies must break down sales and operating profit by:

- continuing operations
- acquisitions acquired in the last financial year
- discontinued operations in the last financial year.

This breakdown provides powerful insight to investors into assessing past actions and 'forming a basis for their assessment of future results and cashflows' (ASB 1992).

The standard essentially abolished extraordinary items from the income statement, or at least confines them to a rare event. Some accountants had a tendency to convert any exceptional item into something extraordinary, the benefit of which was to place extraordinary items after operating profit. This potential for manipulation was removed with FRS 3, allowing only these three items to be reported after operating profit:

- profit or losses on sale or termination of an operation
- costs of a fundamental reorganisation or restructuring of the company
- profits or losses on the disposal of fixed assets.

**IFRS 5 Non-Current Assets Held for Sales and Discontinued Operations** (2005) is essentially the equivalent to FRS 3. It is similar to FRS 3, but it suggests the use of notes and calls for information on both financial performance and financial position.

In the US, an extraordinary item must meet two criteria – it must be:

- unusual in nature
- infrequent occurrence.

The events of the 9/11 terrorist attacks in the US certainly met the above criteria. However, the Financial Accounting Standards Board came to the conclusion that it would be impossible to isolate the financial impact of the attack from the poor economic conditions that prevailed at that time (FASB 2001). It felt that the extent of the losses and the economic disruption that followed could not be adequately captured in one line on the income statement. Accordingly, companies so effected were instructed to report losses among its operating expenses as a 'special charge' and provide a disclosure and discussion to assist users in understanding how 9/11 affected the company. This episode underlines the precision that is required to qualify as an extraordinary item.

## Self-Assessment Question 7

1. The sunny, warm state of Florida in the US is home to a multibillion-dollar orange juice business. Juice harvested today is on European shelves tomorrow. A farm experiences losses due to a frost, having not experienced frost in any of the previous fifteen years. Should these losses be treated as extraordinary? Justify your answer.

### Earnings per share

Referred to as the EPS, it must be disclosed by publicly traded companies on the income statement (P&L) per FRS 14. The international equivalent is IAS 33 Earnings per Share (revised in 2003) and it defines two EPS numbers requiring disclosure:

- **Basic EPS:** Based on ordinary shares currently issued.
- **Diluted EPS:** Based on ordinary shares outstanding *plus* any ordinary shares that may arise from instruments converting into ordinary shares.

It is calculated as follows:

$$\text{operating profit} \div \text{weighted number of ordinary shares}$$

As a financial measure of performance, it is regarded as a somewhat crude indicator of business performance (O'Regan 2001). We will discuss the EPS in Chapter 9 when we interpret financial information.

## Self-Assessment Question 8

NOTE: This self-assessment question contains carriage, or transportation, expense accounts in addition to the discount accounts discussed in earlier chapters. Their inclusion will provide a fuller picture of the financial statements:

- **Carriage inwards:** Transport expenses that are added to purchases.
- **Discounts received:** Regarded as revenues in a way and are added to gross profit.
- **Discounts allowed:** Part of the price of doing business; include in operating expenses.
- **Carriage outwards:** Include in operating expenses.

1. You are provided with the following trial balance of Keeper Ltd as at 31 December 2005. Prepare a balance sheet and an income statement for the year ended 31 December 2005.

|  | Debit | Credit |
|---|---|---|
|  | € | € |
| Ordinary share capital (50c shares) |  | 60,000 |
| 5 per cent preference share capital (€1 shares) |  | 20,000 |
| Sales |  | 80,000 |
| Discount allowed | 400 |  |
| Discount received |  | 200 |
| Carriage inwards | 1,000 |  |
| Carriage outwards | 800 |  |
| Debtors and creditors | 10,000 | 2,000 |
| Stock at 1 Jan 2005 | 10,000 |  |
| 10 per cent debentures 2010 |  | 50,000 |
| Fixed assets at cost | 230,000 |  |
| Accum depreciation – fixed assets |  | 100,000 |
| Purchases | 49,000 |  |
| Administrative expenses | 4,000 |  |
| Staff salaries | 4,000 |  |
| Preference dividend paid | 1,000 |  |
| Profit and loss account balance |  | 8,000 |
| Cash at bank | 10,000 |  |
|  | 320,200 | 320,200 |

Adjustments are required for the following:

(a) Stock at 31 December 2005: €15,000.

(b) Directors' salaries due but not yet paid: €5,000.

(c) Corporation tax for the year: €5,000.

(d) Proposed ordinary dividend: 2.5c per share.

(e) Depreciation charge for the year: €4,600.

(f) Accrual of audit fee: €1,000.

(g) Creation of a plant replacement reserve: €1,000.

Note: Observe that there is a 10 per cent debenture loan, but there is no interest expense listed among the expenses.

## CHAPTER REVIEW

In previous chapters we have used the limited company form without dealing with the presentation demands made by its income statement and balance sheet. By comparing it with another business form, the sole trader, we suggested possible advantages to the limited company that may explain why it is the preferred form of business entity as a business grows. Because it is a separate entity, the formation of a company must meet certain legal requirements. Two documents – the **memorandum of association** and **articles of association** – spell out its objectives, the amount of authorised capital and its internal rules. Once these are in place, the Companies Registration Office (CRO) will issue a Certificate of Incorporation to the company. The duties of the company underline the corporate governance issue in running a company. Maintaining proper books, preparing annual accounts, timely filings with the CRO and holding general meetings reflect the main duties. The ODCE, empowered by the Companies Act 2001, enforces compliance with these duties.

If one of the advantages of the limited company is its ability to attract capital, we find that the handling of capital requires a precise presentation in the income statement (P&L) and the balance sheet. In the P&L, net income before tax is derived and is then disbursed in the following order: taxes, dividends and reserves. This whole section is referred to as the **appropriation** section.

The reserves item describes those profits that are put aside for particular purposes such as plant replacement, or just for general reserve. The balance sheet presentation has as its heading the caption **shareholders' funds and reserves** and will list the following items: ordinary shares, preference shares, share premium, reserves and retained profits.

Capital is raised by issuing either **ordinary** or **preference** shares. If a share is sold for more than its nominal value, then the excess amount is referred to as a **premium**. Ordinary shareholders have a vote and only receive a dividend if one is declared by management. Preference shareholders, on the other hand, do not have a vote but are guaranteed a fixed dividend when a dividend is declared.

The detail in the financial statement presentation reflects the interests of shareholders who, as owners of the business, need to know as much as possible about their investment. Accordingly, the source of sales, perhaps from a major acquisition or whether there has been a fundamental change in the structure of the company, such as a discontinued operation, should be disclosed to the user.

Studying the corporate form sets the stage for accounting of consolidated companies or groups in Chapter 7 and the interpretation of financial statements in Chapter 9.

# SELF-ASSESSMENT QUESTION ANSWERS

## SAQ 1

1. The characteristics that distinguish a limited company as an entity are that it is:
   - owned by one or more individuals, called shareholders
   - a separate legal entity
   - managed by directors who are appointed at the annual general meeting.

## SAQ 2

1. A sole trader owns his or her business, but shareholders own a limited company. If there is a change in ownership with a sole trader, the business must be established as a new entity. However, with a limited company, shareholders come and go and the business continues unchanged.

## SAQ 3

1. **Ordinary** shares are the most common type of share and ordinary shareholders have a vote at company meetings. **Preference** shares receive a dividend before an ordinary shareholder. Assuming that a dividend is declared, preference shareholders will receive a dividend at a fixed rate. In the event of the dissolution of a company, ordinary shareholders will receive whatever funds are left over once all other obligations are settled.
2. The two key legal documents of a company are the memorandum of association and articles of association.
3. A company acting outside its objectives is acting *ultra vires*. Other parties to this transaction may be able to forego their obligation, as the transaction may be rendered void.

## SAQ 4

1. (a) Nominal value of the share is €1.
   (b) Issue price was €1.25.
   (c) Market value is €1.60.

## SAQ 5

1. Because an ordinary share dividend has been declared, preference shareholders must also get paid.

| | | |
|---|---|---|
| Ordinary shares: | 10,000 shares × 5c = €500 | |
| Preference shares: | €6,000 @ 6 per cent = €360 | |
| Total dividend | = €860 | |

## SAQ 6

1. The income statement (appropriation section) of Lanzlot Ltd will look like this:

|  |  |  | € |
|---|---|---|---|
| Net profit before taxation |  |  | 100,000 |
| Taxation (€100,000 × 40 per cent) |  |  | (40,000) |
| Profit after tax |  |  | 60,000 |
| Dividends: |  |  |  |
| Preference dividends: Paid |  | 4,000 |  |
| Proposed |  | 6,000 |  |
|  |  | 10,000 |  |
| Ordinary dividends:  Proposed |  | 22,000 | (32,000) |
|  |  |  | 28,000 |
| Transfer to:           Plant replacement reserve |  |  | (3,000) |
| Retained profits for year |  |  | 25,000 |
| Retained profits from last year |  |  | 44,000 |
| Retained profits |  |  | 69,000 |

## SAQ 7

1. No. Frost is certainly infrequent in Florida, but not unusual in nature.

## SAQ 8

**Keeper Ltd**

**Profit and loss account for the year ended 31 December 2005**

| | | |
|---|---|---|
| Sales | | 80,000 |
| Opening stock | 10,000 | |
| Purchases | 49,000 | |
| Carriage inwards | 1,000 | |
| | 60,000 | |
| Less closing stock | 15,000 | |
| Cost of sales | | 45,000 |
| Gross profit | | 35,000 |
| Discounts received | | 200 |
| | | 35,200 |
| Expenses: | | |
| Administrative expenses | 4,000 | |
| Staff salaries | 4,000 | |
| Directors' salaries | 5,000 | |

| | | |
|---|---:|---:|
| Audit fee | 1,000 | |
| Depreciation | 4,600 | |
| Debenture interest **W1** | 5,000 | |
| Discount allowed | 400 | |
| Carriage outwards | 800 | |
| | | 24,800 |
| Net profit before tax | | 10,400 |
| Corporation tax | | 5,000 |
| Net profit after tax | | 5,400 |
| Transfer to plant repl. reserve | 1,000 | |
| Preference dividend of 5 per cent (paid) **W2** | 1,000 | |
| Ordinary dividend of 2.5c (proposed) | 3,000 | |
| | | 5,000 |
| Retained profit for the year | | 400 |
| Profit and loss account b/d | | 8,000 |
| Retained profits | | 8,400 |

**Keeper Ltd**

**Balance Sheet as at 31 December 2005**

| | € | € | € |
|---|---:|---:|---:|
| **Fixed assets:** | | | |
| Land, buildings, equipment | | | 230,000 |
| Less accumulated depreciation | | | 104,600 |
| | | | 125,400 |
| **Currents assets:** | | | |
| Stock | | 15,000 | |
| Trade debtors | | 10,000 | |
| Cash at bank | | 10,000 | |
| | | 35,000 | |
| **Liabilities falling due within one year:** | | | |
| Trade creditors | 2,000 | | |
| Current tax | 5,000 | | |
| Dividend proposed **W2** | 3,000 | | |
| Accruals **W3** | 11,000 | | |
| | | 21,000 | |
| Net current assets | | | 14,000 |
| **Total net assets** | | | 139,400 |

*continued overleaf*

| Financed by: | | |
|---|---|---|
| **Capital and reserves:** | | |
| Called up share capital: | | |
|    Ordinary 50c shares | 60,000 | |
|    5 per cent €1 preference shares | 20,000 | |
| Plant replacement reserve | 1,000 | |
| Retained profits | 8,400 | |
| | | 89,400 |
| Loans: | | |
| 10 per cent debenture 2010 | | 50,000 |
| | | 139,400 |

**W1:** Interest expense on €50,000 debenture loan at 10 per cent.

Note how the €5,000 is also added to the accrued liability in W3.

**W2:** Preference shareholders have already been paid. We are asked to accrue for the ordinary shareholders, as dividend was declared at year-end but not paid. Both amounts are calculated as follows:

- **Ordinary shares:** €60,000 (50c per share) = 120,000 shares.
  Dividend = 120,000 × 2.5c = €3,000.
  The €3,000 becomes a liability – an accrual – and shows up in the balance sheet. Why? The amount has been proposed or set aside for future payment to the shareholders, so the P&L account has been debited and the liability has been credited.
- **Preference shares:** €20,000 @ 5 per cent = €1,000.

**Please note** that we could easily have included both **taxes payable** and **dividend payable** among the accruals listed in W3. They have been listed separately for greater clarity.

**W3:** The accruals contain obligations of the company:
- directors' salaries of €5,000
- audit fees of €1,000
- interest expense of €5,000 (10 per cent interest on the €50,000 debenture).
  Total = €11,000

The directors' salaries, audit fees and interest expense are captured in the general journal as follows:

| 2005 | | Debit | Credit |
|------|--|-------|--------|
| Dec 31 | Directors' salariees expense | 5,000 | |
| | Audit fees expense | 1,000 | |
| | Interest expense | 5,000 | |
| | Accrued liabilities | | 11,000 |
| *Capturing expenses incurred but not paid* | | | |

The three payables are bundled together and presented in the balance sheet as one amount of €11,000.

# REFERENCES

Accounting Standards Board, *FRS 3 Reporting Financial Performance*, London: ASB 1993 (amended).

Accounting Standards Board, *FRS 14 Earnings per Share,* London: ASB 1998.

Accounting Standards Board, *FRS 18 Accounting Policies*, London: ASB 2000.

Callanan, G., *An Introduction to Irish Company Law*, Dublin: Gill & Macmillan 1999, p. 32.

Committee on the Financial Aspects of Corporate Governance, Cadbury Committee, GEE Publishing 1992.

Companies (Auditing and Accounting) Act 2003, Dublin: The Stationery Office.

Company Law Enforcement Act 2001, Dublin: The Stationery Office.

CRH plc, *Annual Report 2004*, Registered Office: 42 Fitzwilliam Square, Dublin 2 February 2005.

Emerging Issues Task Force, *Accounting for the Impact of the Terrorist Attacks of September 11, 2001*, Issue 11–10, Norwalk: FASB 2001.

Heneghan, J. and O'Regan, P., *Accounting*, Limerick: Centre for Project Management, University of Limerick 2000.

International Accounting Standards Board, *IFRS 5 Non-Current Assets Held for Sales and Discontinued Operations*, London: IASB 2005.

O'Connell, M., *Who'd Want to Be a Company Director? A Guide to the Enforcement of Irish Company Law*, Dublin: First Law 2003.

O'Regan, P., *Introduction to Accounting*, Limerick: The International Equine Institute, University of Limerick 1998.

O'Regan, P., *Financial Information Analysis*, Chichester: John Wiley & Sons 2001.

Office of Director of Corporate Enforcement, *Principal Duties and Powers of Companies, Notice D*, Dublin: ODCE 2002.

# 7

# Limited Companies: Accounting for Groups

C
O
N
T
E
N
T
S

# INTRODUCTION

The creation of a group of companies controlled by a parent has a huge and pervasive impact on a nation's economy. Its emergence is primarily due to the ability of the corporate form to attract funding from external investors through the issuance of shares. The resulting infusion of cash allows it to acquire another company, either a competitor or a player in a complementary market. It could (and does) use the money to buy more equipment, invest in research and development or perhaps spend more on marketing. However, it is the potential to dramatically increase sales and market share and acquire competencies that could otherwise take years to build which makes an acquisition strategy attractive.

Although this chapter explores the principles of group accounting at a very elementary level, its inclusion is warranted for three key reasons. Firstly, students of accounting and finance will almost certainly be faced with a group scenario early rather than later in their careers. In the first half of 2005, almost €5.8 billion was spent by some sixty companies on acquisitions in Ireland (Devine 2005) across all the business sectors (see Figure 7.1). Secondly, it will provide greater insights when we analyse the financial statements in Chapter 9 as companies balance their long-term plans with the demands of day-to-day operations. Thirdly, Irish small to medium-sized enterprises (SMEs) must give serious consideration to growth by acquisition if they are to compete in Ireland, let alone in the international arena. As Figure 7.1 shows, a number of Irish companies have acquired the competency to acquire other companies here and outside of Ireland.

FIGURE 7.1: MERGER AND ACQUISITIONS ACTIVITY IN IRELAND, FIRST HALF OF 2005

| ACQUIRER (top three in each sector) | TARGET | SECTOR TOTAL €, mn |
|---|---|---|
| **Media & Publishing** | | 486.8 |
| Morgan Stanley | NTL Ireland | 325.0 |
| UTV | Wireless Group | 144.8 |
| Radio Kerry | Shannonside/Northern Sound | 6.0 |
| **Health & Pharmaceutical** | | 2,355.5 |
| Waren Acquisition | Warner Chilcott PLC | 2,300.0 |
| United Drug | In2Focus Sales Dev Sces | 18.0 |
| United Drug | UK TD packaging Ltd | 17.0 |
| **IT & Telecoms** | | 461.2 |
| Northgate Information Solutions | Sx3 (owned by Viridian) | 227.0 |
| Alphyra | Post TS UK & TS Spain | 85.0 |

| Redstone | Xpert Group | 37.2 |
|---|---|---|

| **Food & Food Services** | | **310.5** |
|---|---|---|
| Diageo | Bushmills | 300.0 |
| Glanbia | CMP | 10.5 |

(Musgrave and Donegal Creameries also made acquisitions but numbers not available)

| **Leisure & Travel** | | **776.0** |
|---|---|---|
| Prince Alwaleed Bin Talai/BOS | Savoy Hotel | 328.0 |
| Quinn Group | Belfry Golf Club | 270.0 |
| Dr. Smurfit, Gerry Gannon | The K Club | 115.0 |

| **Financial Services** | | **150.0** |
|---|---|---|
| Bank of Scotland Ireland | ESB Retail Business | 120.0 |
| AWD | Chase de Vere (BOI sub) | 30.0 |
| Fexco | BNP Paribas Finance | no numbers |

| **Support Services** | | **147.3** |
|---|---|---|
| IAWS Co-op | Process & energy div of SWS | 64.0 |
| DCC | Pilton | 42.5 |
| DG Distributors & Vendors | King Ireland | 20.0 |

| **Building, Construction, Property** | | **296.8** |
|---|---|---|
| CRH | Half-year acquisitions | 168.0 |
| Kingspan | Century Homes | 98.0 |
| Kingspan | ATC | 30.8 |

| **Industrial** | | **202.9** |
|---|---|---|
| Lundin Mining | Arcon Intl Resources | 94.0 |
| Ardagh Glass | Rexam | 73.0 |
| Aga Foodservice Group | Waterford Stanley | 13.8 |

| **Retail** | | **591.0** |
|---|---|---|
| Select Retail Consortium | Superquinn | 420.0 |
| Alliance UniChem plc | Bairds Chemists | 119.0 |
| Tesco | Golden Island Shopping Centre | 52.0 |

Total €5,778

*Source:* Joe Devine, Ion Equity, for the *Irish Times*, 15 July 2005.

# AN OVERVIEW

It may seem rather strange to start by stating what a group is not. A group is *not* a legal entity. Rather, it is a *conceptual* 'thing' that treats a number of companies as a single entity for financial reporting purposes. How the various companies are *consolidated* into financial statements is the job of acquisition accounting. The result is a financial picture of the group.

A group cannot:
- make contracts
- sue
- be sued.

It is only the individual companies that can enter contracts and create obligations, thus incurring the risk of legal action.

## The parent-subsidiary structure

A **parent** can set about growing by either acquiring another company or by setting up a subsidiary (Pahler 2003). In this latter case, the parent is what is referred to as a **holding company**. A holding company has no operations but is a legal device in which to lay claim to various investments, such as:
- subsidiaries (more than 50 per cent of stock held)
- joint ventures (50 per cent stock held)
- associates (20 to 49 per cent stock held).

Less than 20 per cent is regarded as an investment where the parent is regarded as having no influence on the company invested in.

This parent-subsidiary structure reflects the relationships as the accompanying figures (adapted from Dodge 1996) demonstrate.

FIGURE 7.2: THE GROUP STRUCTURE OF PARENT AND SUBSIDIARY

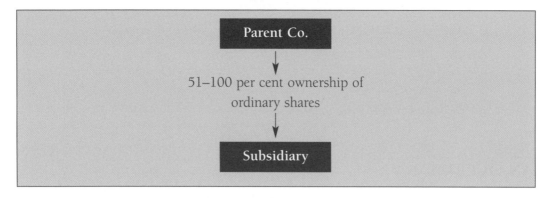

Where there is more than one subsidiary:

FIGURE 7.3: PARENT WITH CONTROLLING INTEREST IN TWO SUBSIDIARIES

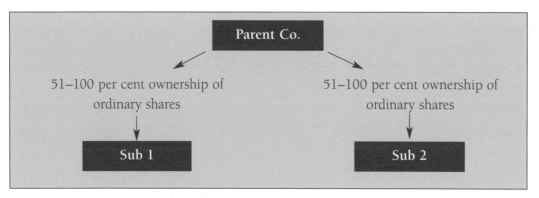

And this:

FIGURE 7.4: SUBSIDIARY CONTROLLING ANOTHER SUBSIDIARY

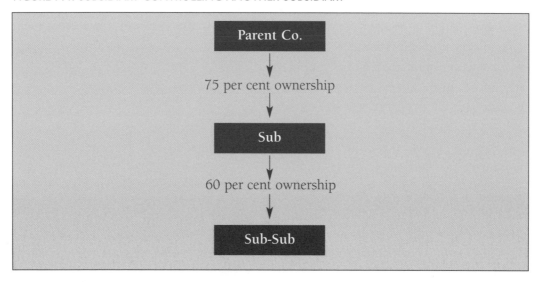

It must be understood that a subsidiary is a separate legal entity, complete with its own board of directors and its own general ledger of accounts. Accounting for groups consolidates all of the accounts of these various arrangements into one set of accounts to provide the consolidated picture. Although the accounting rules for group accounts are very complex, the key principles are accessible and managers should have exposure to them.

## Self-Assessment Question 1

1. Company A acquires 80 per cent of Company B, which in turn acquired 30 per cent of Company C. Company A also acquired 40 per cent in Company C. How should Company C be accounted for?

## Regulatory definitions

The role of regulations is an important aspect in dealing with group accounts. Fortunately for business on this side of the Atlantic, British and Irish FRSs are closely in line with the international standards. **IAS 27 Consolidated and Separate Financial Statements** says that a group exists where one entity directly or indirectly controls another company. Figure 7.4 best reflects this definition. The only circumstance that would allow a subsidiary to be excluded from a consolidation would be where control is temporary and the intent is to dispose of the subsidiary.

As of June 2005, both the International Accounting Standards Board (IASB) and the Financial Accounting Standards Board (FASB) of the US issued a joint draft on business combinations. This is regarded as furthering convergence on one global set of standards.

## The need for a consolidated picture

The company that acquires control of another entity is obliged to combine all of the assets and liabilities of the entity acquired. Anything less may seriously mislead investors or lenders reviewing the financial picture. What are the dangers of less than adequate reporting? In his book on group accounting, Roy Dodge (1996) forwards this scenario whereby a company, Alpha Co., starts business by investing €100,000 in Beta Co. The subsidiary, Beta, proceeds to buy equipment with the €100,000.

This is what Alpha's balance sheet looks like having made the investment:

| | |
|---|---|
| Investment in Beta Co. | €100,000 |
| Share capital | €100,000 |

Very clearly, Alpha controls Beta. Let's now suppose that Beta makes a profit of €30,000 and pays a €10,000 dividend to Alpha. This leaves €20,000 in Beta's cash account. If Alpha incurs €8,000 in expenses, its income statement will show a €2,000 profit (€10,000 dividends − €8,000 expenses) and €2,000 in its cash account. One possible presentation of Alpha's balance sheet might look like this:

| | |
|---|---|
| Investment in Beta Co. | €100,000 |
| Cash at bank | 2,000 |
| | 102,000 |
| Share capital | €100,000 |
| P&L a/c | 2,000 |
| | €102,000 |

But this is misleading. Firstly, the dividend is not a true dividend. On their own, the individual balance sheets may reflect an intercompany transfer of profit by means of the dividend. However, because Alpha controls Beta, the two entities are considered as one entity and a more appropriate presentation is warranted.

| **Consolidated balance sheet:** | |
|---|---|
| Equipment | €100,000 |
| Cash (€20,000 + €2,000) | 22,000 |
| | €122,000 |
| Share capital | €100,000 |
| P&L | 22,000 |
| | 122,000 |

This consolidated picture captures the economic reality of the extent of resources available to Alpha and Beta's contribution to the picture. The addition of Beta's assets to Alpha's makes sense, since the latter controls Beta. We will explore the **control issue** later, but for now, if an entity is controlled by another, then 100 per cent of the assets (and liabilities) of the subsidiary must be included in the consolidated picture.

## Self-Assessment Question 2

1. Why are *all* of the assets and liabilities of a subsidiary added into the consolidated balance of the group?

# ACCOUNTING METHODS FOR CONSOLIDATING

The creation of a group can happen in two ways. Firstly, one company may acquire another. Secondly, two entities may merge to form a new company. The first method will use **acquisition accounting,** while the latter will use **merger accounting**. The latter method is rarely used and under very restricted circumstances. Prior to the 1990s, many acquisitions in Britain and Ireland were accounted for using the merger method even though the reality was of one company controlling another. As we will see, consolidated balance sheets under merger accounting can give a distorted picture.

For the purposes of this chapter we will concentrate on acquisition accounting, but will briefly describe the merger and equity methods so that you will be aware of the complexity involved.

## Acquisition accounting method

When one company acquires another it gains control of the assets of the acquiree, i.e. the subsidiary. This drives the acquisition accounting method, whereby:

- assets and liabilities are added to those of the parent at fair value
- **goodwill** is recognised (goodwill is the excess of the price paid over the fair value).

Only the change in the P&L reserve (the retained earnings) since the acquisition date is included in the consolidation. This prevents a parent from covering up its own losses with the pre-acquisition profits of a subsidiary.

Where ownership is less than 100 per cent (but more than 50 per cent), the percentage owned by others is called the **minority interest**. The **minority interest amount** is listed in the capital section of the consolidated balance sheet.

The fair value concept and the exclusion of pre-acquisition profits give greater credibility to the financial statements.

> The P&L reserve is a term often used to cover the P&L account or the retained earnings account and any other reserves set up by the company.

## Merger accounting method

This method is used where there has truly been a combination of resources, as distinct from a takeover. Two companies, A and B, come together essentially as equals to form Company C. Usually there is no recognition of the fair value of assets and liabilities involved and both balance sheets are added together. Mergers are difficult events to achieve, as they often result in a clash of cultures and egos. In the US, most so-called mergers were in fact acquisitions, and until the adoption of FASB 141 Business Combinations in 2001, such acquisitions were processed using merger accounting. The advantage of using merger accounting was significant. If one entity with profit reserves of €100 million acquired another with reserves of €200 million but completed the consolidation using merger accounting, the profit reserves would show €300 million. Under acquisition accounting, the reserves could not exceed €100 million, as pre-acquisition profits are excluded.

## Equity accounting method

This method is used for accounting of investments in entities where ownership is usually from 20 to less than 50 per cent. It follows along the same lines as acquisition accounting by recognising the fair value of assets invested in and excludes pre-investment profits. For instance, a parent with 25 per cent ownership in a company will recognise that percentage of the fair value of the company in the consolidated balance sheet. The consolidated P&L reserve will have added to it the investor's percentage of the *change* in the investee's P&L reserve since the investment date.

## Self-Assessment Questions 3

1. Distinguish between acquisition accounting and merger accounting.
2. A company acquires 20 per cent of the outstanding shares in another entity together with four of the ten seats on the board of the acquiree. What method of group accounting should prevail with this investment?

# A COMPLETED EXAMPLE

Let's complete a consolidation using simple balance sheets. Ordinarily, the process will entail the use of T-accounts to facilitate the consolidated picture that is completed at least once a year. We must keep in mind that there is no general ledger for the group, but rather it is the bringing together of accounts in the general ledgers of both parent and subsidiary(ies). For our purposes, we will dispense with the T-accounts and concentrate on the bigger picture that elementary statements allow.

## 100 per cent ownership

The parent makes an investment (100 per cent ownership) in its subsidiary on 31 December 2005, resulting in the following balance sheets as of that date:

|  | Parent | Subsidiary |
|---|---|---|
|  | € | € |
| Fixed assets: |  |  |
| Investment in subsidiary at cost | 100,000 |  |
| Property, plant, equipment | 200,000 | 80,000 |
|  |  |  |
| Net current assets | 300,000 | 20,000 |
|  | 600,000 | 100,000 |

| Capital and reserves: | | |
|---|---|---|
| Ordinary share capital | 500,000 | 60,000 |
| P&L reserves | 100,000 | 40,000 |
| | 600,000 | 100,000 |

You will notice that the investment amount in the parent's balance sheet is equal to the book value of the subsidiary. This is rare and accounting principles require that the parent must purchase control at the market value. For now, we will assume that the book value and the fair value are the same. We will complete the consolidation at the same date as that of the acquisition. Using the acquisition method of accounting, the resulting consolidation looks like this:

**Consolidated balance sheet 31 December 2005**

€

**Fixed assets:**

| | |
|---|---|
| Property, plant, equipment (200k + 80k) | 280,000 |
| Net current assets (300k + 20k) | 320,000 |
| | 600,000 |

**Capital and reserves:**

| | |
|---|---|
| Ordinary share capital | 500,000 |
| P&L reserves | 100,000 |
| | 600,000 |

Some important points to note:
- The €100,000 investment by the parent has been offset by the value of the net assets of the subsidiary in the consolidated balance sheet.
- All the net assets of the subsidiary are added to the parent's assets for the consolidated view.

## Self-Assessment Question 4

1. Tar Co. acquired all of the shares of Stone Co. for €44,000. Complete the consolidation as at the date of acquisition using the following the balance sheets.

|  | Tar Co. | Stone Co. |
|---|---|---|
|  | € | € |
| Investment in Stone Co. | 44,000 | 0 |
| Other net assets | 51,000 | 44,000 |
|  | 95,000 | 44,000 |
|  |  |  |
| Share capital (€1 per share) | 70,000 | 40,000 |
| Reserves | 25,000 | 4,000 |
|  | 95,000 | 44,000 |

## Less than 100 per cent ownership

But what if the parent acquired only 80 per cent of the subsidiary? The parent will have a controlling interest, but the remaining 20 per cent, or **minority holders**, belongs to external shareholders known as minority interest holders.

We will use the same balance sheets again, with an adjustment made to the parent investment amount as follows:

|  | Parent |
|---|---|
|  | € |
| **Fixed assets:** |  |
| Investment in subsidiary at cost | 80,000 |
| Property, plant, equipment | 200,000 |
|  |  |
| **Net current assets** | 320,000 |
|  | 600,000 |
|  |  |
| **Capital and reserves:** |  |
| Ordinary share capital | 500,000 |
| P&L reserves | 100,000 |
|  | 600,000 |

Let's confirm the minority interest holding by using this mechanic:

| **Parent's investment** |  | **80,000** |
|---|---|---|
| Subsidiary's net value at acquisition date: |  |  |
| Share capital | 60,000 |  |
| P&L reserve | 40,000 |  |
|  | 100,000 |  |

| Minority interest portion | 20,000 | |
|---|---|---|
| Parent's interest | | 80,000 |
| Goodwill | | 0 |

Again, as in the previous example the subsidiary's book value is equal to its fair value and thus goodwill continues to be zero.

And the consolidated picture:

**Consolidated balance sheet 31 December 2005**

| | € |
|---|---|
| **Fixed assets:** | |
| Property, plant, equipment (200k + 80k) | 280,000 |
| Net current assets (320k + 20k) | 340,000 |
| | 620,000 |
| | |
| **Capital and reserves:** | |
| Ordinary share capital | 500,000 |
| P&L reserves | 100,000 |
| | 600,000 |
| **Minority interest** | 20,000 |
| | 620,000 |

There are two points to note here:

- The parent owns 80 per cent of the subsidiary, yet 100 per cent of the assets are included in the consolidated balance sheet. This is consistent with the concept of control.
- The €80,000 investment acquires the €100,000 net assets of the subsidiary, which is offset by the €20,000 obligation to the minority shareholders.

## Self-Assessment Question 5

1. Ship Co. acquired 32,000 shares of those issued by Boat Co. for €36,000. Complete the consolidation as at the date of acquisition using the following individual balance sheets of the same date.

|  | Ship Co. | Boat Co. |
|---|---|---|
|  | € | € |
| Investment in Boat Co. | 36,000 | – |
| Other net assets | 62,000 | 45,000 |
| Total | 98,000 | 45,000 |
|  |  |  |
| Share capit (€1 per share) | 70,000 | 40,000 |
| Reserves | 28,000 | 5,000 |
| Total | 98,000 | 45,000 |

## Subsequent consolidation

The rules regarding consolidations in the years subsequent to the date of acquisition pay particular attention to the accounting of the consolidated profit. Because of abuses in the 1980s whereby some companies with declining profits camouflaged such losses with the profits of subsidiaries, FRS 2 dealt with this by insisting that pre-acquisition profits be excluded from the consolidation. Only the change in profits since acquisition is permissible.

Let's continue with the parent and subsidiary (100 per cent owned) from our first example and analyse their balance sheets one year later at 31 December 2006.

|  | Parent | Subsidiary |
|---|---|---|
|  | € | € |
| **Fixed assets:** |  |  |
| Investment in subsidiary at cost | 100,000 | – |
| Property, plant, equipment | 220,000 | 80,000 |
|  |  |  |
| **Net current assets** | 310,000 | 30,000 |
|  | 630,000 | 110,000 |
|  |  |  |
| **Capital and reserves:** |  |  |
| Ordinary share capital | 500,000 | 60,000 |
| P&L reserves | 130,000 | 50,000 |
|  | 630,000 | 110,000 |

We notice that the investment of €100,000 continues at its original cost (adhering to the historical cost principle). The parent's P&L reserve has increased, as indeed has that of the subsidiary. We must remind ourselves of two key rules to date, namely:

- 100 per cent of a subsidiary's net assets are added to those of the parent
- only the change in profits since acquisition are added to the parent's amount.

The consolidated balance sheet at 31 December 2006 is as follows:

| Consolidated balance sheet 31 December 2006 | |
|---|---|
| | € |
| **Fixed assets:** | |
| Property, plant, equipment (220k + 80k) | 300,000 |
| **Net current assets** (310k + 30k) | 340,000 |
| | 640,000 |
| | |
| **Capital and reserves:** | |
| Ordinary share capital | 500,000 |
| P&L reserve | 140,000 |
| | 640,000 |

You will notice here that the €10,000 increase in the subsidiary's P&L reserve from €40,000 to €50,000 is added to the parent's amount.

## Self-Assessment Question 6

1. This question addresses the completion of a consolidation years after the acquisition and at ownership of less than 100 per cent. You now have enough knowledge to tackle this.

Solid Co. acquired 15,000 shares in Liquid Co. several years ago when Liquid's P&L account reserve was €12,000. Complete the consolidation using the latest balance sheets below.

| | Solid Co. | Liquid Co. |
|---|---|---|
| | € | € |
| Investment in Liquid Co. | 24,000 | – |
| Other net assets | 83,000 | 28,000 |
| Total | 107,000 | 28,000 |
| | | |
| Share capital (€1 per share) | 82,000 | 20,000 |
| Reserves | 25,000 | 8,000 |
| Total | 107,000 | 28,000 |

# THE ISSUE OF CONTROL

We have referred to control already in this chapter and explore here how it is interpreted. What is critical to ascertain is what level of influence an investment in another entity buys. We will discover that control is essentially binary in function (Seeger 1975). By that we mean that control exists in either yes or no terms: you either have control or you do not. Later, in Chapter 11, we return to control from the perspective of safeguarding the assets of the company and we will find that this binary quality will continue to be fundamental.

## Investment with less than 20 per cent ownership

It is generally agreed that an investment of less than 20 per cent in another entity provides the investor with little or no influence, and accordingly the investment will merely be shown as an asset in the consolidated balance sheet. However, if such an investment gave the investor 20 per cent of the votes on the board, then such an investment constitutes an **associate** and **equity accounting** must be used. What if an investment of less than 20 per cent gave the investor veto power over board decisions? The investee in this case must be regarded as a **subsidiary** and **acquisition accounting** must therefore be applied.

The astute student will clearly discern the potential for 'ducking and diving' by parent companies intent on excluding low-performing investment that they in fact control. Good governance relies hugely on accounting regulation to minimise these possible loopholes and equally on strong oversight to ensure that regulation is applied.

## Investment with more than 20 per cent ownership

In accounting, ownership of 20 per cent but less than 50 per cent gives the investor **significant influence** (Pierce aand Brennan 2003). Even if the investor chooses not to avail of seats on the board, accounting regulations regard the investment as an associate. It would be unlikely that an investor with such a stake would absolve itself from knowing about the plans and operations regarding its investment. Accordingly, **equity accounting** applies, and as noted above, the consolidated balance sheet will capture the percentage of ownership of the fair value of the associate. The consolidated P&L reserve must include the parent's percentage of the *change* in the investee's reserve since the investment date.

Joint ventures are accounted for similarly to associates whereby the consolidation will include 50 per cent of the value of the investment and 50 per cent of the change in profit reserves since the date of investment.

As previously alluded to, we must also inquire as to what control such a level of ownership buys. If 25 per cent ownership gave the parent a majority of votes on the board, then that entity must be regarded as a subsidiary and account for it using the acquisition accounting method.

## Majority ownership (with excess of 50 per cent)

An ownership that exceeds 50 per cent gives the parent or investor a **controlling interest** in that company. Whether or not the parent chooses to take seats on the board of the subsidiary, accounting practice regards control to be complete. The accounting regulations state that the parent has **dominant influence,** thus justifying the acquisition method of accounting to complete the consolidation.

### Self-Assessment Question 7

1. What is the rationale that prevents companies from denying control over subsidiaries they have invested in?

## GOODWILL AND FAIR VALUE

Up to now we assumed that the book value of the assets and liabilities of the subsidiary are also the fair value. This is rarely the case. When the investment amount exceeds the fair value of the entity acquired, the excess is called **goodwill**. It is often referred to as **purchase goodwill**. Of course, it could happen that the goodwill could be negative. Goodwill has featured hugely in recent years, particularly when the so-called dotcom bubble burst in early 2001, forcing many parent companies to expense the goodwill that had accumulated from acquisitions. Essentially, such companies had paid too much for these acquisitions.

### Defining goodwill and fair value

IFRS 3 defines goodwill as 'any excess of the cost of the acquisition over the acquirer's interest in the fair value of **identifiable assets**, liabilities and contingent liabilities acquired as at the date of the exchange transaction should be described as goodwill and recognised as an asset.'

'Identifiable' had previously been defined in British and Irish company law since 1985. It was embraced later in **FRS 7 Fair Values in Acquisition Accounting** (1994) and described as 'capable of being disposed of or settled separately, without disposing of an entity'. How the fair value is arrived at is beyond the scope of this book, but suffice it to say that it avails of professional judgment from other experts. The insistence on identifiable assets and liabilities is meant to maintain a good faith effort in this process. This latter definition provides another demonstration of how the FRSs to date are the basis of the international standards.

IFRS 3 also defines fair value as 'the amount for which an asset could be exchanged or a liability settled between knowledgeable, willing parties in an arm's length transaction.'

Generally we can say that fair value must be first applied in order to calculate goodwill.

## Determining goodwill at acquisition

Let's use our original information and assume that:

● the parent pays €130,000 for the subsidiary
● the subsidiary's property, plant and equipment are valued at €90,000.

The individual balance sheets are as follows:

|  | Parent | Subsidiary |
|---|---|---|
|  | € | € |
| **Fixed assets:** | | |
| Investment in subsidiary at cost | 130,000 | – |
| Property, plant, equipment | 200,000 | 80,000 |
| **Net current assets** | 270,000 | 20,000 |
|  | 600,000 | 100,000 |
| **Capital and reserves:** | | |
| Ordinary share capital | 500,000 | 60,000 |
| P&L reserves | 100,000 | 40,000 |
|  | 600,000 | 100,000 |

Note that the subsidiary is presenting its book value even though the parent has calculated the fair value to be higher.

We can now proceed to calculate the goodwill:

| | | |
|---|---|---|
| **Parent's investment** | | 130,000 |
| Valuation of subsidiary at acquisition: | | |
|    Share capital | 60,000 | |
|    P&L account | 40,000 | |
|    Adjustment for fair value | 10,000 | |
| Fair value of subsidiary | | 110,000 |
| Goodwill | | 20,000 |

This calculation deals with the difference between the book value and the fair value of the subsidiary. We can now proceed to the consolidated picture.

---

**Consolidated balance sheet 31 December 2005**

|  | € |
|---|---|
| **Fixed assets:** | |
| Goodwill | 20,000 |
| Property, plant, equipment (200k + 90k) | 290,000 |
| **Net current assets** (270k + 20k) | 290,000 |
|  | 600,000 |
|  | |
| **Capital and reserves:** | |
| Share capital | 500,000 |
| P&L reserves | 100,000 |
|  | 600,000 |

---

There are a couple points to note here:

- Firstly, the subsidiary's property is included in the consolidated balance sheet at its fair value of €90,000.
- Secondly, goodwill is placed in the balance sheet among the fixed assets. Because it is not something you can hold or touch, we refer to goodwill as an **intangible asset.**

It must also be stated that the goodwill calculation is unique to the acquisition date, therefore in any subsequent consolidations, the goodwill at acquisition continues to be considered.

## *Self-Assessment Question 8*

1. Alto acquires 80 per cent ownership in Bingo, whose book value is €200 million. The assets are assessed at €30 million higher in value than their book value. Alto paid €210 million for the investment. Calculate the goodwill amount in this situation.

## Accounting for goodwill

As shown above, the goodwill amount is calculated at the acquisition date, and as an asset, it will be included in the balance sheet. As with all fixed assets, it is eventually expensed to the income statement. In the past, goodwill was expensed (referred to as amortisation) over the life of an investment. More recently, an **impairment review** process was introduced whereby goodwill or a chunk thereof could be expensed depending on a review of the investment in years subsequent to the acquisition. With the advent in 2004 of IFRS 3 Business Combinations, amortisation of goodwill was prohibited and replaced with the impairment review to be conducted on an annual basis. This means that the goodwill amount could remain unchanged for a number of years or suddenly incur a substantial reduction.

# CONSOLIDATION: A DETAILED EXAMPLE

We have amassed sufficient knowledge to date to attempt a more complex consolidation that will contain a number of the concepts discussed in a single problem. These include:

- date of consolidation years later than the acquisition date
- a subsidiary at less than 100 per cent ownership
- creation of the minority interest account
- consideration of fair value
- calculation of goodwill.

We will now add two more issues to this list:

- declaration of dividends by the parent and/or the subsidiary
- reconciliation of the minority interest account.

The accounting for dividends in group accounting is regarded as comprehensive, as it essentially eliminates manipulation by companies seeking to redress their own losses. It prevents parent companies from getting their hands on pre-acquisition profits. In regard to the minority interest account, we will see that the balance at acquisition will differ from that at any subsequent consolidation. By completing a reconciliation, the student will be able to understand the change.

## Pertinent information of parent and subsidiary

Ash Co. purchased 75,000 shares in Oak Co. several years ago for €200,000. The P&L reserve at Oak Co. was €50,000 at the date of the investment. In addition, the fair value of Oak Co.'s fixed assets was €180,000, or €30,000 above book value. These fixed assets were never adjusted to fair value. The balance sheets for each as at 31 December 2005 are listed below.

|  | Ash Co. | Oak Co. |
|---|---|---|
|  | € | € |
| **Fixed assets:** | | |
| Investment in Oak Co. | 200,000 | 0 |
| Property, plant, equipment | 500,000 | 150,000 |
| | | |
| Current assets | 300,000 | 50,000 |

| Current liabilities: | | |
|---|---|---|
| Dividend payable | 20,000 | 10,000 |
| Net current assets | 280,000 | 40,000 |
| **Total assets** | 980,000 | 190,000 |
| | | |
| **Capital and reserves:** | | |
| Share capital: €1 per share | 630,000 | 100,000 |
| P&L reserve | 350,000 | 90,000 |
| | 980,000 | 190,000 |

The following information is also provided:

1. Ash Co. has not recognised in its profits the dividend declared by Oak Co.
2. An impairment review indicates that goodwill should be reduced by 40 per cent.

You are now in a position to complete a consolidated balance sheet for the Ash Group as at 31 December 2005. The following steps will take you through the process.

## Determine the ownership

Once the size of the ownership is established, then the accounting method to complete the consolidation will also be determined.

Both balance sheets indicate that each share is €1 per share. As Ash Co. acquired 75,000 of Oak Co.'s 100,000 shares, Ash's 75 per cent ownership gives it control over Oak, thus making Oak Co. a subsidiary of the Ash Group. Acquisition accounting will thus apply.

## Calculate the goodwill (if any)

Using the mechanic previously presented, we can proceed as follows:

| Ash's investment | | €200,000 |
|---|---|---|
| Value of Oak Co. at acquisition: | | |
| Share capital | 100,000 | |
| P&L account | 50,000 | |
| Fair value adjustment | 30,000 | |
| Fair value of Oak Co. | 180,000 | |
| Minority interest portion 25 per cent | 45,000 | |
| | | 135,000 |
| Goodwill | | €65,000 |

Now that we have established that there is goodwill of €65,000, we must proceed to reduce it by €26,000 (40 per cent, per the instructions above).

How is this handled? Firstly, goodwill is an asset, therefore it belongs to the balance sheet in its reduced amount. Secondly, the reduction or loss is an expense, and as with all expenses, it goes to reduce the P&L account.

So, in the consolidated balance sheet:

- goodwill will be €39,000 (€65,000 less €26,000 reduction)
- the P&L account will have incurred the €26,000 reduction.

We can now start anticipating the consolidated balance sheet by calculating the P&L account balance.

## Profit and loss account

We begin this with Ash's balance and then add to that the *change* in Oak's reserve since acquisition. What is new here is how the dividend is dealt with. Keep in mind that both companies are entitled to declare a dividend separately, but in a consolidation, both entities are considered as *one* entity, therefore Oak's dividend (75 per cent of it to Ash) is akin to transferring money between pockets. Conceptually, it does not leave the group. Therefore, we must eliminate the dividend. The only complication here concerns the 25 per cent minority interest holders, who as external shareholders must receive €2,500 (10,000 at 25 per cent).

We achieve this by eliminating the €10,000 liability from the consolidation and counter this by adding back €7,500 to the consolidated P&L account and recognising the €2,500 to the minority interest holders.

Having discussed these two issues (the goodwill and Oak's dividend), we can now prepare the P&L account for the consolidated balance sheet.

| P&L reserve | | |
|---|---|---|
| Ash's P&L account | | €350,000 |
| Change in Oak's P&L account (€90k – €50k) | 40,000 | |
| Add Ash's portion of 75 per cent | | 30,000 |
| Add back Oak's div (€10k at 75 per cent) | | 7,500 |
| Less goodwill impairment | | (26,000) |
| | | 361,500 |

Let's proceed now to the consolidated balance sheet.

## Consolidated balance sheet

We finally arrive at the consolidation as of 31 December 2005 for Ash Group.

|  |  | € |
|---|---|---|
| Goodwill |  | 39,000 |
| Property, plant, equipment |  | 680,000 |
| Current assets | 350,000 |  |
| Current liabilities: |  |  |
| Dividend payable (parent) | (20,000) |  |
| Dividend payable (MI) | (2,500) |  |
| Net current assets |  | 327,500 |
|  |  | 1,046,500 |
|  |  |  |
| Share capital |  | 630,000 |
| P&L reserve |  | 361,500 |
|  |  | 991,500 |
| MI (190k + 30 FV adj) at 25 per cent |  | 55,000 |
|  |  | 1,46,500 |

How was the minority interest amount calculated? Oak's book value of €190,000 is increased by the fair value adjustment of €30,000:

| Book value | 190,000 |
|---|---|
| Fair value adjustment | 30,000 |
|  | 220,000 |
| Minority holding | 25 per cent |
|  | €55,000 |

## Reconciliation of the minority interest amount

The minority interest amount has changed from €45,000 at acquisition date to €55,000 in the latest consolidation. How is this explained?

| Beginning balance |  | €45,000 |
|---|---|---|
| Change in P&L reserve | 40,000 |  |
| MI portion of 25 per cent |  | 10,000 |
| Ending balance |  | €55,000 |

This might seem a wasted exercise since we have already determined the MI amount. However, the Enron accountants were found to have hidden loan amounts in the minority interest account when such amounts should have been classified as liabilities. This kept the massive debt and its associated interest expense hidden from analysts and investors and, it would seem, the independent auditor.

## Self-Assessment Question 9

1.  FastLane Co. acquired 16,000 of the 20,000 €1 ordinary shares of SlowDrive Co. on 1 January 2005 for €50,000. SlowDrive's balance sheet at 31 December 2004 showed a proposed dividend of €8,000 out of retained reserves of €24,000. The balance sheets of both companies as at 31 December 2005 are listed below. From this information, prepare the consolidated balance sheet of FastLane Group at 31 December 2005.

Hint: SlowDrive's dividend is from pre-acquisition profits and cannot be taken into group profits. It is dealt with by reducing the investment amount with the parent's portion of the dividend.

|  | FastLane | SlowDrive |
|---|---|---|
| Fixed assets | 70,000 | 29,000 |
| Investment in SlowDrive | 43,600 | |
|  | 113,600 | 29,000 |
| Net current assets | 54,000 | 25,000 |
| Total net assets | 167,600 | 54,000 |
|  |  |  |
| **Capital and reserves:** |  |  |
| Ordinary shares of €1 each | 100,000 | 20,000 |
| Retained reserves | 67,600 | 34,000 |
|  | 167,600 | 54,000 |

# CHAPTER REVIEW

The growth of a company through acquisition of other companies has a huge impact on the economy. It allows a company to acquire or enter markets in an instant instead of working for years to build the competencies organically. The resulting organisation is called a group and even though it is not a legal entity, it must report the financial picture that consolidates the performance and position of each subsidiary into a consolidated P&L and balance sheet. British and Irish accounting FRSs are closely in line with international standards.

The key objective of a consolidation is to capture the economic reality of the extent of resources controlled by a parent company. It is an issue of control in the sense that if a company controls another entity – a subsidiary – it controls the assets and liabilities of the subsidiary, therefore these resources and obligations must be included in a consolidated picture. There are three methods of accounting for a group. Acquisition accounting is used when one company, the parent, acquires a controlling interest (greater than 50 per cent ownership) in another, a subsidiary. A controlling interest is considered as providing the parent with **dominant influence** over the operations of the subsidiary. Merger accounting is used when two companies combine to form a third company. Merger accounting is rare today. The third method is really related to acquisition accounting. This method is used when a company acquires a substantial interest (usually 20 per cent ownership or more but less than 50 per cent) in another entity, referred to in group accounting as an associate. The parent or investor is regarded as having a **significant influence** in the operations of the associate and therefore must include its ownership percentage of the associate's profits in the consolidated P&L reserve.

Accounting regulations require that a subsidiary's net assets must be acquired at their fair value. This usually results in goodwill, whereby the price paid exceeds the fair value of the net assets acquired. Accordingly, goodwill is calculated at the date of acquisition. IFRS 3 Business Combination regulates that goodwill goes through an impairment review annually to determine if it should be expensed.

# SELF-ASSESSMENT QUESTION ANSWERS

### SAQ 1
1. Company C is a subsidiary because Company A owns a total of 68 per cent – 40 per cent directly of Company C and 28 per cent indirectly through Company B (80 per cent of 30 per cent).

### SAQ 2
1. The economic reality is that the parent has 100 per cent control of the subsidiary's resources or its assets. Equally, it is 100 per cent responsible for the subsidiary's liabilities.

### SAQ 3
1. Acquisition accounting is used when one company, the parent, acquires control of another entity, referred to as a subsidiary. Merger accounting is used when two

companies of similar size join to form a third company.

2. Equity accounting will apply. The company invested in is an associate, and although the parent received 40 per cent of the votes on the associate's board for its 20 per cent ownership, the influence is at most significant rather than dominant.

## SAQ 4

1. Consolidated balance sheet for Tar Group:

| | |
|---|---|
| Net assets | 95,000 |
| Total | 95,000 |
| | |
| Capital | 70,000 |
| Reserves | 25,000 |
| Total | 95,000 |

## SAQ 5

1. Consolidated balance sheet:

| | | |
|---|---|---|
| **Establish ownership = 80 per cent** | (32,000 shares ÷ 40,000) | |
| Minority interest = 20 per cent | | |
| | | |
| **Investment in Boat Co.** | | **36,000** |
| Net value of Boat | 45,000 | |
| Less minority interest of 20 per cent | 9,000 | |
| Majority | | 36,000 |
| **Goodwill** | | **0** |
| | | |
| **Consolidated balance sheet of Ship Group** | | |
| Net assets | 107,000 | |
| Total | 107,000 | |
| | | |
| Capital | 70,000 | |
| Reserves | 28,000 | |
| Minority interest | 9,000 | |
| Total | 107,000 | |

## SAQ 6

1.    Ownership = 75 per cent (15,000 shares ÷ 20,000)
      Minority interest = 25 per cent

| Investment in Liquid | | 24,000 |
|---|---|---|
| Value of Liquid at acquisition: | | |
| Share capital | 20,000 | |
| P&L reserve | 12,000 | |
| | 32,000 | |
| Less MI of 25 per cent | 8,000 | |
| | | 24,000 |
| **Goodwill** | | **0** |

| Consolidate the P&L account: | | |
|---|---|---|
| Solid P&L | 25,000 | |
| Change in Liquid's P&L | −3,000 | (€4,000 decrease since acquisition at 75 per cent) |
| | 22,000 | |

**Consolidated balance sheet of Solid Group**

| | | |
|---|---|---|
| Net assets (83k + 28k) | 111,000 | |
| Total | 111,000 | |
| | | |
| Capital | 82,000 | |
| P&L reserves | 22,000 | |
| Minority interest | 7,000 | (25 per cent of €28,000, Liquid's net value) |
| Total | 111,000 | |

## SAQ 7

1. When a parent owns more that 50 per cent of another entity, it has total control. Ownership is measured in parts or 'chunks' (amounts of shares acquired), whereas control exists in yes or no terms. When control exists, then influence by the parent is considered to be dominant.

## SAQ 8

1.

| Cost of investment: | | 210 |
|---|---|---|
| Value of Bingo: | | |
| Net book value | 200 | |
| Add fair value adjust | 30 | |
| | 230 | |
| Less MI 20 per cent | (46) | |
| Majority | | 184 |
| **Goodwill** | | **26** |

## SAQ 9

1. Shareholding in SlowDrive

    16,000 shares ÷ 20,000 = 80 per cent

    Minority interest 20 per cent

    SlowDrive's dividend is from **pre-acquisition** profit and *cannot* be taken into group profits. Instead, it goes to reduce the original investment made by FastLane. Any dividend declared to come out of SlowDrive's 2005 profits will go into consolidated profit, as the subsidiary's profits are then considered **post-acquisition**.

---

**Goodwill:**

| | | |
|---|---:|---|
| Cost of investment | 50,000 | |
| Less parent's share of dividend | 6,400 | (€8,000 @ 80 |
| | 43,600 | per cent) |

SlowDrive's capital and reserves at acquisition date:

| | | |
|---|---:|---:|
| Share capital | 20,000 | |
| Retained reserves (24k − 8k) | 16,000 | |
| | 36,000 | |
| Less MI 20 per cent | 7,200 | |
| | | 28,800 |
| Goodwill | | 14,800 |

**Consolidated reserves:**

| | | |
|---|---:|---|
| FastLane | 67,600 | |
| SlowDrive | 14,400 | (34k − 16k) at 80 per cent |
| | 82,000 | |

**Minority interest:**

20 per cent of 54,000 = 10,800

**Consolidated balance sheet of FastLane Group**

| | |
|---|---:|
| Fixed assets (70 + 29) | 99,000 |
| Net current assets (54 + 25) | 79,000 |
| Goodwill | 14,800 |
| | 192,800 |

| Capital and reserves: | |
|---|---:|
| Share capital | 100,000 |
| Reserves | 82,000 |
| | 182,000 |
| MI | 10,800 |
| | 192,800 |

---

| Reconciliation of MI: | | |
|---|---|---|
| MI at acquisition | **7,200** | |
| Change in SlowDrive's reserves | <u>3,600</u> | (34k − 16k) at 20 per cent |
| MI at 31 Dec 2006 | **10,800** | |

# REFERENCES

Devine, J., 'Outlook for Irish mergers remains positive', *The Irish Times*, 15 July 2005.

Dodge, R., *Group Financial Statements*, London: Chapman & Hall 1996.

Pahler, A., *Advanced Accounting*, 8th ed., Mason: South Western 2003.

Pierce, A. and Brennan, N., *Principles and Practice of Group Accounts: A European Perspective*, London: Thomson Learning 2003.

Seeger, J., *First National City Bank Operating Group*, Boston, MA: Harvard Business School 1975.

# 8
# *Statement of Cash Flows*

C
O
N
T
E
N
T
S

# INTRODUCTION

The life-blood of any business is cash, or to use a more analytical term, **liquidity**. Good liquidity in a company means that it is able to meet its day-to-day operating expenses and at the same time handle long-term obligations such as debt. The cash flow statement provides useful insights on how cash flows into the business and how it is used or flows out. It is not designed to predict cash flow, but rather it confirms that profit, calculated using the accrual method, converts ultimately into cash (Mulford 2002). Yet many investors and creditors look to the statement to determine the company's ability to generate future cash flows. The first group ties the value of their shares to positive cash streams, while the latter, e.g. suppliers and banks, want to be sure that the business can sustain interest and loan repayments into the future.

Many students consider the statement somewhat difficult to grasp. This is understandable, since we have been using the accrual basis of accounting and we must now convert or 'undo' the accrual picture to determine the raw cash picture. The effort is worth it because the student will then be able to confront a phenomenon of financial reporting, namely that a company may report a profit yet have a cash flow problem. We also begin to anticipate the interpretation of financial statements (tackled in the Chapter 9) by showing that in some circumstances a negative cash flow is not necessarily a bad thing. Finally, the student is introduced to an apparent oxymoron, 'free cash flow', demonstrating, perhaps, that accounting is indispensable to investing.

## OBJECTIVES

**When you have finished this chapter, you will be able to:**
- understand the distinction between the accrual and cash basis of accounting
- determine how cash flows in and out of a business
- prepare a cash flow statement
- understand the requirements of the international standard IAS 7 Cash Flow Statements.

# CASH AND ITS ACTIVITIES

The primary purpose of the statement of cash flows is to provide information about cash movements reflected in cash receipts and cash payments. This allows the user to observe the net change in the cash balance between that at the beginning of the period and the balance at the end. As cash can easily be moved into short-term investments and turned back into cash when needed, the term 'cash and cash equivalents' more accurately reflects what we are tracking.

## Cash and cash equivalents

**IAS 7 Cash Flow Statements** is the international standard for dealing with the statement and is comparable to the British and Irish **FRS 1 Cash Flow Statements**. IAS 7 defines the term as follows:

- **Cash** consists of cash on hand and demand deposits.
- **Cash equivalents** are short-term, highly liquid investments that are readily convertible to known amounts of cash and which are subject to an insignificant risk of changes in value.

The standard considers a period no longer than three months for an investment to qualify as a cash equivalent, and because these investments are dedicated to meeting short-term cash commitments, movements between cash and cash equivalents are not tracked separately in the IAS Cash Flow Statement. However, while FRS 1 defines cash similarly as cash in hand and deposits that are available on twenty-four hours' notice, it tracks cash equivalents separately under the apt heading **management of liquid resources.** Both formats are presented in the next section.

What about an overdraft? This is usually the result of the management of cash: the cash account in the 'red' for short periods, perhaps, before going back into the 'black'. Loans, on the other hand, are negotiated infusions of cash and categorised as a financing activity, which is discussed below.

## Activities of cash

These movements or flows of cash *in* and *out* of a company are the result of three fundamental activities:

- **Operating:** These capture the inflows and outflows from operations such as payments received from sales and payments made to suppliers for stock. It also includes payouts for wages, insurance and other operating expenses.
- **Investing:** These include cash paid out for fixed assets such as buildings, equipment and any long-term investments. Acquisitions of other companies are also included here. The proceeds from the sale of fixed assets and investments are captured here as a cash inflow.
- **Financing:** These activities reflect cash acquired to pay for major purchases such as acquisitions and equipment. They include cash inflow from loans and from issuance of shares. Making loan repayments reflects the cash outflow.

The cash flow statement harnesses these activities to reconcile beginning and ending cash balances in a period, and in doing so provides answers to many questions posed by management and investors alike:

- Where did the cash come from during the period?
- What was the cash used for during the period?
- What was the change in the cash balance from the beginning of the period to that at the end?

The answers are not readily discernable due to the financial reports having been prepared in the accrual form. Accruing for items and making estimates on such items as doubtful accounts requires considerable judgment. The cash flow statement redresses that.

## Self-Assessment Question 1

1. What is the primary purpose of the cash flow statement?

### Accrual versus cash method

To appreciate the distinction here, let's look at the income statement produced under the accrual method. A company has these credit sales during 2005 but will not collect the money until early 2006. It also made cash purchases of €30,000 during the year. The accrual method would produce the following statement:

| Income statement for year ended 31 December 2005 | |
| --- | --- |
| | € |
| Sales | 50,000 |
| Less: Cost of sales | 30,000 |
| Gross profit | 20,000 |

With the cash method, however, the figures are *not* based on when the transactions took place, but when cash flowed in and out. This method will produce the following statement:

| Cash flow for the year ended 31 December 2005 | |
| --- | --- |
| | € |
| Cash inflow from sales | zero |
| Cash outflow on purchases | (30,000) |
| Deficit for the year | (30,000) |

The two methods give very different results. One **corporate governance** issue here is that in relying on the accrual method to match the activity with the period, can the user rely on the collectability of the credit sales? We will address this further in Chapter 9 when we interpret the financial statements, including the cash flow statement.

## Self-Assessment Question 2

1. The following information concerns Valley Company for 2005. Calculate the net cash flow of Valley Company for 2005.
   - Cash sales: €20,000.
   - Credit sales: €300,000, of which 40 per cent remains unpaid by debtors.
   - Purchases by cash: €10,000.
   - Purchases on credit: €90,000, of which €30,000 remains unpaid at year-end.

Before creating the mechanical format of the statement, let's consider what we know to be the inflows and outflows experienced in a business.

### Inflows and outflows

**Cash inflows** include:
- cash from issuance of shares to investors (financing)
- cash sales (operating)
- payments from debtors (operating)
- loans from banks (financing)
- rental income (operating)
- cash from sale of fixed assets (investing).

**Cash out** includes:
- cash purchases of fixed assets (investing)
- cash purchases of materials (operating)
- cash paid for rent and all types of bills (operating)
- payments to creditors (operating)
- interest paid on loans (operating)
- taxes (operating)
- dividends paid (financing)
- loan repayments (financing).

Some of these flows deal with day-to-day operations, whereas others are essentially one-time events. For instance, receiving cash from the sale of a product is distinctly different from acquiring cash by way of issuing shares. As we will see below, the format prescribed by accounting standards recognises these distinctions.

## Self-Assessment Question 3

1. Determine the kind of activity in each of the following.
   (a) Issued 100,000 shares for €1 million cash.
   (b) Borrowed €300,000 from a bank for ten years at 7 per cent.
   (c) Paid rent and wages totalling €20,000.
   (d) Received €50,000 for services rendered.
   (e) Purchased a bulldozer for €200,000.
   (f) Purchased a truck with issuance of shares.

# FORMAT OF THE CASH FLOW STATEMENT

The layout prescribed by **FRS 1 Cash Flow Statements** is similar yet distinct from the international standard, **IAS 7 Cash Flow Statements**. Both formats are presented to the student for study due to the prevailing regulations at this time. Small businesses do not have to complete a cash flow statement, while all publicly traded companies must present under IAS 7 for periods beginning after 1 January 2005. Those companies in between must complete the statement under the British and Irish FRS 1. Of course, the net change in the cash balance will be the same number using both formats.

## Layout under FRS 1

The layout under FRS 1 captures the essential activities of operating, investing and financing but breaks them down further into nine categories. Beginning with **net cash inflow/outflow from operating activities**, the categories are presented in bold in Figure 8.1. The cash equivalents that we discussed above are shown under **management of liquid resources** in FRS 1.

The amount calculated in the first line in the statement (net cash inflow/outflow from operating activities) is prepared separately in a note attached to the financial statements. We will examine this note later.

FIGURE 8.1: CASH FLOW STATEMENT FOR THE YEAR ENDED 31 DECEMBER 2006

| | | |
|---|---|---|
| **Net cash inflow/outflow from operating activities** | | XXX |
| | | |
| **Dividends from joint ventures and associates** | | XXX |
| | | |
| **Returns on investments and servicing of finance:** | | |
| Interest received | XX | |
| Dividends paid | (XX) | |
| Interest paid | (XX) | |
| Net cash inflow/outflow from returns | | |
| on investing activities and servicing of finance | | XXX |

**Taxation:**

| | | |
|---|---|---|
| Taxation paid | (XX) | |
| Net cash outflows from taxation | | (XXX) |

**Capital expenditure and financial investment:**

| | | |
|---|---|---|
| Payments for intangible fixed assets | (XX) | |
| Payments for tangible fixed assets | (XX) | |
| Sale of fixed assets | XX | |
| Net outflow/inflows from capital expenditure | | XXX |

**Acquisition and disposal:**

| | | |
|---|---|---|
| Purchase of subsidiaries | (XX) | |
| Sale of business | XX | XXX |

**Equity dividends**    XXX

XXX

**Management of liquid resources:**

| | | |
|---|---|---|
| Purchase of securities | (XX) | |
| Sale of securities | XX | XXX |
| Net cash flow before financing | | XXX |

**Financing:**

| | | |
|---|---|---|
| Issue of shares | XX | |
| Issue of debentures | XX | |
| Redemption of shares | (XX) | |
| Repayment of debentures/loans | (XX) | |
| Issue of expenses for shares/debentures | (XX) | XXX |

**Increase/decrease in cash**    XXX

## Layout under IAS 7

The international standard has a slightly different layout and expressly requires movements in cash to be specified under operating, investing and financing activities. As mentioned earlier, it includes both cash and cash equivalents together. The layout suggested by IAS 7 is shown in Figure 8.2.

FIGURE 8.2: CASH FLOW STATEMENT FOR THE YEAR ENDED 31 DECEMBER 2006

| | | |
|---|---|---|
| Operating profit before tax | | XXX |
| Adjustments for: | | |
| Depreciation | XXX | |
| Loss or gain on disposal | XXX | |
| Interest income | XXX | |
| Interest expense | XXX | |
| Increase/decrease in trade receivables | XXX | |
| Increase/decrease in inventories | XXX | |
| Increase/decrease in trade payables | XXX | |
| Increase/decrease in accrued liabilities | XXX | |
| Cash generated from operations | | XXX |
| Interest received | XXX | |
| Interest paid | XXX | |
| Income tax paid | XXX | XXX |
| Net cash flow from operating activities | | XXX |
| | | |
| **Cash flows from investing activities:** | | |
| Acquisition of subsidiary | XXX | |
| Purchase of plant and property | XXX | |
| Proceeds from sale of plant | XXX | |
| Net cash from investing activities | | XXX |
| | | |
| **Cash flows from financing activities:** | | |
| Proceeds from share issue | XXX | |
| Proceeds from borrowings | XXX | |
| Payment of borrowings | (XXX) | |
| Dividends payments | (XXX) | XXX |
| Net increase/decrease in cash and cash equivalents | | XXX |
| Add cash and cash equivalents at beginning of year | | XXX |
| Cash and cash equivalents at end of year | | XXX |

You will note that the items that make up the first section, **net cash inflow/outflow from operating activities,** are provided in the statement. This differs from the FRS 1 format, where the number is calculated separately. We now turn our attention to preparing the cash flow statement and will commence by examining the methods by which the cash flows from operations are calculated. To do this we must determine what information is available to us.

## Sources of information

Three sources of information are used to prepare the cash flow statement:

- **Comparative balance sheet**: Information in this statement indicates the amount of changes in assets, liabilities and shareholders' funds when comparing end of last year with end of latest year.
- **Current income statement (profit and loss)**: Information in this statement assists in determining the amount of cash provided or used by operations during the period.
- **Additional information**: This includes transaction data needed to determine how cash was provided or used during the period. This may include purchase or disposal of assets or perhaps issuance of shares for cash.

## CALCULATING THE NET CASH FLOW FROM OPERATIONS

The calculation is completed by one of two methods, the **direct** and **indirect** methods. Regardless of the method used, the result is the conversion of operating income under the accrual basis to a cash basis. Both FRS 1 and IAS 7 recommend the direct method in determining cash flows from operations, but allow either method.

The indirect method is favoured by most companies, as it is easier to prepare and is done so by reconciling the operating income to the cash flow from operating activities. This reconciliation is a requirement of FRS 1 and is shown separately in a note. While leaving the choice of method to the company, IAS 7 does insist on including the calculation in the cash flow statement.

This chapter will concentrate on the indirect method. However, both methods are discussed here.

### Self-Assessment Question 4

1. What is the indirect method attempting to reconcile?

### Direct method

Despite its name, the direct method makes great demands on companies to keep track of each type of transaction, particularly as most systems mix accrual and cash transactions. This method identifies cash received from customers, cash paid to suppliers and other cash payments for rent, wages, energy and so on. The information is obtained directly from the cash book and is inserted into the cash flow statement, as the following extract demonstrates:

| Cash flow statement for the year ended 31 December 2005 | |
| --- | --- |
| Operating activities: | |
| Cash received from customers | X |
| Cash payments to suppliers | (X) |
| Other cash payments | (X) |
| Net cash inflow/outflow from operating activities | X |

Although the direct method is recommended by FRS 1, a note reconciling the operating profit to the cash flow from operating activities is also required for users. This is why the indirect method is chosen by most entities, as it also meets the reconciliation requirement.

## Indirect method

The indirect method adjusts the operating profit before taxation, interest and dividends, for those items that do not involve a flow of cash:

- depreciation (remember, it is a non-cash expense)
- profit or loss on sale of an asset (a paper profit)
- increase/decrease in stock
- increase/decrease in debtors
- increase/decrease in creditors.

Calculated in a format called the **reconciliation of operating profit and net cash flows from operating activities**, the reconciliation under FRS 1 is captured in a note to the cash flow statement, but is not required to be part of it. The resulting amount is identical to the amount calculated under the direct method.

## Note to the cash flow statement

The note looks like this:

| Note to the cash flow statement: | |
| --- | --- |
| *Reconciliation of operating profit to net cash flow from operating activities* | |
| Operating profit (per the income statement (P&L)) | €X |
| Depreciation charges | X |
| (Gain)/loss on sale of assets | (X) |
| (Increase)/decrease in stock | X |
| (Increase)/decrease in debtors | X |
| (Decrease)/increase in creditors | X |
| | €X |

An important point regarding the operating profit is that in the income statement the interest expense may already have been included among the operating expenses. If this is the case, it is added back to the operating profit in the reconciliation shown above. The interest expense can then be shown as an outflow in the body of the cash flow statement under the heading **returns on investments and servicing of finance.**

## Understanding changes in the debtors and creditors

Why are the changes in debtors and creditors treated like this in the reconciliation? Notice how an increase in stock or debtors from one year to the next decreases the operating profit, while an increase in creditors increases it. Why is this so?

Consider the movements in the debtors account. We commence with a balance at the end of 2005 of €10,000. The balance at the end of 2006 is higher after processing credit sales and cash receipts for 2006 as follows:

| Consider debtor balance | |
| --- | --- |
| 31 December 2005 | 10,000 |
| Credit sales | 60,000 |
| **Cash received** | **(58,000)** |
| 31 December 2006 | 12,000 |

Although operating profit is ultimately increased by €60,000, the *cash* received *in* is short of that at €58,000. Therefore, we must *reduce* the operating profit in line with the cash flow picture.

In regard to creditors, an increase in the balance from one year to the next means that cash has been kept in the business instead of being paid out to satisfy creditors. Therefore, operating profit in the reconciliation is increased; a decrease in creditors decreases it. Examining the movements in the creditors account will demonstrate this. Assume a balance at the end of 2005 of €20,000 with the following credit purchases and payments made by the company in 2006:

| Consider creditor balance | |
| --- | --- |
| 31 December 2005 | 20,000 |
| Credit purchases | 80,000 |
| **Less payments made** | **75,000** |
| 31 December 2006 | 25,000 |

The operating profit is ultimately decreased with the €80,000 purchases expense, but the *cash* paid *out* was less than that at €75,000. Therefore, the impact on cash flow was less severe to the tune of €5,000, and this is the amount added back in the reconciliation.

## Self-Assessment Question 5

1. Using the indirect method, what is the net cash provided by operating activities when operating profit = €132,000; increase in creditors = €10,000; decrease in stock = €6,000; and debtors increase = €12,000?

## Disposal of an asset

In regard to the disposal of an asset, the gain or loss amount is included in the **reconciliation of operating profit and net cash flows from operating activities**, whereas the proceeds from the disposal are listed in the cash flow statement in the capital expenditure section. Keep in mind that while the proceeds do involve cash, the gain or loss on disposal does not, thus the latter adjusts the operating profit as described.

## Self-Assessment Questions 6

1. Why do you think the gain or loss on the sale of a fixed asset and any proceeds are placed in the cash flow statement, as outlined above?
2. Use the following extracts to prepare the **reconciliation of operating profit to net cash flow from operating activities**.

**Income statement for year ended Dec 2005**

| | |
|---|---|
| Operating income | 500 |
| Interest charges | 100 |
| Net income before tax | 400 |
| Tax | 50 |
| Net income after tax | 350 |
| Divided paid and proposed | 90 |
| Retained income | 260 |

The operating profit of €500 includes, among other items, €60 depreciation expense and a gain on disposal of an asset of €20.

**Current Section from balance sheet, Dec 2005 Dec 2006**

| | € | € |
|---|---|---|
| Stock | 20 | 24 |
| Debtors | 100 | 95 |
| Cash | 14 | 10 |
| | 134 | 129 |
| | | |
| Creditors | 90 | 81 |

# TACKLING AN EXAM QUESTION

You are provided with the income statement and comparative balance sheets of Santo Ltd together with information on the sale of fixed assets during the year ended December 2006. In seeking out numbers to complete the cash flow statement, the balance sheet accounts will provide you with a beginning and end amount; you then apply your understanding of what changes these accounts. For instance, fixed assets were sold, but do we know if fixed assets were also purchased? It may be necessary to use a mechanic that avails of what you know about accounts to answers this question.

And how will we know if the net cash flow number is correct? Find the beginning cash at the end of 2005 and compare it to the overdraft amount at the end of 2006. If the net cash flow number explains the swing from €600 at the end of 2005 to the €16,200 OD in 2006, then the number is correct.

## The begin-add-less and end mechanic

Accountants used this device to squeeze out numbers. We can apply it to determine the movements in and out of a number of accounts, including the plant and machinery account. The balance sheet shows the beginning and end balances for plant and machinery. The additional notes inform us of assets disposed. We can now use the mechanic as follows:

| Plant, machinery and equipment account | |
|---|---|
| Begin balance (2005) | €17,600 |
| Add | ? |
| | ? |
| Less | 5,500 |
| End | €23,900 |

Proceed to 'back into' the missing numbers. Although €5,500 was disposed of, €11,800 must have been purchased. This device will also assist in determining depreciation expense, taxes and dividend paid.

| Santo Ltd profit and loss accounts for the years to 31 December 2006 | | |
|---|---|---|
| | 2005 | 2006 |
| Profit before tax | 9,500 | 20,400 |
| Tax | (3,200) | (5,200) |
| Profit after tax | 6,300 | 15,200 |
| Dividends: | | |

| | | |
|---|---|---|
| Preference (paid) | (100) | (100) |
| Ordinary: interim (paid) | (1,000) | (2,000) |
| final (proposed) | (3,000) | (6,000) |
| Retained profit for the year | 2,200 | 7,100 |

| Balance sheets as of 31 December | 2005 | 2006 |
|---|---|---|
| **Fixed assets** | | |
| Plant, machinery, equipment at cost | 17,600 | 23,900 |
| Less accumulated depreciation | 9,500 | 10,750 |
| | 8,100 | 13,150 |
| | | |
| **Current assets** | | |
| Stocks | 5,000 | 15,000 |
| Trade debtors | 8,600 | 26,700 |
| Prepayments | 300 | 400 |
| Cash at bank | 600 | – |
| | 14,500 | 42,100 |
| | | |
| **Current liabilities** | | |
| Bank overdraft | – | 16,200 |
| Trade creditors | 6,000 | 10,000 |
| Accruals | 800 | 1,000 |
| Taxation | 3,200 | 5,200 |
| Dividends | 3,000 | 6,000 |
| | 13,000 | 38,400 |
| Total net assets | €9,600 | €16,850 |
| | | |
| **Financed by:** | | |
| **Share capital:** | | |
| Ordinary shares of €1 each | 5,000 | 5,000 |
| 10 per cent preference shares of €1 each | 1,000 | 1,000 |
| Profit and loss account | 3,000 | 10,100 |
| | 9,000 | 16,100 |
| | | |
| **Loans** | | |
| 15 per cent debenture stock | 600 | 750 |
| **Total** | €9,600 | €16,850 |

In this example, which is a typical examination question, we capture the mechanics of the statement preparation. As with all successful attempts to solve a problem, you should practise on this and other questions until you can complete the cash flow statement in a reasonable time.

**Additional information:**

During the year to 31 December 2006, fixed assets originally costing €5,500 were sold for €1,000. The accumulated depreciation on these assets as at December 2005 was €3,800.

You are required to prepare a cash flow statement for Santo Ltd for the year ended 31 December 2006 using the indirect method.

**Hint:** The 15 per cent debenture **stock** is not an interest-bearing item (non-cash charge), as distinct from a debenture **loan**, which is interest-bearing.

## Reconciling the operating profit to cash flow from operations

The operating profit before tax and dividends is €20,400. There was no interest on loans so no further adjustment is needed to the opening number. After that we note the straightforward changes to the current assets and liabilities: stocks, debtors, prepayments and the creditors and accruals. All of them have increased from 2005.

### DEPRECIATION

Not all of the fixed assets were disposed of, therefore we assume that there was **depreciation expense**. You will recall from Chapter 5 that when we dispose of an asset, we reduce the accumulated depreciation associated with the disposed asset. The disposed-of asset had an accumulated depreciation of €3,800, which would have reduced the accumulated depreciation upon disposal. Using the same mechanic described above, we can determine the depreciation charge for the year.

| Accumulated depreciation account | |
|---|---:|
| Begin balance (2005) | €9,500 |
| Add depreciation expense | ? |
| | ? |
| **Less disposed** | 3,800 |
| End balance (2006) | €10,750 |

The depreciation charge is therefore €5,050.

### GAIN OR LOSS ON DISPOSAL

Staying with fixed assets, let's see if the disposed asset was sold for a gain or a loss. If the original cost of the disposed asset was €5,500 and its accumulated depreciation was €3,800, then the **net book value** must have been €1,700. The proceeds received were €1,000, therefore it was sold at a loss of €700.

The reconciliation can now be completed.

**Note to the cash flow statement:**

Reconciliation of operating profit to net cash flow from operating activities:

| | |
|---|---:|
| Operating profit before taxation and dividends | €20,400 |
| Depreciation charge | 5,050 |
| Loss on disposal | 700 |
| Increase in stock | (10,000) |
| Increase in debtors | (18,100) |
| Increase in prepayments | (100) |
| Increase in creditors | 4,000 |
| Increase in accruals | 200 |
| | 2,150 |

## The cash flow statement

We will look at the key movements in cash in the order presented in the statement, with the net cash flow from operations on the top line.

### DIVIDENDS

The balance sheets show the two ending liability balances 2005 and 2006 for dividends payable, and the P&L statement shows that dividends were declared in both years. What is key to grasp here is that a dividend declared at the end of 2005 was not paid until early 2006. This is the cash flow. A little complication here concerns the **interim payment**. This is declared *and* paid in the year. The preference share amount is straightforward. It was paid in the year it was declared and is shown separately under the heading **returns on investments and servicing of finance** in the cash flow statement.

Let's put these numbers together in the mechanic to determine the actual **cash flow** – the amount **paid in dividends**:

**Ordinary shares:**

| | |
|---|---|
| Begin balance (2005) | €3,000 |
| Add declared for 2006 | 8,000 (2,000 interim + 6,000 final) |
| | 11,100 |
| Less balance end of 2006 | 6,000 |
| Paid in 2006 | €5,000 |

The €5,000 is included in the statement as **equity dividends**.

Another way of looking at the dividends is to see from the balance sheet that the amount proposed in 2005 of €3,000 was paid in 2006, and when added to the interim paid of €2,000 in 2006, makes up the €5,000 calculated above.

## TAXATION

Determining the taxes paid is similar to dividends paid. Taxes calculated at the end of 2005 are paid in 2006. This, then, is the cash outflow. Using the two ending balance sheet liability balances and the tax expense for 2005, we can 'squeeze out' the taxes paid in 2006:

| Taxes payable: | |
| --- | --- |
| Begin balance (2005) | €3,200 |
| Add charge for 2006 | 5,200 |
| | 8,400 |
| Less balance end of 2006 | 5,200 |
| **Paid in 2006** | **€3,200** |

The €3,200 paid was the amount owed to the Revenue Commissioners at 31 December 2005 but not paid until sometime in 2006.

## CAPITAL EXPENDITURE

We have previously discussed this calculation when introducing the mechanic of 'backing into' missing numbers. So, knowing the amount disposed, here it is one more time:

| Property, plant, equipment: | |
| --- | --- |
| Begin balance (2005) | €17,600 |
| Add | 11,800 (squeezed) |
| | 29,400 |
| Less | 5,500 |
| End | €23,900 |

Both the amount spent (€11,800) and the proceeds of €1,000 from the disposal are listed in the capital expenditure section.

## FINANCING

There has been no issue of shares, but loans have increased by €150.

We are now in a position to prepare the cash flow statement, beginning with the **net cash flow from operating activities**.

**Cash flow statement for the year ended 31 December 2006**

| | | |
|---|---|---|
| Net cash inflow from operating activities | | €2,150 |
| Returns on investments and servicing of finance: | | |
| Dividends paid | (100) | |
| Net cash inflow/outflow from returns on | | |
| investing activities and servicing of finance | | (100) |
| | | |
| Taxation: | | |
| Taxation paid | (3,200) | |
| Net cash outflows from taxation | | (3,200) |
| | | |
| Capital expenditure: | | |
| Payments for tangible fixed assets | (11,800) | |
| Proceeds from sale of fixed assets | 1,000 | |
| Net outflow/inflows from capital expenditure | | (10,800) |
| | | (11,950) |
| | | |
| Equity dividends | | (5,000) |
| | | |
| **Net cash flows before financing** | | (16,950) |
| Financing: | | |
| Issue of debenture stock | | 150 |
| **Decrease in cash** | | **(16,800)** |

We can test to see if the decrease is correct by comparing the beginning and ending cash balances found in the balance sheet:

| | |
|---|---|
| Cash balance as at 31 December 2005 | €600 |
| Cash balance as at 31 December 2006 | (16,200) |
| Net outflow | (16,800) |

The cash position plummeted from a €600 balance in 2005 to an overdraft balance of €16,200 for a total swing downward of €16,800.

## CASH IS KING

A popular book during the early 1990s was aptly titled *Happiness is Positive Cash Flow* by an American entrepreneur, Frederick Adler (1989). It contained advice from many business leaders that mostly centred on control of cash. It did not advocate hoarding money, but advised on anticipating cash needs, negotiating loans and understanding costs and when these costs occurred. The cash flow statement is a useful tool in determining where companies might have applied Adler's advice.

## Is negative cash flow a bad thing?

But if cash flow is negative at the end of a year, is it a bad sign? Consider the 2003 cash flow statement from CRH plc, the international materials group, in Figure 8.3. Going straight to the bottom of the statement, you will notice that the cash flow is negative: it spent more than it took in to the tune of €5.3 million. This might seem like a bad sign, but when we understand how money was spent at CRH, we find that it is quite a satisfactory picture overall.

On running any business, being able to pay the day-to-day expenses is critical. Plans will be 'pie in the sky' if expenses such as payroll on Friday cannot be met. CRH reported a nearly €1.4 billion inflow from its operations, the day-to-day activities. This is what is meant by having the fundamentals in place. Moving down the statement we note that the group spent over €1.4 billion on acquisitions. These purchases essentially guarantee future cash streams in earnings. It also managed to pay out €122.8 million in dividends, thus satisfying shareholders. When analysed in this fashion, the cash flow picture of CRH in 2003 is most satisfactory.

## Cash flow statement as a governance device

Anything that converts the accrual-based performance into cash terms is certainly to be welcomed. Users of statements can only hope that transactions have been classified correctly. However, some caution must be applied. Several US companies have had to settle with the US legislator, the SEC, for such offences as classifying some operating expenses as capital expenditures (Mulford 2003). This inflated the cash flow from operations, thus distorting this component of the cash flow statement.

## Free cash flow?

How can anything be considered free, particularly when relating to cash? Free cash flow is not to be confused with 'free cash'. When looking at the cash flow statement, investors may judge that certain outflows were not necessary and that it would be better to keep the cash than spend it. Consider again the CRH statement. If the group chose not to pay a dividend (a €122.8 million saving) or perhaps if it held acquisitions at €1 billion (a €439 million saving), then the free cash flow would be as follows:

| | |
|---|---|
| Ending net flow | (5.3) |
| Dividends unpaid | 122.8 |
| Acquisitions not made | 439.0 |
| Free cash flow | 556.5 |

It could be viewed that conceivably there was inherently greater cash strength in CRH that a potential takeover investor might avail of.

## Conclusion

In preparing the cash flow statement, we have achieved a greater understanding of the movements in cash. Although the statement is historical, it does cover the short term and is thus essential to controlling a business's liquidity. The indirect method forces the accountant to calculate the net cash flows from operations by considering the other financial statements (the P&L account and the balance sheet) and in this way makes a connection between financial performance and financial position.

FIGURE 8.3: CRH CASH FLOW STATEMENT FOR THE YEAR ENDED 2003

| CRH cash flow statement for the year ended | 2003 | 2002 |
|---|---|---|
| | €m | €m |
| Net cash inflows from operating activities | 1,396.2 | 1,553.5 |
| Dividends received from joint ventures | | |
| and associates | 19.4 | 23.5 |
| Returns on investments and servicing of finance: | | |
| Interest received | 36.1 | 57.7 |
| Interest paid | (140.5) | (183.2) |
| Finance lease interest paid | (0.7) | (0.7) |
| Preference dividends paid | (0.1) | (0.1) |
| | (105.2) | (126.3) |
| Taxation: | | |
| Irish corporation tax paid | (19.6) | (17.2) |
| Overseas paid | (83.3) | (145.1) |
| | (102.9) | (162.3) |
| Capital expenditure: | | |
| Purchase of tangible assets | (402.0) | (367.4) |
| Less capital grants received | 0.1 | 0.1 |
| | (401.9) | (367.3) |
| Disposal of fixed assets | 77.9 | 104.4 |
| | (324.0) | (262.9) |

| | | |
|---|---:|---:|
| **Investments in subsidiary, joint venture and associated undertakings:** | | |
| Acquisition of subsidiary undertakings | (1,439.0) | (793.7) |
| Deferred acquisition consideration | (56.8) | (80.3) |
| Investments in and advances to joint ventures and associates | (79.5) | (22.0) |
| | (1,575.3) | (896.0) |
| **Equity dividends paid** | (122.8) | (111.6) |
| **Cash (outflow)/inflow before use of liquid investments and financing** | (814.6) | 17.9 |
| **Cash (outflow)/inflow from management of liquid investments** | 110.4 | (169.7) |
| | | |
| **Financing:** | | |
| Issue of shares | 13.7 | 13.8 |
| Expenses paid in respect of share issues | (0.1) | (0.4) |
| Increase in term debt | 688.4 | 192.5 |
| Capital elements of finance leases repaid | (3.1) | (5.1) |
| | 698.9 | 200.8 |
| (Decrease)/increase in cash and demand debt in the year | (5.3) | 49.0 |

## Self-Assessment Question 7

1. The following information relates to Arnold Ltd for the year ended 31 December 2005. Using the indirect method, prepare a cash flow statement for Arnold Ltd for the year ended 31 December 2005.

**Profit and loss account for the year ended 31 December 2005**

| | | €000 |
|---|---:|---:|
| Gross profit | | 230 |
| Administrative expenses | 77 | |
| Loss on sale of vehicle | 3 | |
| Depreciation | 35 | 115 |
| Operating profit | | 115 |
| Taxation | | 65 |
| | | 50 |

| | | | | |
|---|---|---:|---|---:|
| Dividends | | | | 25 |
| Retained profits for the year | | | | 25 |

### Balance sheet at 31 December 2005

| | | 2004 | | 2005 |
|---|---|---:|---|---:|
| | | €000 | | €000 |
| **Fixed assets** | | | | |
| Vehicles at cost | | 150 | | 200 |
| Less: Depreciation | | 75 | 75 | 100 | 100 |

| | | 2004 | | 2005 |
|---|---:|---:|---:|---:|
| **Current assets** | | | | |
| Stocks | | 60 | | 50 |
| Debtors | | 76 | | 95 |
| Cash | | 6 | | 8 |
| | | 142 | | 153 |
| **Less: Current liabilities** | | | | |
| Creditors | 60 | | 53 | |
| Corporation tax | 52 | | 65 | |
| Proposed dividends | 20 | 132 | 25 | 143 |
| Net current assets | | 10 | | 10 |
| | | 85 | | 110 |
| **Capital and reserves:** | | | | |
| Ordinary share capital | | 75 | | 75 |
| Retained profit | | 10 | | 35 |
| | | 85 | | 110 |

### Additional information:

During the year the company sold a vehicle for €12,000 in cash. The vehicle originally cost €25,000 and had an accumulated depreciation of €10,000 at the time of disposal. It also purchased some new vehicles during the year.

# CHAPTER REVIEW

The cash flow statement provides information about cash receipts and cash disbursements for a particular period. We discussed the various ways that cash can flow in and out of a business and determined that the sources of information for completing the cash flow are the comparative balance sheet, the current profit and loss account and additional information on items such as the disposal of an asset. We find that a business will have three basic activities: operating, investing and financing. The layout of the statement reflects these distinctions for both IAS 7 and FRS 1.

Two methods, the direct and indirect methods, are used to complete the statement and they differ in the way that they calculate the first line on the statement, described as net cash inflow/outflow from operating activities. The direct method gets information directly from the cash book on cash received from customers, cash paid to suppliers and other cash transactions. The indirect method commences with the operating profit before tax and adjusts this amount back to its cash basis profit. These adjustments are completed in a note called the reconciliation of operating profit and net cash flows from operating activities. Most entities prefer the indirect method.

Cash flow statements are closely scrutinised by investors. As the CRH statement (Figure 8.3) indicates, negative cash flow is not necessarily a bad thing. As long as operations are producing positive flows, then other outflows must be considered for their long-term impact. The CF is the source for free cash flow, a concept that some investors avail of to speculate on what would happen if management refrained from certain expenditures. While the statement converts the accrual picture into raw cash, it must be used judiciously when evaluating corporate governance in a company.

# SELF-ASSESSMENT QUESTION ANSWERS

## SAQ 1

1. The primary purpose of the cash flow statement is to provide information about cash receipts and cash disbursements and to help readers to understand the movements of cash in a business through its operating, investing and financing activities.

## SAQ 2

| | | |
|---|---|---|
| Inflow: | | |
| Cash sales | €20,000 | |
| Credit sales collected (€300k at 60 per cent) | 180,000 | |
| Total inflow | | 200,000 |

| Outflow: | | |
|---|---|---|
| Cash purchases | €10,000 | |
| Paid to creditors (€90k − €30k) | 60,000 | |
| Total outflow | | 70,000 |
| **Net cash inflow** | | **€130,000** |

## SAQ 3

1. (a) Financing
   (b) Financing
   (c) Operating
   (d) Operating
   (e) Investing
   (f) Non-cash activity – not included in the statement

## SAQ 4

1. The indirect method reconciles the operating profit for a period with the actual cash flow resulting from operations in the same period. It is a conversion of the accrual-based profit into the cash equivalent or net cash result.

## SAQ 5

1. 132 + 10 + 6 − 12 = 136

## SAQ 6

1. Any gain or loss from a disposal must be included in the income statement, usually shown after gross profit (if a gain) or among the operating expenses (if a loss). Thus we must factor it in when completing the reconciliation. The proceeds are those resulting from the disposal of a fixed asset, a capital investment, and thus it is appropriate to be shown in the capital expenditure section.

2. **Reconciliation:**

| | |
|---|---|
| Operating income before interest and tax | 500 |
| Depreciation | 60 |
| Gain on disposal | (20) |
| Increase in stock | (4) |
| Decrease in debtors | 5 |
| Decrease in creditors | (9) |
| | 532 |

## SAQ 7

1. **Depreciation:**

    We are given this amount at 35. Asset was disposed, so movement in accum depreciation.

    | | |
    |---|---:|
    | Begin balance | 75 |
    | Add deprec expense | 35 |
    | | 110 |
    | Less disposed | 10 |
    | End balance | 100 |

This works out:

**Movement in fixed assets:**

| | |
|---|---:|
| Begin balance 2004 | 150 |
| **Add purchases** | 75 (squeeze out) (capital expenditure section) |
| | 225 |
| Less disposal at cost | (25) |
| End balance 2005 | 200 |

**Gain or loss on disposal?**

| | |
|---|---:|
| Historic cost | 25 |
| Less accum dep | 10 |
| NBV | 15 |
| Proceeds | 12 (goes to capital expenditure section) |
| **Loss on disposal** | 3 (goes to reconciliation) |

**Taxes paid:**

| | |
|---|---:|
| Tax payable 2004 | 52 |
| Add P&L | 65 |
| | 117 |
| Less tax payable 2005 | (65) |
| **Actual payment in 2005** | 52 (goes to taxation section) |

**Dividends paid:**

| | |
|---|---:|
| Payable 2004 | 20 |
| Add declared | 25 |
| | 45 |

| | | |
|---|---|---|
| Less payable 2005 | (25) | |
| **Actual paid 2005** | **20** (goes to equity section) | |

**Note:**
**Reconciliation of operating profit from operating activities**

| | |
|---|---|
| Operating profit | 115 |
| Depreciation | 35 |
| Loss on disposal | 3 |
| Decrease in stock | 10 |
| Increase in debtors | −19 |
| Decrease in creditors | −7 |
| Net cash flow from operating activities | 137 |

**Arnold Ltd**
**Cash flow statement for the year ended 31 December 2005**

| | | |
|---|---|---|
| Net cash flow from operating activities | | 137 |
| Net cash flow from return on investments and servicing of debt | | 0 |
| Taxation: | | |
| Net cash outflow from taxation | −52 | |
| Capital expenditure: | | |
| Payment for fixed assets | −75 | |
| Proceeds from disposal of fixed assets | 12 | |
| Net cash outflow from capital expenditure | | −63 |
| Financing | | 0 |
| Increase in cash | | 2 |

This is in line with movement in the cash position: 6 in 2004 and 8 in 2005.

# REFERENCES

Accounting Standards Board, *FRS 1 Cash Flow Statements*, London: ASB 1997.

Adler, F., *Happiness is Cash Flow*, New York: Boardroom Reports Inc. 1989.

CRH plc, *Annual Report 2003*, Registered Office: 42 Fitzwilliam Square, Dublin 2 March 2004.

Heneghan, J. and O'Regan, P., *Accounting*, Limerick: Centre for Project Management, University of Limerick 2000.

International Accounting Standards Board, *IAS 7 Cash Flow Statements*, London: IASB 1992.

Mulford, C. and Comiskey, E., *The Financial Numbers Game*, New York: John Witey & Sons 2002.

O'Regan, P., *Introduction to Accounting*, Limerick: The International Equine Institute, University of Limerick 1998.

O'Regan, P., *Financial Information Analysis*, Chichester: John Wiley & Sons 2001.

# 9

# *Interpretation of Financial Information*

# INTRODUCTION

We have spent a considerable amount of time discussing the preparation and presentation of the financial statements and we have now arrived at the point when we can ask what the numbers say. In Chapter 1 we described accounting within the context of an information system. This makes sense, particularly when we consider that users of accounting information ultimately want to make decisions. We are now at the confluence of accounting knowledge and systems and professional judgment, a point at which the true and fair view of financial statements is examined and sometimes contested by users. Relying upon the numbers is a **corporate governance** issue. Using the statements and the numbers they contain reflects the financial decision-making process. As discussed in Chapter 2, reliability and relevance of information are underlying concerns when interpreting accounts.

This chapter brings together the three major statements that you are now familiar with: the income statement (P&L), the balance sheet and the cash flow statement. Analysis will be conducted within and among statements. Financial performance will be linked to financial position as we try to get a handle on the past to somehow anticipate future trends. The accrual basis of accounting has dominated our studies so far, so we must seek out grounds for reliance on today's financial reporting by tying cash flow to profitability. And as the banker's tale below suggests, the role of management is also included for analysis. Accordingly, financial analysis is presented as providing insights into a business, and such insights allowing the professional to make a judgment (Lonergan 1958).

## OBJECTIVES

**When you have finished this chapter, you will be able to:**

- analyse a business's performance by horizontal and vertical analysis
- quantify liquidity, profitability and solvency
- understand the limitations of financial analysis.

## The banker's tale

Let's begin with a vignette that outlines the challenge facing users of financial information. It concerns a lending officer's observation that one of the bank's customers was seriously overdue on its 180-day loan. The customer in question owned and managed a furniture-making business and despite repeated letters and phone calls had done nothing to repay or reduce the debt. This prompted the banker to visit the customer. When she arrived at the plant she observed the place to be a hive of activity, with trucks dropping off materials and other trucks departing filled with finished furniture goods. This picture was at variance with the perception suggested by the overdue payment of the debt.

Three questions arise:
- What is the problem?
- Can it be quantified?
- Where can we find it in the financial statements?

Once you have the answers to these questions, you will then have insights. That is the point at which you can apply judgment.

from Heneghan and O'Regan, *Accounting*, Limerick: Centre for Project Management, University of Limerick 2000.

## FINANCIAL PERFORMANCE AND ANALYSIS

You have essentially been preoccupied to date with the linear flow of the accounting information system:

However, both managers and shareholders are equally preoccupied with another flow or cycle of business activities that highlights key areas of scrutiny (Mores *et al.* 1991). Figure 9.1 demonstrates this flow. The company puts capital to use by investing in assets that hopefully generate sufficient profits to repay loans and satisfy shareholders with dividends. It should also increase its net worth so that it can pay for expansion and continue to grow. This is clearly a dynamic cycle. How well a company does in each of these activities is the subject of financial analysis.

FIGURE 9.1: FLOW OF BUSINESS ACTIVITY

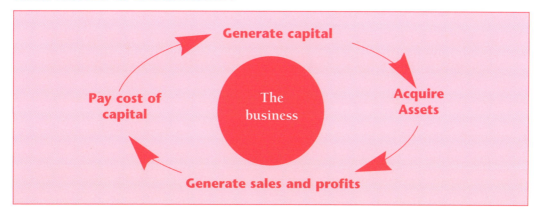

## Overview

Interpreting anything calls for analysis. Analysis allows us to look at something in a number of different ways and thus get a glimpse of the bigger picture. For instance, a company's balance sheet indicates that the cash account has a balance of €100,000, which may seem to be a large amount of money to most people (and it is!). However, if the monthly cash balance on average for the prior six months had been €500,000, then the company may now have a cash flow problem.

Or consider for a moment a company's profit and loss statement showing profit as a percentage of sales at 10 per cent. That appears satisfactory, but what if the industry average is 20 per cent? The situation then looks ominous for this company.

Any analysis of data must include comparisons of that data with other financial data to provide information that is of use. We will examine a number of approaches in this chapter.

However, before we do that let's understand what it is that concerns the business manager when running a business. Firstly, management is concerned about **liquidity**, i.e. a company's ability to pay for its day-to-day expenses. Secondly, it is concerned about **solvency**, i.e. whether the business will be able to meet its debts when they become due. Thirdly, **profitability** is monitored – after all, one of the reasons a business exists is to make a profit. Debtor and stock levels are also monitored for activity. These concerns (see Figure 9.2) are at the heart of the financial analysis effort.

FIGURE 9.2: BUSINESS CONCERNS

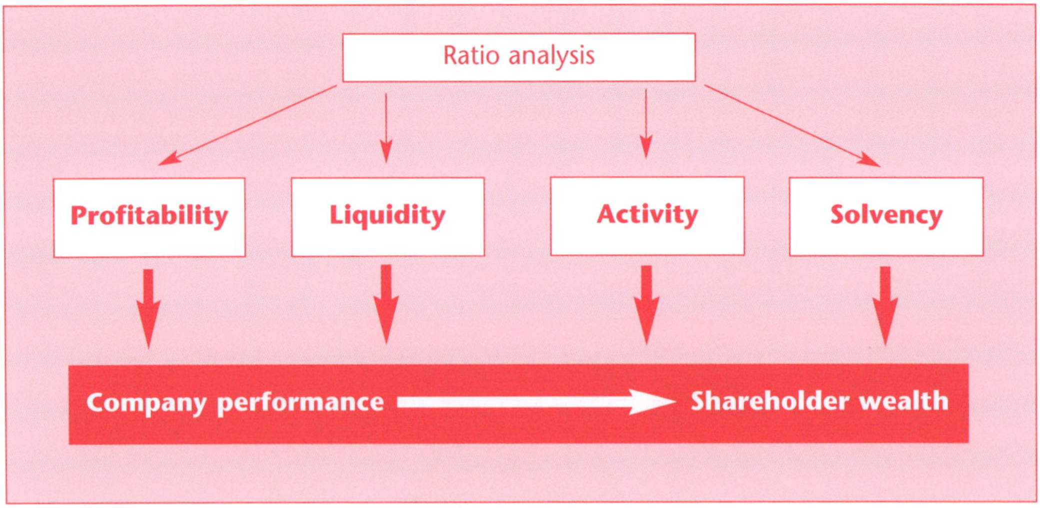

## Comparative analysis

Three types of comparisons can be made:
- **Intracompany basis**: Comparisons within a company are often useful to detect changes

in financial relationships and significant trends. For instance, comparing last year's cash balance with this year's balance will show whether there was an increase or a decrease. Comparing a recent month's operating profit as a percentage of sales with the year to date figure may uncover an error in a recent month's number.

- **Intercompany basis:** Comparisons with other companies provide insight into a company's competitive position. Sales figures and sales growth will not only determine the leaders in an industry, but will also highlight future threats.
- **Industry averages:** Comparisons with industry averages provide information about a company's relative position within an industry.

Now that we have established what we are comparing, we will discuss the three basic tools used in financial statement analysis:

- horizontal analysis
- vertical analysis
- ratio analysis.

The first two are covered in this section, with an overview provided on ratio analysis. The latter is divided up into three sections to cover the three key areas of liquidity, solvency and profitability.

## Self-Assessment Questions 1

1. What are the major bases of comparison for a business?
2. Name the tools used to make comparative analysis.
3. What is the need for comparative analysis?

## Horizontal analysis

This is a technique for evaluating a series of financial statement data over a period of time. Its purpose is to determine the increase or decrease that has taken place, expressed as either an amount or a percentage. Let's look at the following sales of a company in millions:

| 2002 | 2003 | 2004 | 2005 | 2006 |
|------|------|------|------|------|
| 3.0  | 3.2  | 3.5  | 4.0  | 3.6  |

If we assume that 2002 is the base year, we can measure all percentage increases or decreases from this base-period amount with the formula:

$$\frac{\text{current year amount} - \text{base year amount}}{\text{base year amount}}$$

We can determine that sales increased approximately 7 per cent from 2002 to 2003, and from 2002 to 2006 sales increased by 20 per cent.

Although there is an upward trend with each year increasing when compared to 2002, the drop in sales for 2006 causes the percentage increase to drop too:

| 2002 | 2003 | 2004 | 2005 | 2006 |
|------|------|------|------|------|
| 3.0  | 3.2  | 3.5  | 4.0  | 3.6  |
| n/a  | 7%   | 17%  | 33%  | 20%  |

We can analyse this a little differently by looking at each year as a percentage of the base period:

| 2002 | 2003 | 2004 | 2005 | 2006 |
|------|------|------|------|------|
| 3.0  | 3.2  | 3.5  | 4.0  | 3.6  |
| 100% | 107% | 117% | 133% | 120% |

Over the long term there is a definite upward trend, although the drop in 2006 should get the company's attention.

Applying horizontal analysis further to the financial statements offers up important insights, as illustrated with a look at the financial statements of a company for a two-year period.

**Oregon Forest Company**
**Balance sheet as of 31 December**
**(in millions)**

| | 2006 | 2005 | Increase/decrease Amount | % |
|---|---|---|---|---|
| **Assets** | | | | |
| Current assets | 1,528 | 1,429 | 99 | 6.9% |
| Plant assets | 2,932 | 2,784 | 148 | 5.3% |
| Other assets | 588 | 201 | 387 | 192.5% |
| Total assets | 5,048 | 4,414 | 634 | 14.4% |
| | | | | |
| **Liabilities and shareholders** | | | | |
| Current liabilities | 2,200 | 1,265 | 935 | 73.9% |
| Long term | 1,568 | 1,558 | 10 | .6% |
| | | | | |
| Common stock | 202 | 183 | 19 | 10.3% |
| Retained earning | 3,981 | 3,769 | 212 | 5.6% |
| Treasury stock | (2,903) | (2,361) | 542 | 23.0% |
| | 5,048 | 4,414 | 634 | 14.4% |

The comparative table shows a number of changes from 2005 to 2006. Current assets increased by €99 million, or 7 per cent, plant assets by €148 million and other assets 192 per cent. This last increase may be due to purchase or acquisition of trademarks, trade names or goodwill.

*Treasury stock is common stock or share capital bought back from shareholders.*

Plant assets increased, yet there is little increase in the share capital or long-term debt. Current liabilities have increased rather dramatically, allowing us to speculate that the plant acquired was financed primarily with short-term debt. Such a situation, if true, would put pressure on the supply of day-to-day funding requirements.

When change is expressed in percentage form, it is easier to grasp the true magnitude of the change.

Here is the income statement (P&L) in comparative form.

| (In millions) | | | Increase/decrease | |
|---|---|---|---|---|
| | 2006 | 2005 | Amount | % |
| Net sales | 6,676 | 7,003 | (327) | (4.7%) |
| Cost of goods sold | 3,123 | 3,177 | 54 | 1.7% |
| Gross profit | 3,553 | 3,826 | (273) | (7.1%) |
| Selling and adm | 2,458 | 2,566 | 108 | 4.2% |
| Non-recurring charges | 136 | 421 | 285 | 67.7% |
| Operating income | 959 | 839 | 121 | 14.4% |
| Int expense | 66 | 63 | (3) | (4.8%) |
| Other income | (33) | 21 | (54) | n/a |
| Income before taxes | 860 | 796 | 64 | 8.0% |
| Income tax expense | 329 | 306 | (23) | (7.5%) |
| Net income | 531 | 490 | 41 | 8.3% |

A significant observation here is that sales and gross profit decreased while net income increased. The achievement of the net income increase in a period of falling sales was due mainly to the reduction in non-recurring expense in 2006, possibly early retirement packages. Is the company undergoing some structural change?

As these examples show, the financial position and operating results are compared and significant changes **flagged** for investigation to determine the reason for the changes.

## Self-Assessment Question 2

1. Chopper Ltd reported net sales of €300,000, €330,000 and €360,000 in the years 2004, 2005 and 2006, respectively.
   (a) If 2004 is the base year, what is the percentage trend for 2005 and 2006?
   (b) If the company's performance exceeds the industry levels, what basis of comparison is being used?

### Vertical analysis

Vertical analysis is a technique for calculating financial data that expresses each item in a financial statement as a percentage of a base amount. For example, on a balance sheet we might say that current assets are 22 per cent of total assets (total assets being the base amount). Or in the income statement we might say that selling expenses are 16 per cent of net sales (net sales being the base amount).

These percentages should be investigated for differences either:

● across years in the same company or
● in the same year across different companies.

A benefit of vertical analysis is that it facilitates a comparison with companies that vary in size.

## Self-Assessment Question 3

1. In vertical analysis, what base amount would you choose for each of the operating expenses?

### Ratio analysis

Ratio analysis provides quantitative insight into the financial position and performance of a business. Clues to underlying conditions that may not be apparent from an initial inspection of the financial statements are uncovered. On its own a ratio may not throw much light on an entity, but if discussed in the context of meaningful comparisons with the industry or with previous years, then ratios are a powerful tool. Ratios are divided into three groups, reflecting the fundamental concerns of a business, namely liquidity, solvency and profitability. A section is dedicated to each of these three ratio groups (see Figure 9.3).

FIGURE 9.3: RATIO GROUPS

| Profitability | Liquidity | Activity | Gearing |
|---|---|---|---|
| • Net profit margin | • Current ratio | • Stock turnover | • Debt/equity ratio |
| • Gross profit margin | • Quick ratio, a.k.a | • Debtors turnover | • Times interest |
| • Return on capital | acid-test ratio | • Asset turnover | covered |
| employed | | | |

Recall our banker's tale from the beginning of this chapter. What is her concern? The bank has not been paid. If the company is insolvent, the bank will not get its money. Banks are not in the business of making furniture and closing down businesses is a last resort. But the plant appears to be busy, so perhaps it is an operational situation and the lack of funds is temporary. Ratio analysis will provide insights to the business and help the banker and us to get to the root of the problem.

Before we examine each set of ratios, you should be aware that textbooks and teachers often vary in their definition of many of them. The ratios presented here are the generally understood items, although many companies create or adapt ratios to the demands of their operations. The issue really is whether the ratio in question interprets a company's performance adequately.

# LIQUIDITY RATIOS

The ability of a business to pay for its current obligations is of keen interest to the creditors of that business. Bankers and creditors will assess the liquidity position so that they can be certain that loans will be repaid and supplies can be paid for. A quick look at the balance sheet will allow the user to determine working capital, which we define as the excess of current liabilities over current assets. Ratios reveal the behind-the-scenes nature of working capital (Hampton 1982). A multiyear business plan will seem academic if there is not enough cash to pay the electricity bill or cover the weekly payroll. And that is before unanticipated cash needs.

The following ratios evaluate a business's liquidity:

- current ratio
- acid-test ratio
- debtors turnover ratio
- average collection period
- stock (inventory) turnover ratio
- average days stock.

## Current ratio

This compares the current assets with current liabilities. We divide the current assets by the current liabilities to determine the amount of current assets available to cover each euro of current debt.

If a company has €1.2 million in current assets and €1 million of current liabilities, then the company has a current ratio of 1:2, as follows:

$$\frac{\text{current assets}}{\text{current liabilities}} = \frac{1,200,000}{1,000,000} = 1:2$$

For every €1 of debt there is €1.20 available to cover the debt. Is this number good or bad? In general, a current ratio greater than one is satisfactory. However, it depends on the type of industry the company is in. High-tech companies, for instance, produce products that have ever-shortening lives and therefore must continue to pour cash into research and development, marketing and highly paid employees; a current ratio of 5:1 may be required. On the other hand, retail supermarkets may face stiff competition in their industry, but in general their operations are stable, and because they have few debtors, a current ratio of less than one is tolerable.

A weakness in the current ratio is that it does not consider the composition of current assets. For instance, what is the actual amount of cash in the business? Is too much tied up in slow-paying debtors, or is the level of inventory excessive? The acid test, also known as the quick ratio, addresses this shortcoming.

### ACID-TEST RATIO

The **acid-test ratio** measures the immediate short-term liquidity. It takes the cash and near-cash amount (investments and debtors) and divides it by the current liabilities. Comparing this number with the industry average provides some indication of a company's liquidity strength.

$$\frac{\text{cash} + \text{cash equivalents} + \text{debtors}}{\text{current liabilities}}$$

## Debtor turnover and age

The **debtor turnover ratio** measures the number of times that debtors are collected from during the year. The net sales figure is divided by the average debtor balance. The average trade debtors balance is usually calculated by means of a simple average (add opening and closing debtor balances and divide by two). However, if the closing balance is representative of the overall period, then it is the closing balance that is used instead of the average balance.

What is a good number in this instance? A lot will depend on the business you are in, but in general, the faster the turnover, the greater the reliance on the current and quick ratios will be. Fast-moving debtors may place greater demands for products and services and in turn cause the business to increase activity with creditors.

$$\frac{\text{net sales}}{\text{average debtors}}$$

This is linked to calculating the **age** of the debtors (see below).

## DEBTOR AGE (AVERAGE COLLECTION PERIOD)

The age of debtors, also called the **average collection period ratio,** continues from the debtors turnover ratio. If a company has a debtor turnover of five for the year, then we divide that number into 365 days to determine the average age of the debtors to be seventy-three days. Is this good or bad? Clearly a collection period of thirty-five days is preferable to seventy-three days, but the ratio varies between industries. High-volume, high-turnover businesses such as retail grocery outlets will have shorter collection periods than those selling luxury cars or haulage equipment.

$$\frac{365 \text{ days}}{\text{debtors turnover ratio}}$$

## Self-Assessment Question 4

1. Lamont Company has the following balance sheet items for 2006.
   (a) What is the current ratio?
   (b) What is the acid-test ratio?

| | |
|---|---|
| Cash | 8,200 |
| Short-term investments | 1,900 |
| Debtors | 12,500 |
| Inventories | 14,800 |
| Other current assets | 5,300 |
| Total current assets | 42,700 |
| Total current liabilities | 44,800 |

## Stock (inventory) turnover and age

**Stock (inventory) turnover ratio** measures the number of times on average that stock balance is sold or turned over during the year. It is calculated by dividing the costs of goods

This is linked to calculating the **age of the stock** (see below).

sold by the average stock. The average stock is easily calculated, as the P&L account will contain the opening and closing stock amounts. The two amounts are added and the sum is divided by two.

$$\frac{\text{cost of goods sold}}{\text{average stock}}$$

### AGE (AVERAGE DAYS STOCK)

As with the debtors, the age of the stock over a year is derived by dividing the stock turnover into 365 days. This puts an age on the stock, and by assessing it against the industry average, you can judge whether or not it is slow moving.

$$\frac{365 \text{ days}}{\text{stock turnover ratio}}$$

That completes our review of the liquidity ratios. Maintaining sound liquidity is one of management's most important responsibilities. In Chapter 11 we will discuss techniques for controlling and managing cash. For now, we will summarise by stating that a timely reporting system, combined with strong collections procedures, will maximise cash flow so that emergencies are covered and discounts from suppliers are availed of.

## Activity ratios

The liquidity ratios just discussed give an indicator of the position of working capital or available cash for operations. Because the debtor turnover number and stock turnover number are often referred to as **activity ratios,** they give a glimpse of how quickly (or slowly) debtors are paying and stock is shifting. Strong management will keep these indicators at a minimum.

## Cash and operating cycles

Additional insights into day-to-day operations can be gleaned from combining some of the ratios just explained.

### OPERATING CYCLE

This is the time between the purchase of stock and the cash received from the sale of those goods. It is calculated by adding the stock days to age of debtors. If an entity's stock days are forty and age of debtors is forty-five days, then the operating cycle is eighty-five days.

### CASH CYCLE

This encompasses creditor days by subtracting the age of creditors from the operating cycle (debtors and stock days). The age of creditors is calculated by dividing the average creditor balance into cost of goods sold to give the creditor turnover. This number is then divided into 365 days to come up with the age in days. If creditor days is sixty-five, then the cash cycle is as follows:

$$\text{stock days} + \text{debtor days} - \text{creditor days} = \text{cash cycle}$$
$$40 + 45 \qquad - 65 \qquad = 20 \text{ days}$$

A positive number has resulted, which means that creditors are paid twenty days before the cash payment from sales is received. This is not a desirable outcome.

## SOLVENCY RATIOS

Solvency ratios measure the ability of a business to survive over a long period. In other words, can it meet its obligations now and over the long term? They deal with the fundamental financial question of whether the business has a future. For most companies, this means being able to repay its debts on time. Solvency also focuses on the business's total assets to determine how well they are being used and how they are made up. The **going concern principle** (see Chapter 2) reflects this issue of survival and solvency.

There are three ratios that assist the user to gauge solvency:
- debts to total assets ratio
- debt to equity ratio
- times interest earned.

### Debts to total assets ratio

This ratio measures the percentage of total assets provided by creditors. It is calculated by dividing the total of all debt (including current and long-term liabilities) by total assets.

$$\frac{\text{total debt}}{\text{total assets}}$$

It provides some indication of the risk faced by creditors and the ability of a business to repay its obligations. For instance, a 75 per cent ratio carries a greater risk that the company will be unable to repay its debt than that associated with a 25 per cent ratio.

### Debt to equity ratio

Referred to as the gearing ratio, it compares the use of borrowed funds with the resources invested by the owners. The argument on whether to acquire more equity (and give away ownership) or take on more debt (repayments in good times

This is often referred to as the **gearing ratio**.

and bad) comes into focus here and is the subject of study beyond the scope of this book. It is calculated as follows:

$$\frac{\text{long-term loans}}{\text{shareholders' funds} + \text{long term loans}}$$

## Times interest earned

Also called the **interest cover,** it indicates the company's ability to meet interest payments as they come due. It is calculated by dividing income before interest expense and income taxes by interest expense.

$$\frac{\text{income before interest expense and income taxes}}{\text{interest expense}}$$

What constitutes a good number? To answer this requires a comparison with industry averages. Certainly a company with a lot of debt will maintain confidence if its income can cover the interest expense ten times over.

### Self-Assessment Question 5

1. State whether each of the following changes is good or bad for a company.
   (a) Decrease in inventory (stock) turnover ratio.
   (b) Increase in debt to total assets ratio.
   (c) Decrease in times interest earned ratio.

## PROFITABILITY RATIOS

Profitability reflects the fundamental performance of the business. It inspires confidence in its day-to-day operations and in its future plans for growth. Liquidity and solvency are strengthened and lenders and creditors will feel more comfortable in doing business with the company.

### The DuPont model

The ratios presented here reflect the many factors that affect profitability, so it is important to see how the ratios are related. Their relationships are illustrated below in the DuPont model (Gitman 1998).

FIGURE 9.4: THE DUPONT MODEL

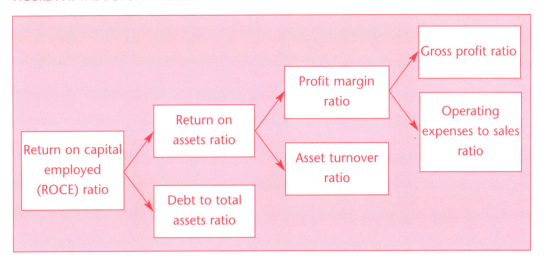

We'll cover each of these below, except the **debt to total assets ratio**, which we've already dealt with.

### RETURN ON CAPITAL EMPLOYED RATIO

**Return on capital employed (ROCE) ratio** shows how many euro of profit have been earned by the business for its owners. It is calculated by dividing income before taxes by average shareholders' funds.

> If the closing shareholders' funds are representative of the overall period, then the **closing amount** is used.

$$\frac{\text{net income before taxation}}{\text{average shareholders' funds}}$$

Some users, however, view capital employed as also including long-term loans; they will use this formula:

$$\frac{\text{net income before taxation and before loan interest}}{\text{average shareholders' funds} + \text{long-term loans}}$$

### RETURN ON ASSETS RATIO

**Return on assets (ROA) ratio** measures the overall profitability of assets. It is calculated by dividing the net income before taxation by average total assets. As Figure 9.4 above suggests, this ratio affects the **return on capital employed ratio**. The percentage derived is the return earned by each euro invested in assets. The strength of the number can only be gauged by comparing it with a competitor and with the industry average.

Also affecting the **return on capital employed ratio** is the **debt to total assets ratio**, a measure which deals with **leveraging**. Leveraging means using debt to

> **Leveraging** is often referred to as **gearing**.

increase the returns to owners. Debt, of course, has a cost; to determine whether a business should have more or less debt is the subject of many studies and is beyond the scope of this book. We can say, however, that if the cost of debt is less than the return on assets, the business is **trading on the equity at a gain**. If the opposite is true, **the trading on the equity is at a loss**.

### PROFIT MARGIN RATIO

**Profit margin ratio is often referred to as the rate of return on sales.**

**Profit margin ratio** is calculated by dividing the net income by net sales. It tells us the percentage of each euro of sales that results in net profit.

A feature of some businesses, such as grocery retailers and other high-volume retailers, is their low profit margins. Low-volume businesses such as shipbuilding or jewellery stores experience high profit margins.

### ASSET TURNOVER RATIO

**Asset turnover ratio** measures how efficiently a company's assets are used to generate sales. It is calculated by dividing net profit by average total assets. It shows the amount of sales produced by one euro of assets for the period.

The DuPont model suggests an important insight into the **return on assets (ROA)** by examining the composition of the ROA:

| Profit margin | $\times$ | asset turnover | = | return on assets |
|---|---|---|---|---|
| $\dfrac{\text{income before tax}}{\text{net sales}}$ | $\times$ | $\dfrac{\text{net sales}}{\text{average total assets}}$ | = | $\dfrac{\text{income before tax}}{\text{average total assets}}$ |

Take a company that has an ROA of 10 per cent in 2005, a ratio regarded by the company's management as below comparable market performance.

| profit margin | $\times$ | asset turnover | = | return on assets |
|---|---|---|---|---|
| $\dfrac{10}{200}$ | $\times$ | $\dfrac{200}{100}$ | = | 10% |

If management feels that this has to be addressed immediately, then waiting for sales to grow or investing in more assets may take too long (and growth is not guaranteed!).

It may spend less on marketing, reduce its sales force and cut operating expenses – that may reduce sales, but with the reduction in expenses, it may also increase net income. Suppose the 2006 numbers are:

| profit margin | × | asset turnover | = | return on assets |
|---|---|---|---|---|
| $\dfrac{20}{150}$ | × | $\dfrac{150}{100}$ | = | 21% |

Notice that the ROA has increased without the assets changing from one year to the next.

### GROSS PROFIT RATIO

**Gross profit ratio** is calculated by dividing the gross profit by net sales. You will recall that gross profit is net sales less the cost of goods sold. The rate reflects a business's ability to maintain an adequate selling price above its costs. In an increasingly competitive environment, the gross profit ratio of a business will become less as it responds to the price cutting of competitors.

$$\frac{\text{gross profit}}{\text{net sales}}$$

### OPERATING EXPENSES TO SALES RATIO

**Operating expenses to sales ratio** measures the costs incurred to support each euro of sales and is calculated by dividing operating expenses by net sales.

$$\frac{\text{operating expenses}}{\text{net sales}}$$

Availing of new technologies or restructuring operations may change or reduce the operating costs of a business and thus affect this ratio.

## Share price performance

We stated in Chapter 6 that earnings per share was a crude measurement of share value. Yet share price is perhaps the most readily produced indicator by most investors. It is believed that with the efficient movement of information today, share prices almost instantaneously react to information. The following are the most used ratios regarding shares:

- earnings per share (EPS)
- price-earnings (P-E) ratio
- dividend cover.

## EARNINGS PER SHARE (EPS)

**Earnings per share (EPS)** measures the net income earned on each share of common stock. If there are preferred shares in the company's capital, preferred shares dividends must be removed from the net income figure to provide the net income available to common shareholders.

$$\frac{\text{income before tax available to common shareholders}}{\text{average number of shares outstanding}}$$

As a ratio for industry and competitor comparison, it is limited in value because the number of outstanding shares will vary among companies.

## PRICE-EARNINGS (P-E) RATIO

**Price-earnings (P-E) ratio** is the ratio of the market price of each share of common stock to the earnings per share and is calculated by dividing the market price per share by the earnings per share. It is probably the most used ratio, primarily because it reflects investors' opinion of a company's future performance.

$$\frac{\text{stock price}}{\text{earnings per share}}$$

## DIVIDEND COVER RATIO

**Dividend cover ratio** measures the amount of earnings distributed in the form of cash dividends and is calculated by dividing cash dividends for common shareholders into net income.

---

### *Self-Assessment Question 6*

1. Which ratios should be used to answer each of the following questions?
   (a) How efficient is a company in using its assets to produce sales?
   (b) How near to selling is the inventory on hand?
   (c) How many euro of net income were earned for each euro invested by the owners?
   (d) What is a company's ability to meet interest charges as they fall due?

---

## Linking profitability with liquidity

How good are any company's operating profits? After all, they are prepared using the accrual basis of accounting. You will recall from Chapter 8 that we determined the **net cash**

**flow from operations** which was the conversion or 'undoing' of operating profit back into the raw cash picture. We can calculate the **quality** of the operating profit by dividing it into the net cash flow from operations. Consider Tesco's profits and cash flow from 2004, as follows:

$$\frac{\text{operating cash flow}}{\text{operating profit}} = \frac{£2,942 \text{ million}}{£1,600 \text{ million}} = £1.84$$

This means that for every £1 in operating profit, Tesco had £1.84 in raw cash, a most satisfactory level of quality profits.

## EXTENT AND LIMITATIONS OF FINANCIAL ANALYSIS

Ratios and trend analysis are not ends in themselves. They may indicate that perhaps there is a problem with cash flow, but they also say something about management and its response to a dynamic marketplace. We discussed how strong management can minimise the age of debtors or keep stock levels low. This may not be enough for some companies, as there are limits to how tight margins can become. New business models that combine technology and re-engineering of activities sometimes make quantum leaps in performance that show up in ratios.

### Technology

Until the arrival of Dell Computers, manufacturers of computers essentially ran assembly lines and stored computers in warehouses. Even if just-in-time inventory was in use, warehouse costs at front and back-end – the bricks and mortar – continued to be high. Dell introduced a new business model that waits for orders to be received before building a computer, receives payment by credit card at the time of the order and dispatches the computer upon completion. This means that warehousing costs are minimised, and with payment by credit card, age of debtors in some of Dell's markets is as low as sixteen hours.

### The banker's tale

And how about our banker's story mentioned at the beginning of the chapter? Can we apply any of the skills and tools learned in this chapter? The activity at the plant seemed to indicate a busy workplace. In many businesses, managers often mistake delivery of orders for money in the bank. Let's see how this might manifest itself in the financial statements.

A balance sheet has this situation:

| Current assets: | | Current liabilities: | |
|---|---|---|---|
| Debtors | 10,000 | Creditors | 15,000 |
| Cash | 5,000 | | |
| Total | 15,000 | Total | 15,000 |

Current ratio is 1:1 (15,000 ÷ 15,000) and this is generally good. However, if sales for the year are €50,000, then we find that the debtor turnover is not good:

| Debtor turnover | $\dfrac{50,000}{10,000}$ | = | 5 times |
|---|---|---|---|
| Average collection period | 365 ÷ 5 | = | 73 days  (not good) |

This is most likely the problem with the bank's customer. If the customer paid attention to collecting money owed to it, and converted half of the debtor balance into cash, the current ratio would still be the same, but the debtor turnover would improve as follows:

| Debtor turnover | $\dfrac{50,000}{5,000}$ | = | 5 times |
|---|---|---|---|
| Average collection period | 365 ÷ 10 | = | 37 days  (a big improvement!) |

A wise banker will spot the danger early on and guide the customer before the situation gets out of hand. The correct insight means that the bank should continue to have a thriving (and fee-paying) customer.

## Limitations

The techniques discussed here reflect the common approaches to analysing financial information, and when combined with trend analysis, they do assist investors and credit managers alike. However, there are some limitations.

Firstly, management makes **estimates** on such things as doubtful debtors, depreciation timeframes and contingent losses. If these prove to be inaccurate, then the ratios will also be defective.

Secondly, inflation may make comparisons between periods ineffective. A 10 per cent increase in sales today may not be comparable to a 10 per cent increase five years ago, particularly if prices also increased by 10 per cent. In addition, assets are valued at their historical costs, which, over time, may be under- or overvalued.

Thirdly, the different methods available to applying accounting principles make comparability difficult. For instance, depreciation can be by straight line or by the accelerated method. Inventory can be expensed using either the first-in-first-out (FIFO) method or the last-in-first-out (LIFO) method. This calls for adjustments that may be difficult if not impossible to complete.

Financial analysis combined with prudence is the best approach.

## Self-Assessment Question 7

1. Comment on the financial position of Late Ltd for the year 2006. Calculate appropriate ratios.

| Income statement for Late Ltd: | 2005 | 2006 |
|---|---|---|
| | € | € |
| Sales | 100,000 | 100,000 |
| Cost of sales | 50,000 | 60,000 |
| | 50,000 | 40,000 |
| Expenses | 30,000 | 30,000 |
| Operating profit | 20,000 | 10,000 |
| Dividends | 10,000 | 10,000 |
| | 10,000 | 0 |
| Retained profits b/d | 2,500 | 12,500 |
| Retained profits | 12,500 | 12,500 |

| Balance sheets | | |
|---|---|---|
| Land/bld/equip | 44,500 | 74,000 |
| **Current assets:** | | |
| Investments | 25,000 | 40,000 |
| Stock | 27,500 | 32,500 |
| Debtors | 20,000 | 25,000 |
| Bank | 1,500 | – |
| | 74,000 | 97,500 |
| **Current liabilities:** | | |
| Creditors | 20,000 | 30,000 |
| Proposed dividend | 10,000 | 10,000 |
| Bank OD | 0 | 2,000 |
| | (30,000) | (42,000) |
| Total assets | 88,500 | 129,500 |

| Shareholders and reserves: | | |
|---|---|---|
| Ordinary €1 shares | 20,000 | 25,000 |
| Share premium | 6,000 | 7,000 |
| Retained profits | 12,500 | 12,500 |
| | 38,500 | 44,500 |
| Debenture loan 10 per cent | 50,000 | 85,000 |
| | 88,500 | 129,500 |

## CHAPTER REVIEW

It should be of some satisfaction to you that you are now at the point where you can interpret the information in the financial statements. By including the cash flow statement with the income statement and the balance sheet, we get a sense of the quality of a company's performance and how in reporting the accrual picture we can rely on it because we also have a sense of the cash position.

The three concerns of running a business – liquidity, solvency and profitability – determine the extent of the effort to analyse the statements. We can compare financial information in one of three ways:

● intracompany
● intercompany
● industry averages.

The comparisons can be completed using analysis that is horizontal, vertical or by ratios. Horizontal analysis means comparing an item such as yearly sales over a number of years. Using vertical analysis, we express items in the financial statements as a percentage of some base amount. For instance, we can calculate each expense as a percentage of net sales or debtors as a percentage of total assets.

Ratio analysis provides the user with quantitative insight into financial performance. Liquidity ratios measure the short-term ability of an entity to pay its current obligations; the current ratio is the most prominent of these. Solvency measures the ability of the entity to meet its long-term obligations and thus its ability to survive; the debt to assets ratio and the times interest earned are the main ratios. Profitability is the fundamental driving force behind any business endeavour. While there are many ratios that measure profit, return on capital employed (ROCE), profit margin (rate of return on sales) and price-earnings ratio are monitored closely by users.

Interpreting financial information is of equal importance to both internal and external users, and although there are limitations, the key concerns of running a business can be addressed adequately.

# SELF-ASSESSMENT QUESTION ANSWERS

## SAQ 1

1. Bases of comparison are intracompany, intercompany and industry averages.
2. Tools used to make comparison are horizontal analysis, vertical analysis and ratio analysis.
3. Comparative analysis evaluates a business's liquidity, solvency and profitability. It detects changes in financial relationships and significant trends and provides insight into its position in terms of the competition and the industry.

## SAQ 2

1. (a)

| 2004 | 2005 | 2006 |
|------|------|------|
| 300 | 330 | 360 |
| n/a | 10% | 20% |

(b)  Comparative analysis by industry averages.

## SAQ 3

1. Net sales is the preferable base amount when completing vertical analysis on the P&L statement.

## SAQ 4

1. (a)   current ratio:   $\dfrac{\text{current assets}}{\text{current liabilities}} = \dfrac{42,700}{44,800} = .95 \text{ to } 1.0$

(b)   Acid-test ratio:   $\dfrac{\text{cash + investments + debtors}}{\text{current liabilities}} = \dfrac{22,600}{44,800} = .5 \text{ to } 1$

## SAQ 5

1. (a) **Bad:** This may mean that inventory is obsolete.
   (b) **Bad:** This may put greater pressure on a business to repay the interest.
   (c) **Bad:** This may mean that operationally the business will have difficulty servicing its debts.

## SAQ 6

1. (a) Efficiency:                Asset turnover ratio.
   (b) Age of inventory:          Average days inventory.
   (c) Return to shareholders:    ROCE.
   (d) Demands of debt:           Times interest earned.

## SAQ 7

1. Sales are flat from 2005 to 2006 but cost of sales has increased. Gross profit has fallen from €50,000 to €40,000. This is worrisome. Why have these costs increased? This has filtered through to the ROCE, which has dropped dramatically from 28 per cent to 14 per cent. Profitability looks vulnerable.

   The increase in the equipment was probably financed by a loan – loans have increased. Such a long-term commitment also makes demands in the short term, as interest expense will be expected to increase accordingly. The ability of profit to cover interest expense has decreased from five to two, putting pressure on liquidity and ultimately on solvency. The new equipment, however, may assist in increasing sales and creating synergies that may reduce operating expenses.

   The current ratio continues to look okay despite the small decline. However, the age of debtors is alarming, having increased to 92 days, and management must reduce that if the threat to liquidity is to be minimised. On the positive side, operating expenses remain unchanged, so management should be able to concentrate on the cost of goods problem and collections activity.

The 5 represents the 10 per cent interest on the debenture and is added back to operating profit. Similar situation in 2006.

---

**Ratio analysis on Late Ltd**

| | 2005 | 2006 |
|---|---|---|
| ROCE: | $\frac{20 + 5}{88.5} = 28.2\%$ | $\frac{10 + 8.5}{129.5} = 14.3\%$ |
| Gross profit % | 50/100 = 50% | 40/100 = 40% |
| Net profit | 20/100 = 20% | 10/100 = 10% |
| Sales to capital employed | 100/(38.5+50) = 1.13 | 100/(44.5+85) = .77 |
| Return on owners equity | 20/38.5 = 52% | 10/44.5 = 22% |
| Return on assets | 20/88.5 = 23% | 10/129.5 = 7.7% |
| Gearing ratio | 50/(38.5+50) = 56.5% | 85/(44.5+85) = 65.6% |
| Current ratio | 74/30 = 2.4:1 | 97.5/42 = 2.3:1 |
| Acid test | 46.5/30 = 1.55:1 | 65/42 = 1.55:1 |
| Debtors turnover | 5 | 4 |
| Average collection period | 365/5 = 73 days | 365/4 = 92 days |
| Creditors turnover | 2.5 | 2 |
| Stock turnover | 50/27.5 = 1.82 | 60/32.5 = 1.85 |
| Average days stock | 201 days | 198 days |
| Dividend cover | 2 | 1 |
| Times interest earned | (20 + 5)/5 = 5 | (10 + 8.5)/8.5 = 2.18 |

Note: In the ROCE, the interest expense is added back to profit.

# REFERENCES

Gitman, L., *Principles of Managerial Finance*, New York: Addison-Wesley Educational Publishers 1998.

Heneghan, J. and O'Regan, P., *Accounting*, Limerick: Centre for Project Management, University of Limerick 2000.

Lonergan, B.J.F., *Insight: A Study of Human Understanding*, New York: Philosophical Library and Longmans 1958.

Morse, W., Davis, J. and Hartgraves, A., *Management Accounting*, 3rd ed., New York: Addison-Wesley Publishing 1991.

O'Regan, P., *Introduction to Accounting*, Limerick: The International Equine Institute, University of Limerick 1998.

O'Regan, P., *Financial Information Analysis*, Chichester: John Wiley & Sons 2001.

# 10

# *The Nature of Corporate Governance*

C O N T E N T S

# INTRODUCTION

Throughout the preceding chapters, concepts and issues in accounting we
and applied to the accounting process. The implications for governan
discussed, even at the introductory stages, so that the student would see early on that
governance permeates the whole accounting environment. When we discuss it at any point
along the accounting cycle, beginning with the initial transaction right through to the
preparation of the financial statements, or plan for it at management levels, be it junior
entry right through to CEO, we are acknowledging corporate governance to be an *oversight*
issue. This chapter will present the structure that formalises this oversight. Having taken
the approach we have, governance will be seen not as a detached concept but as something
that is integral to good accounting practice and financial reporting.

---

## OBJECTIVES

**When you have finished this chapter, you will be able to:**
- understand the various theories in governance
- understand the concerns of the participants
- become familiar with the combined code
- understand the role of the board of directors.

---

# THEORIES IN CORPORATE GOVERNANCE

There are a number of theoretical approaches to governance. At best, theories give an
insight to the concept, but where there are a number of them, the study of governance may
become unduly complicated. **Agency theory** has the obvious quality of directors acting on
shareholders' behalf. **Stakeholder theory,** however, embraces a wider group of players
who are impacted directly and indirectly by the actions of companies. A third theory,
**transaction costs,** reflects the economic argument that the corporate structure of a board
and an executive management team offers the most efficient means of running a company
in any economy. In looking at these theories separately, the student should be mindful that
the environment that a company operates in today is distinctly different from prior periods.
Companies are viewed as corporate citizens, and corporate social responsibility has
become a concern of both boards and shareholders alike.

## Agency theory

This stems from the structure whereby shareholders elect directors to represent them in the
running of the company. Historically, many investors invested funds into an entity,
preferring someone else to run it. In owning shares in the business, these investors

ɔceeded to appoint directors to act on their behalf. As a company grew, the responsibility of running the entity was divided into two roles, the strategic and operational. In time, directors delegated the operational role to executive managers who took care of the day-to-day running of the entity. Today, a triangular relationship has arisen that typifies the governance structure of the modern corporation, as Figure 10.1 shows.

FIGURE 10.1: CORPORATE GOVERNANCE

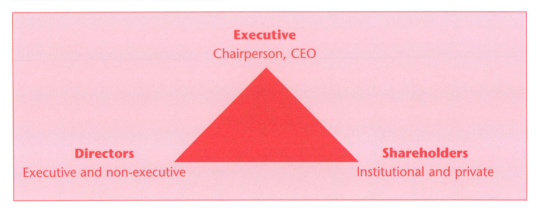

Thus, the shareholders as principals appoint directors as their agents. The directors in turn hire managers to run the business. This description might seem to contradict the apparent equality that the triangular arrangement suggests. Two points must be made here. Firstly, in virtually all companies the chief executive officer (CEO) or managing director (MD) is also a board member. Secondly, boards have an obligation to support their CEOs in good times and bad. Events such as a downturn in the global economy may depress a share price and survival may depend on strong leadership from the CEO. The reality is obvious. Shareholders may not like the loss in value of their shares, but the CEO is at the wheel, as it were. Pragmatism and fair play demand that this situation should be tolerated for a period of time.

The corporate governance issue thrown up by agency theory is that shareholders cannot always rely on boards to do exactly what shareholders want. For instance, shareholders would like to see their shares increase in value and receive dividends every year. The directors may decide on a long-term strategy that perhaps requires conserving cash flow and thus refrain from declaring a dividend. More acute tension arises when shareholders feel that they have not been adequately informed of the financial picture of the company.

## Self-Assessment Question 1

1. How is agency theory related to governance?

## Stakeholder theory

The company, be it public or private, has many relationships other than that between its board and shareholders. Employees, suppliers, lenders, customers and the communities in which the company is located represent important constituents that it relies upon to do business. This can be represented by another triangular design that captures these relationships (Muckenberger 1997), as shown in Figure 10.2.

FIGURE 10.2: SOCIETAL GOVERNANCE

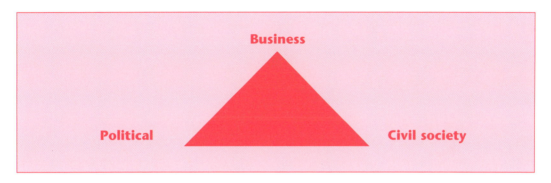

In this picture we should expect that good corporate governance will add value to a company by their dealings with these participants. Employees should expect a safe and healthy workplace together with an adequate wage. Suppliers should expect to be paid on time and banks should be able to rely on financial information provided by the company. Companies generate revenues by attracting customers who believe they are getting value for money. What of communities that cater for businesses by providing workspace and workers? A company in any community has an obligation to safeguard the environment from pollution and other contaminants, as is required of all citizens. The concern, however, is that globalisation places 'economic power and political power in a relationship of conflict' (Villeneuve 1997) and that perhaps as companies seek lower costs, they will abandon communities for countries less demanding compliance-wise.

The **governance challenge** that arises for a company is how to meet its social responsibilities while at the same time run a profitable business. No company can guarantee life-long employment and on occasion it may be necessary to lay off workers in order for the business to survive. Innovative products may expand markets and employment opportunities, while competition will demand efficiency and attention to cost control.

Generally, though, stakeholder theory reflects relationships more than anything else. Most commentators agree that as economies become more service oriented, maintaining good relationships with all stakeholders becomes critical.

## Self-Assessment Question 2

1. What governance issue arises for a company under the stakeholder theory?

### Transaction cost theory

The successful running of a business will always incur costs and the strong control of those costs. Transaction cost theory suggests that the driving force in the governance of any business is the presence of costs incurred in the pursuit of revenues. The cost structure will include costs that enhance good governance, such as:

- accounting systems with solid controls
- sufficient staff to facilitate segregation of duties
- hiring independent auditors
- investing in training and good hiring practices.

These costs represent the result of what is best described as proactive action. Other costs have a more reactive quality about them. For instance, with greater emphasis on compliance, whereby directors are now responsible for 'all relevant obligations' (Companies Act 2003), additional legal and professional advice is now sought by company boards.

The corporate governance issue here concerns whether the benefits derived in achieving better governance is greater than the costs incurred in increased compliance.

### The OECD view

In 1999, the Organisation for Economic Co-operation and Development (OECD) defined corporate governance as

a set of relationships between a company's board, its shareholders and other stakeholders. It also provides the structure through which the objectives of the company are set, and through which the means of attaining those objectives and monitoring performance, are determined.

This clearly acknowledges both agency and stakeholder theories. The OECD also included in its 1999 document a number of principles that reflect the main concerns of corporate governance. It highlighted:

- the rights of shareholders
- the equitable treatment of shareholders
- the role of stakeholders in corporate governance
- disclosure and transparency
- the responsibilities of the board.

Debates and discussion have essentially centred around these points, primarily because they are at the heart of the oversight function carried out by directors. Addressing them and creating a compliance mechanism to improve governance is the subject of the next section.

## THE GENESIS OF THE COMBINED CODE

On this side of the Atlantic, British and Irish companies that are publicly traded in the London or Irish stock exchanges must adhere to the combined code. The term 'adherence' is used reservedly in this sense that through statements of compliance and appliance, companies will accompany their declaration of compliance with that of any exceptions to the code. The code is a collection of recommended practices as suggested by a series of reports that began with the Cadbury Report in 1992. The code was revised in 2003 and is often referred to now as the **revised combined code**. It is worth starting our review of the code by briefly examining the reports that provided the practices.

### Cadbury Report 1992

Headed by Sir Adrian Cadbury, it advocated the key issues in governance to be **transparency, disclosure** and **responsibility**. If we add accountability to these, we have today the fundamental concerns of corporate governance. The report centred on four areas in its final form:

- **Board of directors:** Proper accountability is best achieved by not having the same person hold the functions of chairman and CEO.
- **Executive directors:** It recommended that contracts should not exceed three years without shareholder approval. This underlined that executive directors were accountable to the shareholders.
- **Non-executive directors:** A more proactive role and a more independent stance by non-executives strengthens corporate governance. Apart from their fees and shares, they 'should be independent of management and free from any business or other relationship that could materially interfere with the exercise of their independent judgment.' They should also dominate audit and remuneration committees.
- **Reporting and controls:** It stated that the responsibility of directors is 'to present a balanced and understandable assessment of the company's position.' It also stated that in addition to the audited financial numbers, a narrative that described the company's performance and future prospects should also be included.

It is difficult to believe that these suggestions were regarded as radical when they were made in 1992. The emphasis on a strong audit committee and the operating and financial review that are now standard practice in today's annual report were the results of the Cadbury Report.

## Greenbury Report 1995

This committee was headed by Sir Richard Greenbury, which issued **directors' remuneration** in 1995. It made four recommendations:

- **Remuneration committee:** Remuneration of executive directors should be decided by a committee made up of non-executive directors.
- **Disclosure and approval provisions:** Pensions, share options and other entitlements to directors should be disclosed in the annual report.
- **Remuneration policy:** Remuneration packages should be consistent with industry standards.
- **Service contracts and compensation:** The period of notice required under service contracts should generally be one year or less.

The London Stock Exchange included the key points of Greenbury in its listing rules.

## Hampel Report 1998

Toward the end of 1998, Sir Ronald Hampel chaired a committee that issued a report called *Committee on Corporate Governance: Final Report,* which essentially reiterated in stronger terms the Cadbury and Greenbury reports. It explicitly recommended that:

- the positions of chairman and CEO were to be filled by different people
- a senior non-executive director should be nominated to liase with shareholders and address their concerns.

The Hampel Report made a subtle but important distinction when reviewing the work of the board when it said 'corporate governance is concerned with the way corporate entities are governed as distinct from the way business within those companies are managed.'

What this means is that a company can decide, for instance, to open up a new international market, but if it does, shareholders should be informed of the outcome of that action, be it good or bad. The disclosure makes for good corporate governance.

All of these reports were put together, or combined, so that by 1998 the combined code was in place. As we discuss below, it was revised in 2003 without any change to its fundamental structure.

### Self-Assessment Question 3

1. Explain why the combined code was an evolving process.

## Turnbull Report 1999

Headed by Sir Nigel Turnbull, this committee issued *Internal Control: Guidance for Directors on the Combined Code* in 1999. It was prompted by concern for the integrity of information and management's responsibility in providing the internal control system to safeguard that information. Turnbull emphasised that directors are responsible for proper controls and that controls are crucial in dealing with risk. Its articulation of the role of risk in running any business is of acute relevance today. Risk is inherent in:

● maintaining financial strength
● maintaining operations
● meeting compliance in legal and health and safety issues.

The Turnbull Report was cited in the aftermath of a number of world events since 2000. The 9/11 bombings of the World Trade Center in New York City in 2001 and the huge fraud in 2002 at Allied Irish Banks' subsidiary Allfirst in Baltimore in the US were two such events. The 9/11 horror put the focus on safeguarding people and information systems and the ability of organisations to respond when hit with either a natural or manmade catastrophe. The issue of internal controls in minimising risk was the key feature at Allfirst. In early 2005, it was reported that the Securities and Exchange Commission (SEC) in the US was examining the principles in Turnbull in the ongoing response to the financial scandals there. Clearly, the recognition of risk and the management of it are central to achieving good corporate governance.

# THE REVISED COMBINED CODE

The combined code was revised in 2003 with the Higgs Review, headed by Sir Derek Higgs. It incorporated into its recommendations suggestions from the Smith Report, the work of a Higgs subcommittee. The Smith Report dealt with the audit committee, which you will recall was first signalled by Cadbury as an important instrument in good governance.

The recommendations from the various reports just described were placed in a structure made up of two parts. The first outlines the principles under five headings. The second part provides provisions of best practice through which the principles are applied.

## Part 1: Principles of good governance

This first part contains the principles of good corporate governance for:

● directors
● directors' remuneration
● relations with shareholders
● accountability and audit
● institutional shareholders.

The student may be puzzled that there are two sets of principles dedicated to shareholders. There are indeed two issues here. Firstly, shareholders are a constituent player of the corporate world; they are, after all, the owners of the company. In a dynamic economy, they seem powerless in having a say other than buying or selling their holdings. And when the company does badly, shareholders suffer loss in value to their shares. The combined code suggests the appointment of a senior independent non-executive director to liase with shareholders. This will call for great tact on the part of the individual taking up the position. Indeed, critics of this proposal have voiced the fear of conflict that this might generate between the CEO and the senior director.

The other issue reflects the reality that many pension funds and large investors own significant chunks of shares in companies. The concerns of these institutional investors are distinctly different from those of the small shareholders, and while the latter have been very vocal in their criticisms of boards at annual general meetings, the fact is that the institutional shareholders hold the majority shares and boards respond accordingly. The combined code suggests that institutional shareholders engage companies in dialogue that is 'based on mutual understanding of objectives'. It also recommends that these investors pay strong attention to 'board structure and composition'. Of course, the institutional shareholders can simply sell their shares and invest elsewhere. The code, however, makes the point that they have a responsibility to 'make considered use' of their voting power, clearly implying that positive change at a company may result from invoking such powers.

## Part 2: Code of best practice

This part of the code is designed to provide practical steps in applying the principles. For instance, in Part 1 the first principle relating to **directors** proceeds to list seven sub-principles, A1 to A7. The first of these, **A1**, deals with the **board** and states that 'every listed company should be headed by an effective board'.

In Part 2 of the code there are seven **provisions** or **practices, A.1.1** to **A.1.7**, relating to the **board**. In A.1.1 the code advises that the board should:

- set the company's strategic aims
- ensure that the necessary financial and human resources are in place
- review management performance.

The remaining practices recommended for A1 encompass holding regular meetings, maintaining a formal schedule of matters reserved for its decision, making non-executive directors responsible for setting appropriate levels of remuneration and establishing internal controls. In this last item, the code made it clear that directors 'should satisfy themselves that financial information is accurate and that financial controls and systems of risk management are robust and defensible' (A.1.4). We will return to this interconnection between controls and risk in the next section.

Interestingly, the code suggests that non-executive directors meet regularly as a group without executives present; such meetings are to be led by the senior independent director **(A.1.5)**. In companies that have grown spectacularly under the leadership of a dynamic CEO, there may be a hesitancy to embrace such a practice.

In all, there are **eighty-four** recommended practices supporting the **eighteen principles** listed in Part 1. The future of the code is speculated upon at the end of the section.

## Accountability and audit

Of particular importance to accountants and their involvement in corporate governance are the principles relating to **accountability and audit**, Section D in Part 1 of the code. Very early on in the governance debate, Cadbury had referred to the importance of a strong audit committee. Also hovering over the debate was the emergence of the role of the non-executive director (NED) that has evolved further to be known as the independent NED. The Smith Report that accompanied the Higgs Review recommended that the audit committee should be made up of at least three independent NEDs and that it should:

- monitor the integrity of the financial statements
- review the internal control system
- recommend the appointment of the external auditor.

Smith also recommended that the committee should monitor the independent auditor's independence and objectivity. These guidelines were fed into the revised combined code. A look at accountability and audit in Part 1 shows three sub-principles relating to:

- **D.1: Financial reporting:** 'The board should present a balanced and understandable assessment of the company's position and prospects.'
- **D.2: Internal control:** 'The board should maintain a sound system of internal control to safeguard shareholders' investment and the company's assets.'
- **D.3: Audit committee and auditors:** 'The board should establish formal and transparent arrangements for considering how they should apply the financial reporting and internal control principles and for maintaining an appropriate relationship with the company's auditors.'

The code provisions in Part 2 are strident in applying the principles. D.1.2 recommends that the board present a balanced and understandable assessment in its reporting, and the internal control provisions recommend that the directors 'at least annually conduct a review of the effectiveness of the group's system of internal control and should report to the shareholders that they have done so' (D.2.1).

The audit committee is called upon in Part 1 to 'establish formal and transparent arrangements for applying reporting and internal control principles'. How this might be achieved is suggested in the corresponding provision, D.3.1: 'The board should establish an audit committee of at least three directors, all non-executive, all independent.'

This clear-cut direction reflects the fundamental tenet of the audit function – that a sense of independence must be given to those responsible for it.

## Self-Assessment Question 4

1. Explain the practice suggested to implement the principle in **accountability and audit** (Part 1, Section D) concerning the audit committee.

### Future of the combined code

What is the future of the combined code? Is it here to stay? As a moral force there is no doubt that it has had an impact on corporate behaviour. Its growth in blocks of practices commencing with Cadbury in 1992 may well have been its strength, as it allowed board attitudes to evolve over time. Cadbury's suggestion that the roles of chairman and CEO be held by separate individuals was regarded as controversial at the time. Today, there is general agreement with **Principle A.2 Chairman and Chief Executive** in the revised version, which spells it out that 'there should be a clear division of responsibilities at the head of the company' to ensure 'that no one individual has unfettered powers of decision'. Although the London Stock Exchange requires adherence to the code or steps toward adherence, it is primarily a recommended practice. Therefore, its general acceptance reflects its moral authority. This is perhaps its greatest strength. It is the opinion of this author that the absence of a comparable code in the US may have contributed to the scandals there. The combined code will continue to be a positive force in Irish and British publicly traded companies and indeed for private entities also.

## THE STRUCTURE OF THE CORPORATE BOARD

From what we have examined so far in this chapter, it is clear that the role of the directors is vital to good governance. How they delegate their various responsibilities among themselves and the structures they develop are closely monitored by regulators and investors alike. We will describe these responsibilities and the structure used to implement them. Our final heading will include a look at a suggested structure based upon a perusal of Tesco plc's annual report for 2004.

### Directors' duties

These duties are essentially derived from two sources, that of the legislative process or the Companies Acts and secondly, common law or decisions made in the courts. The legislation covers the Acts from 1963 to 2003 and the requirements made of companies are the responsibilities of directors. The main duties are as follows.

- **Maintain proper books of account:** Transactions are correctly recorded and adequately explained. Financial position is determined with reasonable accuracy.
- **Prepare annual returns of accounts:** The financial statements such as the balance sheet, profit and loss account and cash flow that together 'give a true and fair view of the state of affairs of the company'.
- **Facilitate an annual audit:** Carried out by an independent auditor. Auditor provides an opinion on whether the financial statements give a true and fair view of the affairs of the entity and whether the same statements agree with the accounts in the general ledger.
- **Maintain registers and other key documents:** Registers of shareholders, directors and secretaries, their holdings and/or their interests, loan holders, directors' contracts.
- **Document filings:** With the Registrar of Companies. These include annual return, changes in registered office, change of director and/or secretary.
- **Disclosures:** Register of directors and secretaries to contain name, address, date of birth, nationality, occupation and any other directorships. Shares held by directors, service contracts of directors.
- **General meetings:** An annual general meeting (AGM) must be convened or no more than fifteen months must pass since the previous meeting. An extraordinary meeting (EGM) may also be called where circumstances warrant.

> The term 'true and fair view' is not defined but is generally regarded as met when both legislation and accounting principles are deemed adhered to.

These represent the key legislative requirements, most of which were set by the Companies Act 1990. However, the completion of a **directors' compliance statement** by directors, as required by Companies Act 2003, adds significantly to directors' duties. This compliance statement must contain information regarding a company's 'policies respecting compliance with its relevant obligations' (Section 45, Companies Act 2003). What these relevant obligations are and how they are to be met has not been specified in the legislation.

Duties prompted by **common law** reflect the reasonable expectations found in most professions. Directors must:

- act in good faith and in the interests of the company as a whole
- carry out their duties with due skill, care and diligence
- maintain independent judgment
- avoid making undisclosed profits from their position as directors
- attend meetings when it is reasonably expected of them.

Duties of loyalty to the company and consideration of the interests of third parties may also be added to the above. In the event that a director is found negligent in his or her duties, the director may face a restriction or disqualification from holding a directorship. It must be pointed out that the duty of care is required of all directors, both executive and non-executive.

## Board committees

The modern public company has many demands made of it, from marketing its services to maintaining staff to meeting compliance. To manage these demands, the corporate board delegates its responsibilities into subcommittees. We have already discussed some of these as prompted by the combined code, namely the remuneration, nomination and audit committees. The establishment of the audit committee is the only committee required by the Irish Companies Act 2003. It spells out the responsibilities of the committee and stipulates that it consist of independent non-executive directors only. Once we have reviewed these committees, we can then speculate on what a good governance structure may look like.

*Known as the Companies (Auditing and Accounting) Act 2003.*

- **Remuneration committee:** Decides on the pay of executives. The issue of executive pay has been a contentious one, especially for shareholders. A comparison of UK executive pay with that in the US shows that the former are paid far less than their American peers. In recent years, UK CEOs earned approximately forty times the average working wage, whereas CEOs in the US earned in excess of 400 times the US equivalent. The combined code recommends that this committee should consist of at least three independent non-executive directors who decide on executive remuneration, including pension rights and compensation packages. These arrangements should be transparent and the names of the committee members disclosed in the annual report.

- **Nomination committee:** Responsible for choosing board members. A good board will have a balance of skills, expertise, knowledge and experience among its members. It will also have a balance between executive and non-executive directors. As the list of duties indicates, the modern director cannot be nonchalant regarding his or her responsibilities. The combined code recommends that the majority of members in the committee should be independent non-executive directors. The committee should evaluate the levels of skills and experience on the board and thereby inform itself when seeking new board members.

- **Audit committee:** This is the most important subcommittee, primarily due to its inclusion in the Companies Act 2003. It was the subject of a special review in the Smith Report that accompanied the Higgs Review in 2003. Because of its impact and key role in governance, it is examined in more detail under the next heading.

---

### Self-Assessment Questions 5

1. List the duties of directors.
2. What underlines the importance of the audit committee?

## The audit committee

In its introduction, the Smith Report states that the 'audit committee has a particular role, acting independently from the executive, to ensure that the interests of shareholders are properly protected in relation to financial reporting and internal control.' This explains why the accountability and audit section of the revised combined code recommends that the committee should consist of non-executive directors, *all* independent. The Companies Act 2003 in Ireland embraces this understanding by requiring Irish companies that qualify to establish audit committees. In Section 42 (subsection 2) of the Act, it provides the following responsibilities for the committee:

- review the annual accounts *before* they are presented to the board for approval
- determine whether the accounts give the true and fair view
- determine whether the group accounts (parent and subsidiaries) give the true and fair view

  *The true and fair view is not defined.*

- review the directors' compliance statement and determine whether it is 'fair and reasonable and is based on due and careful enquiry'
- recommend to the board whether or not to approve the annual accounts and the compliance statement
- monitor the performance and quality of the auditor's work and independence from the company
- provide a report on the committee's activities for inclusion in the directors' report
- perform any other functions relating to the company's audit and financial management that are delegated to it by the board of directors.

The Act does not explicitly use the term 'independent non-executive director' to qualify a director for the audit committee, but it does state that the individual must not have been an employee for at least three years prior to the appointment. An individual or director so described is not an executive, and as a result, Irish legislation has 'brought the recognition of the non-executive director into Irish company law for the first time' (Deloitte & Touche 2004). The three-year time period is in line with the combined code that regards a 'material business relationship with the company' (A.3.4) during that time as undermining independence.

## The independent non-executive director

The non-executive director does not have a contract of service and will usually serve on the board on a part-time basis. This director is considered independent when the board determines that he or she is independent in character and judgment (combined code 2003) and that 'there are no relationships or circumstances which could affect, or appear to affect, the director's judgment' (A.3.4). We have already seen the demands now being made of the non-executive. In the audit committee, this person must possess a high level of financial competency if they are to fulfil the legislative requirements. The recommendation for the appointment of a senior independent non-executive director who will communicate with shareholders ratchets up the skill requirement even further.

## Self-Assessment Question 6

1. If the code recommends that companies determine the independence of their directors, is such a determination arbitrary?

## A RECOMMENDED STRUCTURE

Now that we have a sense of the various committees that the board of directors avails of to fulfil its duties, we can speculate on what an effective governance structure might look like. The danger for many companies when responding to the concerns of shareholders and other stakeholders is that the resulting structure essentially pays lip service to recommended practices. Any structure then must reflect something of the governance spirit espoused by the combined code.

### Weak governance

The combined code is essentially a recommended practice and research suggests that problem companies, those in need of best practice, are least likely to embrace non-mandatory provisions (Brennan and McDermott 2004). We have seen a growing recognition of the combined code, mainly due to the insistence of the London Stock Exchange. However, it is not a legal requirement and almost by definition it must offer certain flexibility. The use of the appliance and compliance statements, for instance, allows a company to declare that it is in compliance, and where it is not, to state those exceptions. From this we can detect a number of potential areas of weakness in the corporate structure (Brennan and McDermott 2003):

- creating board subcommittees without demonstrating how they feed back to the board
- failure to appoint a senior non-executive director
- appointing a senior non-executive director without delegating explicit duties or producing a report on this director's activities
- creating an audit committee without appointing an internal audit department
- varying definitions of what constitutes an independent director
- role of chairman and CEO held by the same person
- a retiring CEO proceeding to become chairman of the same board.

The lack of agreement on what constitutes an independent director has particular relevance for Irish companies. Brennan and McDermott's report (2003) concluded that only 60 per cent of Irish publicly traded companies could be regarded as independent. It also concluded:

- Only 51 per cent complied with recommendations for separate audit, remuneration and nomination committees.
- Almost 20 per cent did not have a separate audit committee.
- Fourteen per cent of directors had more than nine years' service, a threshold beyond which independence is considered impaired per the Higgs Review.

The audit committee statistic is a moot point now as the Companies Act 2003 requires the creation of an audit committee.

Governance codes do influence the behaviour of boards, but Brennan and McDermott (2003) concluded that investors' desire for strong growth earnings had the greater influence on boards. This should be a reminder to stakeholders to look more closely at how companies portray themselves, particularly in the annual report.

## An evaluation of Tesco's governance structure

An evaluation of the governance structure of the UK-based Tesco Group gives some indication of what such structures should aspire to. The figures below provide a graphical layout of the structure and are the result of an interpretation of Tesco's annual report, issued in February 2004.

Figure 10.3 lays out the key committees: remuneration, audit and nominations. Virtually all publicly traded entities have these in place and most will disclose the composition regarding directors' names, executive or non-executive and those who are independent. As required by the London Stock Exchange, these companies include a corporate governance statement in the annual report. The statement acknowledges risk as a key concern to the business and outlines the role of the audit committee in dealing with it. Many statements, however, do not go beyond that.

FIGURE 10.3: TESCO'S BOARD AND COMMITTEES

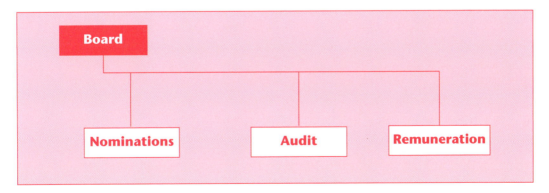

The Tesco statement seems to make an extra effort to show *how* it manages risk. Its audit committee is responsible for the usual items, such as the internal control system, accounting policies and the annual financial statements. It also reviews compliance with the combined code. The addition of two further committees, however, gives a sense of how risk is handled operationally, as shown in Figure 10.4.

- **Compliance committee:** Run by the executive and senior management to ensure compliance with all necessary laws and regulations.
- **Corporate social responsibility (CSR) committee:** Run by senior management from all parts of the business to identify threats and opportunities and highlight emerging issues.

FIGURE 10.4: TESCO'S AUDIT COMMITTEE

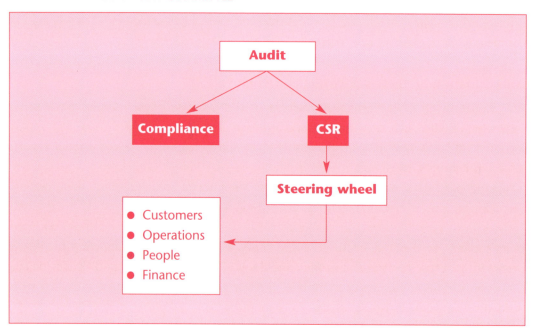

The CSR uses **key performance indicators** to track performance quarterly, and these indicators are then fed into what Tesco calls its **steering wheel monitoring system**. Tesco describes this monitoring system as its balance scorecard that targets:

- customers
- operations
- people
- finance.

An observer of business will quickly determine that these four items will figure among the concerns of any board.

The corporate governance statement does not state that the compliance and CSR committees report directly to the audit committee, but on reading the responsibilities of the latter, the layout in Figure 10.5 is a reasonable interpretation.

FIGURE 10.5: TESCO'S GOVERNANCE STRUCTURE

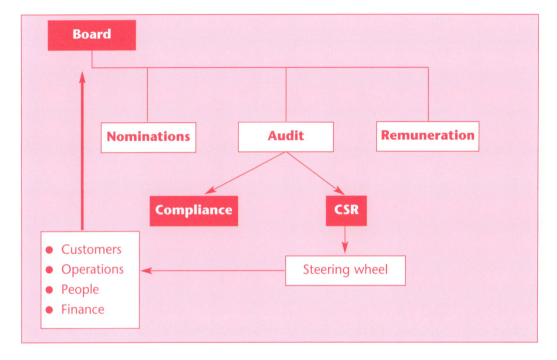

## Commitment to corporate governance

What constitutes adequate governance structures and disclosures will vary from one business to the next. Merely describing committees or proclaiming what risk is constitutes nothing more than ticking off boxes, and many companies are perceived as such. The Tesco presentation certainly addresses the fundamental issues in corporate governance, but how it defines the roles of its committees and integrates structures into the relationships among these committees suggests a strong commitment to governance. This may be a quality most desired by stakeholders.

## Self-Assessment Question 7

1. Suggest how the Tesco structure may combat a potential weakness(es) in company board structure.

# CHAPTER REVIEW

Corporate governance is the oversight mechanism in a company. The number of governance theories reflects the dynamics that exist in a business. In agency theory, directors act on behalf of shareholders, although the latter cannot be guaranteed that the directors will always do what shareholders want. The emergence of corporate governance in business today probably has a lot to do with stakeholder theory, which reflects the concerns of other parties associated directly or indirectly with a company, from lenders to customers to communities at large. Transaction costs theory has to do with the economic cost in providing oversight and fulfilling compliance requirements. The relationship between the executive, directors and shareholders, central to agency theory, dominates much of the debate.

Some important contributions to what good governance should be come from the OECD, and in Britain and Ireland the creation of the combined code has provided generally accepted practices. Beginning with the Cadbury Report in 1992, the code was revised in 2003 and places emphasis on independent non-executive directors. It is made of two parts, Part 1 containing the principles and Part 2 covering best practices for implementing the principles. The suggestion of an audit committee consisting entirely of independent non-executive directors only strengthens the accountability and is a noted feature of the revised code. This puts it in line with the Companies Act 2003, whereby for the first time the audit committee is part of Irish corporate legislation.

Board structures and directors' responsibilities are articulated in companies' annual reports. The challenge for a publicly traded company is to demonstrate that it takes governance seriously. The analysis of the Tesco model suggests a commitment to oversight and contends that such a commitment is a quality of good corporate governance.

# SELF-ASSESSMENT QUESTION ANSWERS

### SAQ 1

1. Agency theory is the dominant theory in governance by virtue of the appointment of directors as agents for shareholders who, as principals, own the company. The duty of the directors is to put structures in place that oversee the effective running of the entity. Corporate governance is an oversight issue.

### SAQ 2

1. The challenge for a business is to meet its social responsibility to employees and customers, to society generally and at the same time maintain profitability.

### SAQ 3

1. The sequence of reports beginning in 1992 with the Cadbury Report and followed by

Greenbury in 1995 and Hampel in 1998 identified all of the essentials that make up the code today. Some issues implied in Cadbury were made explicit in later reports. As we will see later, earlier suggestions of having a majority of non-executive directors on committees gave way to recommending committees to consist of non-executive directors only.

## SAQ 4

1. The principle states that 'the board should establish formal and transparent arrangements for considering how they should apply the financial reporting and internal control principles and for maintaining an appropriate relationship with the company's auditors' (D.3). The practice as stated in Part 2 says that an audit committee consist 'of at least three directors, all non-executive, all independent' (D.3.1). This reflects the stridency of the revised combined code.

## SAQ 5

1. The following duties are required by the Companies Acts 1963–2003:
   - maintain proper books of accounts
   - prepare annual returns of accounts
   - facilitate an annual audit
   - maintain registers and other key documents
   - complete document filings with the Registrar of Companies
   - disclose key information on directors and secretaries, such as name, address, date of birth, nationality, occupation, other directorships, shares held and service contracts
   - hold annual general meetings
   - complete directors' compliance statement.

   Duties arising from court cases or common law are:
   - act in good faith
   - use due skill, care and diligence
   - maintain independent judgment
   - avoid making undisclosed profits
   - attend regular meetings, as can be reasonably expected.

2. The audit committee was explicitly mentioned in the Companies Act 2003, marking the first time that any board committee was included in legislation.

## SAQ 6

1. The combined code requires the director who qualifies to be independent in character and judgment. It suggests a guideline that 'there are no relationships or circumstances

which could affect, or appear to affect, the director's judgment' (A.3.4). This guideline eliminates any arbitrariness, and as it is not a legal document, companies must abide by the spirit of the code.

## SAQ 7

1. Although complete knowledge of Tesco's corporate structure is not provided, the corporate governance structure does suggest a flow that collects information through the committees and feeds it back to the board itself. It appears to pursue a good faith attempt to understand the key stakeholders, such as customers and staff.

## REFERENCES

Brennan, N. and McDermott, M., *Are Non-executive Directors of Irish plcs Independent?* Dublin: Institute of Directors 2003.

Cadbury, Sir Adrian, *Report of the Committee on the Financial Aspects of Corporate Governance*, London: Gee Publishing 1992.

Committee on Corporate Governance, *The Combined Code on Corporate Governance* (revised), London: Gee Publishing 2003.

Companies (Auditing and Accounting) Act 2003, Dublin: The Stationery Office.

Company Law Enforcement Act 2001, Dublin: The Stationery Office.

Deloitte & Touche, *Responsibilities of Directors in Ireland*, Dublin: Deloitte 2004.

Greenbury, Sir Richard, *Directors' Remuneration*, London: Gee Publishing 1995.

Higgs, D., *Review of the Role and Effectiveness of Non-executive Directors*, London: The Stationery Office 2003.

Muckenberger, U., 'Toward institutionalising urban time policy', *Quarterly of the European Trade Union Institute*, III/4 (1997).

O'Connell, M., *Who'd Want to Be a Company Director? A Guide to the Enforcement of Irish Company Law*, Dublin: First Law 2003.

O'Regan, P., *Financial Information Analysis*, Chichester: John Wiley & Sons 2001.

Smith, R., *Audit Committees – Combined Code Guidance*, London: The Financial Reporting Council 2003.

Tesco plc, *Annual Report and Financial Statements 2004*, Registered Office: Tesco House, Delamere Road, Cashunt, Hertfordshire February 2004.

Villeneuve, R., 'Europe and territories: emerging processes', *Quarterly of the European Trade Union Institute*, III/4 (1997).

# 11

# *Control of Accounting Systems*

# INTRODUCTION

It is the responsibility of the financial controller of a company to safeguard the company's assets and to maintain the integrity of the financial data. This is arguably the greatest challenge facing an accounting professional, focusing as it does on the issue of adequate controls for the accounts, and generally referred to as the internal control system (ICS). It is a structure that now attracts close scrutiny in the aftermath of the Enron and WorldCom scandals with the introduction of the Companies Act 2003 in Ireland and Sarbanes Oxley (2002) in the US. Most corporate governance proponents welcome the legislation, primarily because it highlights responsibility and accountability, key qualities that are integral to control and the corporate governance debate. Businesses on both sides of the Atlantic complain, with some justification, about the increase in cost for this compliance. However, the lamentable fact is that the internal control model presently advocated for businesses was introduced in the US as early as 1992 by the Committee of Sponsoring Organisations (COSO) of the Treadway Commission. The years since then are a useful reminder of how good practices and principles become redundant when compliance is not enforced.

In this chapter we will examine the internal control system and understand how its mechanical processes are designed to minimise risk. We will understand that while it cannot be eliminated, risk can be reduced and managed. This is why controlling is a fundamental activity of all managers. All assets have internal controls in place and in this chapter we will concentrate on the controls for cash to demonstrate how internal control objectives are met by the application of internal control principles. At the end, this internal machination must allow a company to assert the true and fair view of its state of affairs. In Chapter 12 we will study how the external audit process challenges that assertion.

## OBJECTIVES

**When you have finished this chapter, you will be able to:**
- understand the role of risk in internal control
- identify the principles of internal control
- identify the components of the internal control system (ICS)
- understand how principles of internal control are applied to cash.

# THE ENVIRONMENT OF INTERNAL CONTROL

Internal control in any business is more than a set of procedures and computers. It is a world of processes and people that provides reasonable assurance in three key areas (Turnbull 1999):

- effectiveness and efficiency of operations
- reliability of financial reporting
- compliance with required laws and regulations.

One commentator also views it as a 'totality of methods' introduced by management to avoid unwanted outcomes (Chambers 2002). This is appropriate when one considers that half of all companies are victims of fraud more than once a year (Rezaee 2002). Generally, 25 per cent of staff are honest, 25 per cent are dishonest and 50 per cent are easily swayed. Thus the threats to a company's resources are significant. In addition to dishonest employees, controls must contend with:

- incompetent employees
- mistakes
- poor internal controls
- weak cash or unpredictable cash flow.

This is before the threats from competition, changing tastes and markets and the unending developments in technology are taken into consideration. Dealing with aggressive growth and adapting to it successfully places stress on a business to apply controls and keep them up to date. We can add to that the impact of perhaps a very domineering CEO, and from the outside, the compliance demands of regulators. The control environment is therefore a dynamic world, and as we will see in Chapter 12, it requires rigorous testing by an independent auditor to give stakeholders some level of assurance.

## Identifying risk

If reasonable assurance is the best that a control system can give, then clearly risk is a factor to contend with. External auditors are hugely sensitive to risk and the international standards of auditing (ISA) issued by the International Auditing and Assurance Standards Board (IAASB) provide us with useful definitions that company management can also embrace.

- **Inherent risk:** 'Susceptibility of an account balance or set of transactions to material misstatement' (ISA 400). While some transactions may have been omitted in error, at WorldCom and Enron revenues were fraudulently inflated to meet analysts' expectations. We can expand inherent risk to cover:
  - managerial competence – is it in line with growth?
  - complex transactions – can they handle them?
  - age of debtors – is anybody watching it?
    Management's emphasis on controls will minimise the risk in these additional areas.

- **Control risk:** 'That a misstatement could occur in an account balance or class of transactions and would not be prevented, or detected and corrected on a timely basis' (ISA 400).

Many of the threats listed above indicate a danger from within, prompting a company's management to view prevention and detection as first and second lines of defence, respectively. This is why inherent risk and control risk will have a major impact on the eventual internal control mechanism or structure.

### The binary aspect of control

You will recall from Chapter 7 that we discussed control as binary in function, i.e. it provides an answer in yes or no terms (Seeger 1975). We must not lose sight of this very intuitive point as we prepare to study the COSO model, complete with its mechanisms and conceptual thinking. Questions posed on a timely basis, such as 'Are the books balanced?' or 'Are there two authorised signatures on outgoing cheques?', should trigger unambiguous answers that inform management of the state of things. Applying controls in this way means that the focus is on performance, and any detection of problems early on will minimise stress.

---

### *Self-Assessment Question 1*

1. In what way does inherent risk differ from control risk?

---

## THE INTERNAL CONTROL SYSTEM (ICS) – COSO MODEL

The report published by COSO in 1992 was called *Internal Control – An Integrated Framework* and it identified five components of internal control:
- control environment
- risk assessment
- control activities
- information and communication
- monitoring.

The report placed heavy emphasis on assessing the effectiveness of control systems – what works, what does not work. Its broad application of control makes the report relevant for all systems in a company, not just the accounting system (Porter *et al.* 2003), and its undated 2002 report demonstrates this graphically in Figure 11.1. It applies across the control of operations, financial reporting and compliance.

FIGURE 11.1: COMPONENTS OF INTERNAL CONTROL: COSO REPORT

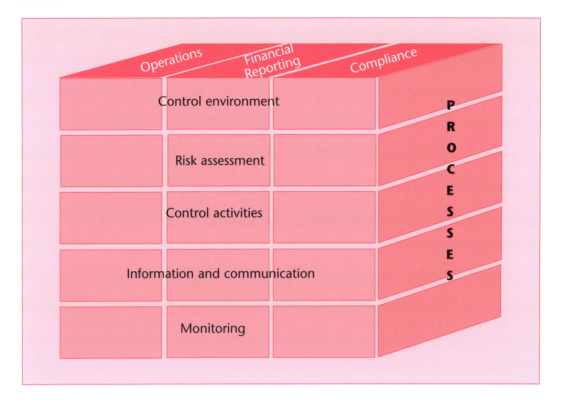

## Control environment

What we are looking at is the leadership in a company that aspires to the ethical values of integrity and competence. The following characteristics capture the criteria for assessing a committed management:

- commitment to competence and integrity
- communication of ethical values
- appropriate organisational structure to manage objectives
- appropriate delegation of authority with accountability.

Very clearly, directors and senior management set the tone for behaviour in any company. This may explain why some commentators have presented **control environment** as an umbrella covering the other components (Arens *et al.* 2005).

## Risk assessment

We have already identified risk from both internal and external sources as inherent in the running of any business. Good governance recognises risk as primarily financial, operational and compliance related. Therefore, assessing it is a constant activity. Three criteria for effectiveness in managing risk are recommended (Arens *et al.* 2005):

- identification of the key risks
- likelihood of risks crystallising
- allocation of resources for meeting control objectives.

These recommendations are very much in line with the UK's Turnbull Report of 1999.

## Control activities

These represent the mechanism, the nuts and bolts if you will, of applying controls in a practical way. The challenge here is to match authority with responsibility so that exposure to loss is minimised. It is appropriate here to remind ourselves of the **objectives** of internal control:

- safeguard all assets from theft, robbery and unauthorised use
- enhance the accuracy and reliability of accounting records by reducing the risk of errors and irregularities.

To achieve these control objectives, a company follows a number of **internal control principles**. Specific control mechanisms or approaches may vary from one company to the next, but these principles (see Figure 11.2) will apply to most business environments. They are:

- establishment of responsibility
- segregation of duties
- documentation procedures
- physical, mechanical and electronic controls
- independent internal verification
- other controls.

FIGURE 11.2: INTERNAL CONTROL PRINCIPLES

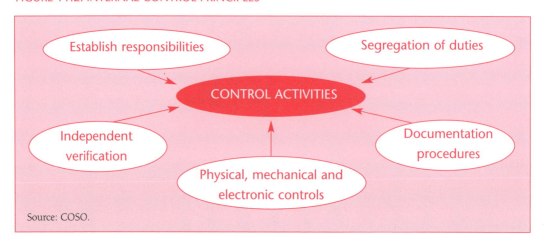

Source: COSO.

In examining these more closely, we will see how issues such as limiting exposure to losses, reliability of information, good record keeping and routine and random checking are the basis of a culture of good controls and good habits.

*As you examine each principle, try to relate it to the internal control objectives.*

## Self-Assessment Questions 2

1. What are the objectives of internal control?
2. Identify the principles of internal control.

### ESTABLISHMENT OF RESPONSIBILITY

This calls for assigning responsibility to a specific individual. Control is most effective when only one person is responsible for a given task.

An important element of this is the inclusion of authorisation to approve transactions. For instance, in considering selling goods on credit, the sales department should be able to establish the criteria allowing such sales. In this way, accountability is matched with responsibility and the sales department is held accountable for its actions.

### SEGREGATION OF DUTIES

This principle is applied in two ways:

- the responsibility for related activities should be assigned to different individuals
- the responsibility for keeping the records for an asset should be separate from the physical custody of that asset.

When completed by the same person, related but distinct activities, such as ordering goods and receiving and paying for the goods, facilitate the risk of theft. For instance, goods might be ordered from friends or suppliers who give kickbacks, or payments might be approved for fictitious invoices. Similarly, sales-related activities should be assigned to different individuals.

Another example of segregating the duties is where the bookkeeper of asset records does not have access to the assets. Equally, the person in charge of the asset should not maintain or have access to the accounting records for that asset. An employee in charge of cash is not likely to make personal use of the cash if somebody else is maintaining the accounting for the cash.

### DOCUMENTATION PROCEDURES

Procedures should be established for documentation. Firstly, documents should be pre-numbered and all documents should be accounted for. Second, source documents for accounting entries should be promptly forwarded to the accounting department to help ensure timely recording of the transaction and of the event. This directly affects the accuracy and reliability of the accounting records.

### PHYSICAL, MECHANICAL AND ELECTRONIC CONTROLS

Physical controls relate primarily to the safeguarding of assets and include safes and vaults, secure warehouses and cabinets and computer facilities with security key access. Mechanical and electronic controls safeguard assets and enhance the accuracy and reliability of the records. These include computer security and back-up, alarm systems, TV monitors, photo sensors, time clocks and air-conditioning systems.

Computer security is particularly challenging. There are the natural dangers to secure against, such as black-outs, brown-outs and obsolete technology in addition to manmade threats such as hacking, viruses and data manipulation. Firewalls and virus protection should be installed and updated regularly. Access should be restricted by an ever-changing password system. The 9/11 terrorist attack in New York City has emphasised disaster recovery as standard in emergency planning. If there was a fire or flood damage to a company's premises, how many hours would it take to have vital systems back up and running?

### INDEPENDENT INTERNAL VERIFICATION

This principle involves the review, comparison and reconciliation of data prepared by employees. It usually requires verification to be made periodically or on a surprise basis and carried out by a person independent of the individual responsible for the information. This independent person can be an employee from another department; if the verification is a large task, an external accounting professional can fulfil the role. A large organisation will almost certainly have its own internal auditing department where regular verification constitutes a significant part of the work.

Any discrepancies or exceptions should be reported to a senior management level, capable of corrective action.

*A register is a document containing a list of fixed assets with date of purchase, cost, estimated usage life and location in the plant or office.*

An example of a verification might be having somebody verify a company's register of fixed assets against existing assets, or have somebody reconcile the cash balance in the books with that of the bank statements. The interaction with outside professionals anticipates our study of external controls in Chapter 12, but it must be stressed that effective internal control is maximised when it possesses an element of external control.

### OTHER CONTROLS

Additional controls may include:

- **Bonding of employees who handle cash:** This involves obtaining insurance protection against misappropriation of assets by dishonest employees.
- **Rotation of duties and insistence on holidays:** That may make concealment of embezzlement or theft difficult to sustain.

## Self-Assessment Question 3

1. Identify the principle of internal control being followed in each of these situations.
   (a) Employees in charge of assets do not have access to accounting records.
   (b) The assets on hand are compared with accounting records by an internal auditor every month.
   (c) A pre-numbered shipping document is prepared for each shipment of goods to customers.

## Information and communication

At the heart of accounting information is the accounting system itself, and today, virtually every company uses a computer software package to store this information. In fact, this component brings us full circle because the question to be addressed here is whether the system processes transactions using the same principles and methods that you studied in the earlier chapters of this book. Does it capture transactions by class, such as sales, purchases and sales returns? Will it balance the general ledger and thus facilitate preparation of the financial statements? This system must produce reliable information that is up to date so that management can monitor activities and advance to meeting financial objectives. Good systems will also compare actual with budgeted performance and with prior years' activity. The criteria that we are seeking here are:

- performance indicators that monitor business and financial activities, risks and progress on objectives
- systems which communicate relevant, reliable and timely information.

We can add to these the regular use of information by an active management team, monthly board and/or executive meetings, daily cash flow reporting and age analysis of debtors and creditors.

## Monitoring

The recent legislation concerning responsibilities of directors in companies will leave no board in doubt about its priorities. They will want at least reasonable assurance that there is an adequate system of control in place. It is not enough to have a report on past events, and boards will want to know the status of projects and progress in plans already launched. They will also want to anticipate or even forecast events, particularly those that may increase risk of losses, such as a pending lawsuit. Effectiveness can be assessed with the following steps:

- Processes in place to provide reasonable assurance to the directors that appropriate control procedures are in place.
- Identification of changes in the business requiring updates to the internal control system.
- Formal procedures for reporting weaknesses and for taking corrective action.
- Adequately compensating directors for committing to such statements on their part.

In Chapter 10 we discussed the significant demands now being made of directors, not the least of which is a declaration that the company is compliant with its 'relevant obligations' (Companies Act 2003). We can expect that the audit committee will emphasise quality of control performance and that the internal auditing function will receive greater prominence.

### Limitations of internal control

How much control is enough? The best that we can say is that a system of internal control can only provide a reasonable assurance that assets are properly safeguarded and that records are reliable. The concept of reasonable assurance was always predicated on the guideline that the costs of such controls should not exceed the benefits derived. And there are limitations to steps used to protect a business. For instance, shoplifting would be eliminated if all customers were searched upon leaving a store, but such treatment would be abhorrent to most customers. A good control system may be rendered useless through employee carelessness or boredom. Collusion is always a possibility.

There is no doubt but that higher levels of assurance will cost significantly more. The guidance provided by the PCAOB in the US for the internal control section alone of the Sarbanes Oxley Act exceeds 210 pages, with an additional twenty-seven pages of appendices. In December 2004 Ireland's ODCE published a forty-plus-page paper as a guide to complying with the directors' compliance statement (CA 2003, Section 45). Even with that there is considerable anxiety over the scope of the Act's 'relevant obligations' and what exactly it includes. Perhaps holding a directorship will not have the same lure as it once had.

### Self-Assessment Question 4

1. Explain how recent legislative changes have underlined the importance of the monitoring component.

# CONTROL AND MANAGEMENT OF CASH

Of all the assets of a company, cash is the most susceptible to loss or wrongful use. It is the beginning of a business's operating cycle and therefore it is the first place in which to institute internal controls. Where there is a large volume of cash transactions, the risk of error is great in executing and recording transactions. Therefore, to enhance accuracy and protect cash, effective internal control is imperative.

## Cash and its equivalent

So that we are perfectly clear on what we mean by cash, and specifically on what we report as cash in the financial statements, let's look at it more closely.

The current assets section of the balance sheet will usually list cash in these instances as **cash and cash equivalent**.

Cash is made up of coins, notes, cheques, money orders, money on hand and money in the bank or similar institution. There is also a distinction made for those items that are investments nearing maturity and that are highly liquid. Financial instruments such as ten- to thirty-day investment funds, and those that can be converted to cash prior to maturity (for a fee, of course), make up this group and they are referred to as cash equivalents (IAS 7). Companies with excess cash can increase income by investing in these short-term funds.

Sometimes cash is restricted in its use, as in the case of a loan requirement whereby the lender insists on a growing cash balance to assist the eventual repayment of the loan. If the restricted amount is availed of within a year, then the amount is listed as **restricted cash** in the current assets section of the balance sheet. It is listed in the long-term assets section if the restriction is longer.

Let's now look at internal controls for cash.

## Internal control over cash receipts

Cash is received from a number of sources:
- cash sales
- collections from debtors
- interest, rents and dividends
- cash infusions from investors
- bank loans
- sales of fixed assets.

Let's see how the principles of internal control that we listed earlier can be applied to cash:

| Establishment of responsibility | Specific individuals are authorised to handle receipts. |
|---|---|
| Segregation of duties | Different people receive cash, record cash and deposit cash. |
| Documentation procedures | Use of numbered receipts and issuance forms, tapes, advice slips. |
| Physical, mechanical and electronic controls | Use of safes, vaults and cash registers, limited access to cash areas. |
| Independent internal verification | Other staff or supervisors to confirm cash receipt totals. Accounting department to compare bank receipts with total receipts. |
| Other controls | Minimising cash on premises, bonding staff, regular vacations. |

## Self-Assessment Question 5

1. Identify the internal control principle that is applicable to each procedure.
   (a) All over-the-counter receipts are registered on cash registers.
   (b) All cashiers are bonded.
   (c) Daily cash counts are made by cashier department supervisors.
   (d) The duties of receiving cash and recording cash are assigned to different employees.
   (e) Only cashiers may operate cash registers.

## Internal control over cash disbursements

Cash is disbursed to pay for expenses, wages, settling with suppliers or buying equipment. Payment by cheque certainly enhances internal control over disbursements. A cheque issuance is usually the result of a number of procedures designed to protect the business, and of course the cheque acts as proof of payment. Even then, dangers such as fictitious creditors or staff slipping in relatively small personal expenses for payment may not be detected.

Some expenses are such that payment by cheque is not practical. Payment for newspapers, tea and coffee and taxi expenses are usually small amounts and are paid for out of the petty cash fund. Access to this fund (very often a box in somebody's desk drawer) should be restricted and balanced out regularly by somebody independent of its custodian.

How are the internal control principles applied to cash disbursements?

| | |
|---|---|
| Establishment of responsibility | Designated individuals are authorised to sign cheques. |
| Segregation of duties | Different people approve and make payments. Cheque signers do not record the disbursements. |
| Documentation procedures | Use of pre-numbered cheques, used in sequence (missing cheques to be accounted for). Each cheque must have an approved invoice attached. |
| Physical, mechanical and electronic controls | Keep blank chequebook in a safe. Restrict access to petty cash box. |
| Independent internal verification | Reconcile bank statements monthly. Compare cheque and invoice. Examine blank cheque run for stolen cheques. |
| Other controls | Encourage use of electronic funds transfer (EFT). |

## Self-Assessment Question 6

1. Identify the internal control principle that is applicable to each procedure.
   (a) Company cheques are pre-numbered.
   (b) The bank statement is reconciled monthly by an internal auditor.
   (c) Blank cheques are stored in a safe in the financial controller's office.
   (d) The financial controller and the office manager must both sign cheques.
   (e) Cheque signatories are not allowed to record cash disbursement transactions.

### BANK RECONCILIATION

Reconciliation of the bank account is mentioned above as a key control over cash. As most people know how to reconcile their own bank statements, an in-depth reconciliation will not be done here. Some points, however, are warranted:

- The bank statement acts as a second control to the company's record of cash transactions.
- The reconciliation is an effective device when it is done by somebody other than those receiving and disbursing cash.
- Items such as returned cheques and bank fees are isolated and thus processed for posting to the books.

## The management of cash

As we discussed in Chapter 9 when examining liquidity, achieving sound cash flow is essential to running a business. It is often referred to as the **life-blood** of any endeavour, be it profit or non-profit, and managing it successfully is one the greatest challenges for any organisation.

The managing of cash invariably centres around the operating cycle of a business and is calculated as follows:

$$\text{stock days} + \text{debtor days} - \text{creditor days} = \text{cash cycle}$$

For a manufacturing business, the cycle is longer than that for a retail business, which buys inventory and resells it quickly and thus can expect cash flow in and out much more quickly than the manufacturer. The challenge for each is to collect cash from sales as quickly as possible so that suppliers in turn can be paid on time.

While lack of sales is a major reason why liquidity is poor, bad management of debtors can also jeopardise liquidity, even when sales are terrific. There are instances where entrepreneurs with a great product or service mistake a sale for money in the bank. Visionaries with great marketing ideas but lacking in strong back-office support often fall into this trap.

There are several principles for managing cash (O'Regan 1998):
- speed up the collection of debtors' balances
- maintain low inventory levels
- delay payment of liabilities
- plan the timing of major expenditures
- invest idle cash.

### SPEED UP THE COLLECTION OF DEBTORS' BALANCES

This is pursued in two ways: maintaining regular and consistent contact with debtors and preventing bad habits from arising. If the payment period is agreed at thirty days, then always call on the thirty-first day if payment has not been received. If there is a problem, it is better to find out early, encouraging debtors to avail of discounts if they pay earlier. This is suggested particularly if competitors are offering longer repayment periods.

## MAINTAIN LOW INVENTORY LEVELS

Large amounts of inventory tie up cash in addition to increasing warehouse costs, space requirements and exposure to obsolescence. At the other end of the argument is the danger of running out of inventory and thus losing sales. This is a delicate balance and much depends on the pacing in usage and the nearness of suppliers.

## DELAY PAYMENT OF LIABILITIES

A business should use the full period available to it for paying its bills. Not paying its bills too early, and yet not risking its credit rating by paying late, is the balance to be achieved.

## PLAN THE TIMING OF MAJOR EXPENDITURES

Purchase of major assets often characterises growth in businesses. While most capital expenditures are financed by loans, the installation and integration of such assets can be a drain on cash flow. It is therefore recommended that a major purchase should take place when there is excess cash.

## INVEST IDLE CASH

Cash is usually kept in bank accounts that earn little or no interest on balances. Managers of cash should be able to anticipate excess levels and invest in short-term investments accordingly. By virtue of technology in use in banks today, many banks offer investment accounts that transfer amounts into current accounts only when cheques are presented.

There are other opportunities in this area. In his role as a CFO, this author replaced fifteen suppliers of the main inventory with three suppliers. This arrangement achieved considerable discounts and an attractive repayment period for the company in return for each supplier increasing their share of the business to one-third. And how do you avoid doing business with a possible cartel? You simply buy from a fourth supplier periodically.

# Cash budgeting

We have dealt with many of the key elements in controlling cash, ranging from protecting it to discussing the best ways to manage it. When we discussed cash receipts and disbursements, we essentially anticipated the topic of cash budgeting, an important activity for planning the company's cash needs. In this section we will discuss only the very basics; you are advised that budgeting is itself a subject of many textbooks.

The cash budget is made of three sections:

- **Cash receipts section:** Includes expected receipts from revenue (cash and credit), interest, dividends and proceeds from the sale of fixed assets.
- **Cash disbursement section:** Includes payments for materials, labour, electricity and heating, taxes, interest, dividends, investments and purchase of assets.
- **Financing section:** Reflects expected borrowing and repayment of borrowed funds.

If a company determines that it needs a minimum cash balance of €30,000 to operate, it will create a budget that typically will look like this:

**Cash budget**

| | |
|---|---:|
| Beginning cash balance | €100,000 |
| Add cash receipts | 80,000 |
| Total available cash | 180,000 |
| | |
| Less cash disbursements | 160,000 |
| Excess (or deficiency) of available | |
| cash over disbursements | 20,000 |
| | |
| Financing needed | 10,000 |
| Ending cash balance | €30,000 |

When a cash budget is prepared, detailed sub-budgets that forecast sales and timing of collections of credit sales are also prepared.

### Self-Assessment Questions 7

1. What are the principles of cash management?
2. Command Co. wants to maintain a minimum monthly cash balance of €15,000. On 1 March, the cash balance is €16,500; expected receipts for March are €210,000; disbursements are expected to be €220,000. How much cash, if any, must be borrowed to maintain the desired minimum monthly balance?

Many departments often feel pestered by the seeming red-tape mentality of the accounting department, with its insistence on correct signatures, copies of everything and specific times for cheque runs and end-of-month transactions. Yet this must be understood in light of the two objectives that we stated at the outset: safeguarding the assets and maintaining reliable information. Only when good internal controls are in place is good cash management possible.

## CHAPTER REVIEW

In this chapter we commenced our study by restating that the key responsibility of an organisation's accounting system is to:

- safeguard all assets from theft, robbery and unauthorised use
- enhance the accuracy and reliability of its accounting records by reducing the risk of errors and irregularities.

This calls for control measures and systems that are established internally and that can be tested both internally and externally. Although no system can guarantee the integrity of accounting information and the safety of assets, constant vigilance and updating can minimise the risks of error and fraud.

We addressed the threats to a business, whether from dishonest employees or just from poor internal controls, and suggested six principles of internal control to combat these threats. Principles such as segregation of duties and physical, mechanical and electronic controls are designed to maximise protection from fraud, but unfortunately they cannot prevent collusion among staff members. Independent internal verification is highly desirable and can be carried out by other staff members or outside people. This latter option anticipates the usefulness of external control, which is implemented mainly by the completion of an audit by external auditors.

We concentrated on the internal controls relating to cash, as this asset is the most susceptible to loss. Controls can be applied to cash receipts, and disbursements and devices such as monthly bank reconciliations and the use of electronic fund transfer enhance controls.

In addition to protecting cash, we saw that internal controls complement the management of cash. Cash is the life-blood of any business and it demands strong controls and solid management. We listed five principles for managing cash; any test of internal controls would include a review of the application of these principles.

## SELF-ASSESSMENT QUESTION ANSWERS

### SAQ 1

1. Inherent in an accounting system is the possibility that a transaction or account balance will be materially misstated. Control risk is concerned with the possibility that misstatements will not be detected or prevented.

### SAQ 2

1. There are two primary objectives of internal control:
   - to safeguard a business's assets
   - to enhance the accuracy and reliability of its accounting records.
2. There are essentially six principles of internal control:
   - establishment of responsibility
   - segregation of duties
   - documentation procedures
   - physical, mechanical and electronic controls
   - independent internal verification
   - other controls.

## SAQ 3

1. (a)  Segregation of duties.
   (b)  Independent verification.
   (c)  Documentation procedures.

## SAQ 4

1. The Companies Act 2003 brought the audit committee into legislation for the first time, whereby directors will be held responsible for complying with 'all relevant obligations'. The monitoring by the board will include procedures on reporting processes, identifying weaknesses and taking corrective action. Generally a more involved approach is required of the board.

## SAQ 5

1. (a)  Documentation procedures.
   (b)  Additional controls (there are probably never enough).
   (c)  Independent verification.
   (d)  Segregation of duties.
   (e)  Establishment of responsibility.

## SAQ 6

1. (a)  Documentation procedures.
   (b)  Independent verification.
   (c)  Physical control.
   (d)  Establishment of responsibility.
   (e)  Segregation of duties.

## SAQ 7

1. The principles of cash management:
   - speed up the collection of debtors' balances
   - maintain low inventory levels
   - delay payment of liabilities
   - plan the timing of major expenditures
   - invest idle cash.

2.  Cash budget:

| | € |
|---|---|
| Beginning cash balance | 16,500 |
| Add receipts for March | 210,000 |
| Total available cash | 226,500 |
| Less cash disbursements for March | 220,000 |
| Excess of available cash over disbursements | 6,500 |
| Financing | **8,500** |
| Ending cash balance | €15,000 |
| | |
| Command Co. must borrow | €8,500 |

## REFERENCES

Arens, A., Elder, R. and Beasley, M., *Auditing and Assurance Services*, Upper Saddle River, NJ: Pearson Education Inc. 2005.

Bisk, N., *Auditing from CPA Comprehensive Exam Review*, Tampa, FL: Fox Gearty 1993.

Chambers, A., *Corporate Governance Handbook*. London: Reed Elsevier 2002.

Company Law Enforcement Act 2001, Dublin: The Stationery Office.

Committee of Sponsoring Organizations of the Treadway Commission (COSO), *Internal Control – Integrated Framework*, New Jersey: AICPA 2002.

IAASB, *Handbook of International Auditing, Assurance and Ethics Pronouncements*, New York: International Federation of Accountants 2005.

International Accounting Standards Board, *IAS 7 Cash Flow Statements*, London: IASB 1992.

O'Regan, P., *Introduction to Accounting*, Limerick: The International Equine Institute, University of Limerick 1998.

Porter, B., Simon, J. and Hatherly, D., *Principles of External Auditing*, 2nd ed., Chichester: Wiley 2003.

Rezaee, Z., *Financial Statement Fraud: Prevention and Detection*, New York: John Wiley & Sons 2002.

Seeger, J., *First National City Bank Operating Group*, Boston, MA: Harvard Business School 1975.

Turnbull, N., *Internal Control: Guidance for Directors on the Combined Code*, London: ICAEW 1999.

# 12

# *The Audit Process*

**C O N T E N T S**

# INTRODUCTION

The audit by an independent auditor is a key component of the overall reporting process. It has many aspects to it, some of which are complex and sometimes contradictory. The choice of auditor is suggested by management and placed before the shareholders for approval at the AGM. Although the report is provided to the shareholders, it is the management who pays the auditor for the service. The student, having stayed the course to this point, must now make some vital connections with a number of concepts previously discussed. The statements were prepared according to accounting principles. Transactions were processed and accounted for in a system that culminated in a periodic report. Along the way we discussed control issues, governance issues and whether the business will survive. We must now step back from this headlong rush forward and look back at the system in its entirety and ask: can the user rely on what is reported? This is what the audit attempts to answer.

**PCAOB**: Public Company Accounting Oversight Board, established by Sarbanes Oxley Act 2002. Sets and/or adopts auditing standards. Reports to the Securities and Exchange Commission (SEC).

The audit process calls upon companies to show a firm commitment to **accountability** for the obvious reason that they are direct participants (DiPiazza and Eccles 2003) in the corporate governance structure. The audit looks very closely at the internal control system, a fact which prompted the insightful comment by W.J.M. MacKenzie (1966) that 'without audit, no accountability, without accountability, no control'.

An unwitting boost to the interest in corporate governance occurred as a result of the demise of Arthur Andersen, one of the largest accounting firms in the world. It was the independent auditor for Enron, and yet it proceeded to take on the role of internal auditor, a violation of a fundamental principle! This contributed to its loss in credibility and triggered the mass departure of its clients. The auditing profession was further rocked with the loss of self-regulation on both sides of the Atlantic. The PCAOB in the US oversees the accounting profession, and in Ireland, Irish accountancy bodies are supervised by the IAASA per the Companies Act 2003.

**IAASA**: Irish Auditing and Accounting Supervisory Authority. Established in response to Irish scandals: Ansbacher, DIRT, NIB, Beef Tribunal findings.

## OBJECTIVES

**When you have finished this chapter, you will be able to:**

- understand auditing as a means of external control
- understand the auditing standards
- understand the audit process
- understand the auditor's report and opinions
- understand the components of the annual report.

# THE NATURE OF THE INDEPENDENT AUDIT

In Chapter 11 we examined the internal approach to safeguarding the assets of the business. A business relies on internal controls and management's ability to enforce those controls. An external audit entails a review of those same controls, the accounting systems and the transactions with outsiders to ensure that the financial statements have been prepared in accordance with accounting principles. These auditors should be expert and independent so that investors, lenders and revenue officials can rely on their report. The primary guidance for auditors is provided by the international standards on auditing (ISA), which are issued by the Council of the International Federation of Accounting (IFAC) and are similar to the UK and Irish statements of auditing standards (SAS). We will refer to the ISAs, as these are increasingly recognised since the introduction of the international accounting standards in January 2005.

## Definition and purpose

An audit is defined as an independent review whose objective is to enable auditors to express an opinion on whether the financial statements are prepared, in all material respects, in accordance with an identified financial reporting framework (ISA 200).

The framework referred to here is the international accounting standards.

We can also describe auditing as 'a systematic process of objectively gathering and evaluating evidence relating to assertions about economic actions and events' generated by a business (American Accounting Association 1973).

The focus of much of the auditor's attention includes not only the financial statements – the profit and loss account, the balance sheet and the cash flow statement – but also the notes, reconciliations and estimates associated with the statements. Accordingly, in the report to the shareholders, the auditor must state whether:

- the auditor has had access to all records and information considered necessary
- the balance sheet and profit and loss account are in agreement with the accounts in the general ledger.

This should allow the auditor to meet its obligation to express an opinion on whether:

- the accounts give a true and fair view (or **present fairly**, if using IASs) of the state of the company's financial affairs at the end of its financial year, and of its profit and loss account for the year ended on that date
- the balance sheet and the profit and loss account comply with the legal requirements contained in the various Companies Acts
- proper books of account (general ledger) have been kept.

The purpose of the audit, then, is to allow the various stakeholders to rely on the financial statements prepared by a company's management. The auditor effectively acts as a check on management, and by bringing qualities of objectivity and independence to the job, inspires confidence in the reported numbers. However, the auditor does *not* guarantee accuracy. In this regard, he or she can only provide '**reasonable assurance**' that the statements are not impacted by fraud or error (ISA 240).

## Self-Assessment Question 1

1. How does the auditor disclose that he or she was able to adequately pursue the audit?

## What is meant by true and fair?

The term '**true and fair**' does not a have a statutory definition and an understanding of it is very much dependent upon case law. Indeed, it is particularly difficult to apply it in an auditing and accounting context, since one person's view may differ from another. It is a qualitative judgment regarding a company's state of affairs and not simply an 'arithmetic compliance' (Jones 2005) with accounting standards. What exacerbates matters has been the translation difficulties encountered in attempting to incorporate the term into the various EU Directives on auditing.

One explanation by Lee (1970) is often used, whereby 'true and fair' is generally understood to mean:

- a presentation of accounts drawn up according to accepted accounting principles
- using accurate figures as far as possible and reasonable estimates otherwise
- to show as objective a picture as possible free from all wilful bias, distortion, manipulation or concealment of material facts.

As this is an explanation and not a definition, it may underline the difficulty of ever agreeing on a definition. Adding to the debate is the term '**present fairly**', advocated by international accounting standards (IAS 1). The Financial Reporting Council, the accounting regulator in the UK, has stated that even with the advent of the IASs, 'the concept of the *true and fair* view remains the cornerstone of financial reporting and auditing in the UK' (August 2005). We will assume that this guidance will also apply to Ireland and for our purposes we will consider both terms to be essentially the same.

## Agency: A governance issue

Before we examine the auditing standards, let's remind ourselves of the corporate governance issue at the heart of the auditor's role. The shareholders, while owners of the company, are separated from its control. The problem for owners, then, is that they cannot be certain the directors will always act in the shareholders' interests. The auditor enters the fray as an agent, acting on behalf of the shareholders, and in this way provides a control against an imbalance in available information that may detract from quality reporting (Jones 2005). Once that is in place, investors can only rely on the auditor's independence and professional judgment. In effect, auditors are 'part of the corporate governance mosaic' because they monitor the quality of the financial reporting process (Beasley and Salterio 2001).

## Self-Assessment Question 2

1. What are the key characteristics of an audit?

## AUDITING STANDARDS AND GUIDELINES

Auditors are provided with auditing standards that inform them of the standard of work required and that assist the profession to protect its reputation (Porter *et al.* 2003). UK and Irish auditors used the SASs as developed by the Auditing Practices Board until 2004. From 2005, the EU, in its drive for harmonisation of markets, recommended the ISAs for all statutory audits. As with the SASs, the ISAs are mandatory and their use reflects due care on the part of the auditor. An advantage accrues to the British and Irish auditing profession, as the SASs form the basis for the international standards.

### Concepts of auditing

The standards are formed on what is generally accepted as four concepts of auditing:
- credibility
- audit process
- reporting
- standards of performance.

Within each of these concepts are themes around which the standards are built. Figure 12.1 shows the graphical picture of this configuration. Of the four concepts, **audit process** represents the mechanics, or 'rolling up the sleeves', of completing the audit. We will address a number of these themes and it will be apparent that all of them require use of judgment, the hallmark of any professional.

FIGURE 12.1: CONCEPTS OF AUDITING

| Credibility | Audit process | Reporting | Standards of performance |
|---|---|---|---|
| ● Independence. <br> ● Competence. <br> ● Ethical conduct. | ● Evidence. <br> ● Materiality. <br> ● Audit risk. <br> ● Judgment. <br> ● Scepticism. | ● Adequacy. <br> ● Disclosure. | ● Due care. <br> ● Quality control. |

## Audit risk

This is the risk that the auditor may express an inappropriate opinion on financial statements that are not correct (FRC 2005). This could come about as a result of inherent risk and control risk, previously discussed in Chapter 11. **Audit risk** is essentially a sequence of three risk factors. If a set of transactions is not processed properly **(inherent risk)** and subsequently not corrected **(control risk)**, then there is the **detection risk** that the auditor will not detect the mistake. Of course, we are assuming that these misstatements failing detection are material. Materiality is therefore a crucial theme here.

## Materiality

Information is considered material if its omission or misstatement could influence economic decisions made by users relying on the financial statements (FRC 2005). It does depend on the size of a transaction amount or circumstance involved. Clearly, a €1,000 error in the creditors account of a street corner coffee shop is material, but an insignificant error perhaps at a multinational company. For this reason, the ISAs suggest that 'materiality provides a threshold or cut-off point' (FRC 2005) for transaction amounts to be audited. At the end of the day, would you, the user, have made a different decision if you had received the omitted information? If you would have, then it was material.

## Audit evidence

Audit evidence covers all the information used by the auditor to reach conclusions on which the audit opinion is based (FRC 2005). It includes information from the accounting records underlying the financial statements. However, it is more than just collecting numbers or verifying balances. As Porter *et al.* point out (2003), citing Anderson (1977), auditors' observations and perceptions also add to the picture. The fixed assets register may list the cost of each item and assist in verifying the assets' existence. But what about the quality of those assets? Are machines maintained regularly? Skill levels and competencies of staff also provide an insight into the running of a company. If these skills are perceived to be inadequate or management is lackadaisical, then perhaps the auditor may look more closely at how well procedures are followed. Auditing evidence, therefore, includes all of the facts and impressions that auditors gather to facilitate an opinion on the truth and fairness of the financial statements (Porter *et al.* 2003).

Auditing standards suggest that auditors should obtain **sufficient** and **appropriate** evidence to draw reasonable conclusions. The two terms are interrelated:

- **Sufficient**: Enough evidence to meet audit objectives and enough to be representative.
- **Appropriate:** Has two further elements, *relevance* and *reliability*. Evidence must be pertinent and it must be trustworthy.

There is a caveat, however, to gathering and using evidence. In the modern audit environment, evidence is at best persuasive, *not* conclusive. The auditor cannot look at every transaction, a vulnerability to the auditor that can only be tackled with experience and judgment.

## Self-Assessment Question 3

1. List the concepts of auditing and explain what distinguishes one of them in particular from the others.

### ISA structure

Now that we have made our way through the concepts and related themes, we can proceed to how the ISAs are structured to assist auditors in practice (IFAC 2004). The list below contains a numbering system itemising practical advice and can be expanded to add new practices. For instance, the **evidence** theme just studied contains a number of related standards, a few of which are in this snapshot:

### International Standards on Auditing (ISA)

| | |
|---|---|
| 100/199 | Introductory matters |
| 200/299 | Responsibilities |
| 300/399 | Planning |
| 400/499 | Internal control |
| 500/599 | Evidence |
| 600/699 | Using work of others |
| 700/799 | Audit conclusions and reporting |

**Audit Evidence**

| | |
|---|---|
| ISA 500 | Audit evidence |

| ISA 501 | Audit evidence – additional considerations for specific items |
| ISA 505 | External confirmations |
| ISA 560 | Subsequent events |
| ISA 570 | Going concern |

The ISAs complement the international accounting standards. Both UK and Irish auditors should feel comfortable in using them.

As stated, compliance with the ISAs is mandatory for publicly traded companies. Non-public entities that require audits will continue to use the APB-sponsored SASs, at least for the next few years. Due to the similarity with ISAs, this will not be a problem. The APB released two additional sets of guidelines as prompted by emerging issues in business and auditing practices:

- **Practice notes** assist auditors in applying SASs to particular circumstances and industries.
- **Bulletins** provide auditors with timely guidance on new or emerging issues.

Being merely a guide and reflective in nature, they are not mandatory.

## Errors and fraud

A good system of internal control will minimise, but not eliminate, fraud and error. However, there are limitations on the effectiveness of the system and no system can guarantee the efficient administration and the completeness and accuracy of the records. Activities such as collusion by staff members, especially on the part of those holding positions of authority and trust, are extremely difficult to defend against.

It is important to distinguish the different types of errors and acts of fraud. An experienced auditor will recognise these main classifications of errors (Bisk 1993):

- **Errors of omission:** For example, failing to capture the transaction relating to the disposal of a fixed asset.
- **Errors of commission:** For example, treating a credit sale as a cash sale.
- **Errors of principle:** For example, treating a payment in advance as a sale instead of as a liability.
- **Compensating errors:** For example, plugging in numbers to make the trial balance agree.

Fraud, on the other hand, includes (but is not limited to) theft, forgery and manipulation of figures or of accounts. The manipulation described here is often perpetrated by collusion among staff members. Acts such as misappropriating a payment from a customer and applying a subsequent receipt to the first customer requires continuous monitoring if the fraud is to be minimised. Fictitious creditors or ghost employees may involve collusion with outside parties or involve innocent parties such as banks or other cheque-cashing facilities.

### THE AUDITOR'S RESPONSIBILITY

It must be emphasised again that the primary function of an audit is not to detect fraud and error, but rather to obtain sufficient appropriate audit evidence to form an opinion on the financial statements. However, the auditor is bound to exercise due care in the conduct of an audit, and a well-planned and carried out audit would be expected to uncover material fraud. Guidance from IAASB through ISA 240, dealing with fraud and error, specifies that auditors should be conscious of the possibility of fraud and error occurring and that may result in a significant misstatement of the accounts (IFAC 2004). They should therefore plan and perform their work accordingly. As long as the audit procedures provide for a **reasonable** expectation of detecting material error or fraud, then the auditor is not liable for failing to detect immaterial error or fraud.

An overemphasis on detection of fraud and error might result in additional costs as well as directing attention away from the primary statutory responsibility of the auditor.

### Self-Assessment Question 4

1. We stated earlier that evidence collected is at best persuasive and not conclusive. Does this support or detract from the auditor's approach to the possibility of fraud and error?

### CONDITIONS FACILITATING ERROR AND FRAUD

ISA 240 provides a checklist of conditions that may increase the risk of error and fraud occurring. Here is a brief synopsis of the areas of concern that alert the auditor to possible dangers:

- previous experience or incidents that call into question the integrity or competence of management
- particular financial pressures within an entity
- weaknesses in the design and operation of the accounting and internal controls system
- unusual transactions
- problems in obtaining sufficient appropriate audit evidence.

It must be repeated that it is the responsibility of the directors to take such steps as are open to them to prevent and detect fraud. This clearly implies the setting up of effective systems of financial and other internal controls. The auditor assesses the risk an audit procedures so as to have a **reasonable expectation** of detecting misstatem from fraud and error, material to the financial statements. We will discuss these in the Audit Process section below.

## Code of conduct

Most professions have codes of conduct and most will contain similar principles and values. The Institute of Internal Auditors, for instance, regards integrity, objectivity, confidentiality and competency as key to its code of ethics. UK and Irish accountants subscribe to the Guide to Professional Ethics, which is similar to the IFAC code. The Guide contains statements that cover both personal and professional behaviour and how accountants should conduct themselves in their relationships with clients and the public. Independence and competency feature highly in the work of accountants. Independence in mind and action is a prerequisite if conflicts of interests are to be avoided. When combined with caution, reasonable skill, care and due diligence are the essential traits of a competent auditor.

## THE AUDIT PROCESS

As we have discussed, the external auditor is required to give an opinion on the financial statements. The statements are assertions made by management that each account is correct and that when combined they reflect the true and fair view of the company's finances. The audit process confronts or questions those assertions. How does the auditor proceed to accomplish this? The auditor must start with an audit plan that describes the expected scope and conduct of the audit (ISA 300). This will include a set of objectives (listed below) for each account, and by means of substantive tests the audit will determine if these objectives can be met.

## Scope of the audit

This pursuit of the objectives can be approached in two main ways (O'Regan 1998):

- **System approach:** This means evaluating the internal control system by means of **compliance tests** and **substantive tests**. Compliance tests are essentially a test of the controls, not of the transaction itself. Substantive tests, on the other hand, examine transactions and balances to provide evidence of the completeness, accuracy and validity of the information contained in the accounting records or in the financial statements. They will usually start at the beginning of a transaction and follow it through to the financial statements.
- **Direct verification approach:** This requires detailed testing of items in the financial statements, so the opinion is based on the auditor's ability to obtain relevant and reliable

evidence from a number of sources. This approach will usually start with the year-end balance and backtrack to the original transactions.

The nature, extent and timing of tests in the **systems approach** are a matter of judgment for the auditor. Where the auditor places reliance on evaluating the internal control system, and where that evaluation provides assurance that the controls are working adequately, the auditor will limit the number of substantive tests to be carried out.

Where there are weaknesses in the internal control system, the auditor will need sufficient evidence that material errors or omissions have not occurred in the financial statements. In this situation, the auditor should not limit the substantive tests, but rather give way to the **direct verification approach**, where testing encompasses substantive testing.

The key advantage of the systems approach is that when the internal control system is deemed to be reliable, the number of tests is greatly reduced.

## Self-Assessment Question 5

1. How does a compliance test differ from a substantive test?

## Auditing objectives

The following list captures the objectives to be pursued for each account:
- completeness
- existence
- accuracy
- valuation
- occurrence (cut-off)
- obligations and rights
- presentation.

The audit process will test to see if, for example, the debtors making up the ending balance in the account do in fact *exist* or that a purchase transaction on credit did in fact make it into the creditors balance to make it *complete*.

## Substantive tests

Also referred to as **substantive procedures**, they are comprised of two types of tests:
- **tests of details** regarding transactions and account balances
- **analytical procedures** are carried out by comparing recent account balances with previous years' balances. Relationships between accounts in a year are also included here. An example: How did the gross margin this year compare with last year?

Tests of details provide the audit evidence and may involve the following procedures:

- **Observation and enquiry:** Does management carry out specific procedures, such as stock counts, or are regular reconciliations performed?
- **Reperformance and recomputation:** Apply or redo client procedures or computations.
- **Confirmation:** Obtain audit evidence from a third party in support of a fact or a condition. Call or write to debtors or creditors to determine if they exist and that they agree with what the company says are the outstanding balances.
- **Physical inspection:** Examine and count the physical assets underlying the amounts in an account.
- **Examining documentary evidence:** The existence or validity of a recorded item or balance.
- **Reviewing minutes of meetings:** Board's approval of significant corporate actions.
- **Letters of enquiry to solicitors:** Additional assurance as to active, pending or expected litigation.

## Self-Assessment Questions 6

1. What objective(s) is met when the physical inspection test is carried out on stock?
2. If the evaluation of the internal control is a positive one, what impact will this have on the pursuit of substantive tests?

### EXAMPLES OF TESTS

Looking at controls in place for purchases, the auditor can expect that invoices presented for payment will have been authorised by the responsible official. This official's signature should appear on the purchase invoice. The **compliance test** is whether the invoice has the signature or not.

A **substantive test** of a transaction such as a sale calls for an examination of the sales order received by the business, following it through to the sales account appearing in the profit and loss account. Calculations are checked, multipart forms are pursued through to their respective destinations, delivery documents are compared with sales invoices and sales postings to the accounts are confirmed.

Of help to the auditor is the use of the **audit trail**, which is defined as a number of documents and records allowing the auditor to find a particular document or to pursue a transaction from beginning to end. It is useful to both management and the auditor:

- inquiries from customers and suppliers
- auditors' queries
- facilitates tracing and vouching of documents.

es an audit trail is difficult to track due to advances in technology, and if a on cannot be tracked back to its genesis, substantive tests may not be possible.

## Tracing and vouching

**Tracing** is a substantive test method whereby the auditor starts at the beginning with the original transaction and follows it right through to the account balance. It is a test for *completeness* and the possibility that if a transaction(s) does not go through to a proper conclusion, the account balance will be understated.

**Vouching** is also a method of substantive testing and it starts at the end balance by choosing final entries there and working back. This tests for *existence*, and by verifying that amounts from transactions do in fact belong to an account, the threat of overstatement is minimised.

## THE AUDITOR'S REPORT

The auditor's report represents the culmination of the audit process. It contains the auditor's opinion on whether or not the financial statements reflect the **true and fair view** (or **present fairly**, if using the IASs). The opinion is the ultimate test in professional judgment for the auditor.

## Opinion types

There are a number of positions that the auditor can take depending on the conclusions reached. The most desirable opinion is an **unqualified opinion** and is recognised with the following wording: 'In our opinion the financial statements give a true and fair view of the state of affairs of the company at 31 December 200X and of the profit and cash flows of the company for the year then ended.'

Circumstances may arise that necessitate a **qualified opinion,** as shown below. Having limited access to account information, for instance, constitutes a scope limitation, or a disagreement with management may also prevent the auditor from expressing an unqualified opinion.

FIGURE 12.2: DETERMINING A QUALIFIED REPORT

| Circumstances | Limitation of scope | Disagreement |
|---|---|---|
| Form of qualification | Except for | Except for |
| | Disclaimer | Adverse |

## A qualified opinion

A scope limitation and a disagreement between management and auditor may qualify an opinion. What the auditor must first decide is whether these circumstances are material, and secondly, how extensive they are.

### LIMITATION OF SCOPE

Both circumstances must trigger a material impact if a qualified opinion is to be considered. Let's say that the auditor does not have access to a subsidiary's stock records (the subsidiary is located in a war-torn country) and such stock is approximately 10 per cent of total stock. The size of the limitation is certainly material, but contained enough to express: '**Except for** restricted access to a subsidiary's stock located abroad, the financial statements do reflect the true and fair view…'.

If the limitation is greater than that due perhaps to severe damage to information systems, then the auditor may state that 'due to considerable damage to information systems, we are unable to issue an opinion on the financial statements.' This is called a **disclaimer**.

### DISAGREEMENT

A disagreement usually arises over the application of an accounting principle. The auditor may discover that a portion of reported revenue has yet to be earned (a violation of the matching principle) and request management to adjust accordingly. If management refuses to budge, and depending on the size of the amount, the auditor may qualify the opinion with an 'except for' or issue an **adverse** opinion: 'The financial statements do not reflect the true and fair view.' This is obviously the most damaging of possible opinions for a company.

## Issue of going concern

A fundamental concept that is central to the auditor's report is whether the company can continue as a going concern. Unless we are informed to the contrary, the business is expected to continue into the foreseeable future. However, a situation could arise where a lawsuit threatens the existence of an otherwise healthy company. The company is confronted with what is referred to as a **fundamental uncertainty** and it must be reported as such. The situation is outlined in a separate paragraph (sometimes called an **emphasis of matter**) in the auditor's report under the heading '**fundamental uncertainty**'. What will the opinion be? If management agrees with the auditor's assessment and disclosure is adequate, then an unqualified opinion will be issued. On the other hand, if management does not agree with the auditor, then an adverse opinion will ensue.

## Self-Assessment Question 7

1. Examine each of the following *independent* situations and determine the type of opinion to be expressed.

   (a) The auditor did not observe the entity's physical inventory and is unable to become satisfied as to its balance by using other auditing procedures.

   (b) The financial statements fail to disclose information that is required by generally accepted accounting principles.

   (c) The auditor is asked to report only on the entity's balance sheet and not on the other basic financial statements.

   (d) Events disclosed in the financial statements cause the auditor to have substantial doubt about the entity's ability to continue as a going concern.

## Advantages and disadvantages of an audit

There are certain inherent advantages in having financial statements audited:

- A major change in ownership is facilitated if past accounts contain an unqualified audit report, e.g. where two businesses merge to form a partnership.
- Applications to third parties for finance may be enhanced by audited accounts.
- An auditor may well discover major errors and fraud during the audit, even though such discovery is not the primary objective of the audit.
- The in-depth examination of the business may enable the auditor to give constructive advice to management on improving the efficiency of the business.

Disadvantages of an audit are basically twofold:

- Audits can be costly, involving as they do the services of a professional. However, these costs should be small in comparison with the benefits derived.
- Disruption of the work of employees is unavoidable, as an audit requires management and staff to spend time providing information to the auditor.

## The role of the internal auditor

As we noted earlier, an **internal auditor** is often employed in medium to large companies to install and maintain internal controls. It is impossible for top management in large organisations to exercise direct control and supervision of operations. Exacerbating this further is the remoteness that evolves in growing businesses, facilitating misrepresentation, misunderstanding and misjudgment. An internal auditor is able to bridge the gap that may emerge in controls and in a sense provide an independent check of the accounting records and other operations of the company.

While the scope of the internal auditor is defined by management, maximum benefit is

obtained if the auditor's duties extend beyond mere checking for accuracy of fun
records to cover all aspects of financial and non-financial matters. In order to do
internal auditor must be completely divorced from executive responsibility and al
investigate any area of the organisation's activities. This independence is underlined if the
internal auditor reports directly to the audit committee in keeping with good governance
practice.

The external audit can be assisted by the internal auditor in minimising disruption and
in assessing internal controls on a timely basis.

FIGURE 12.3: CONTRASTING THE INTERNAL AND EXTERNAL AUDITOR

| Areas of difference | Internal auditor | External auditor |
|---|---|---|
| Scope | Determined by management. | Determined by statute. |
| Approach | Ensure that accounting system is efficient and that it provides management with accurate and material information. | Ensure that financial statements presented to shareholders present a true and fair view. |
| Responsibility | To management. | To shareholders. |

## Self-Assessment Question 8

1. In the context of the audit, distinguish between the role of management and that of the external auditor.

## THE ANNUAL REPORT

The annual report of a publicly traded company contains a number of reports required by
legislation, including the accounts and the auditor's opinion. It is primarily a
communications device and is the responsibility of the directors. In recent years it has been
expanded to include a number of statements, including statements from the chairperson
and the CEO and a review called the **operational and financial review (OFR)**. This last
item has evolved to the point that beginning in January 2005, the OFR is required by
accounting regulation. But in a stunning reversal in December 2005, the UK government
decided that the OFR was not mandatory. All this additional narrative is accompanied with
glossy photographs and imagery that has turned the annual report into a marketing event
that competes with the enclosed financial information. While the financial results are
announced to the public often within days of the year-end, the annual report is prepared

in time for the annual general meeting that is scheduled, usually between sixty and ninety days after the end of the year. It can exceed eighty pages and is thus a showcase for the company.

## The emergence of narrative of content

The requirement to produce accounts and a directors' report prompted the independent auditor's report of the accounts, and taken together all three formed the genesis of the annual report. Numbers on their own were always insufficient and in time narrative content emerged to try and address investors' inquiries and concerns (O'Regan 2001).

Today we can describe the annual report as made up essentially of four components:

- **Introductory content**: Graphs, financial highlights, colour photographs.
- **Operational reports and reviews:** Chairperson's and CEO's statements, OFR, corporate governance statement (required by London Stock Exchange if publicly traded).
- **Accounts section:** Includes financial statements and notes, accounting policies, directors' report and auditor's report, *all* of which are mandatory.
- **Shareholders' information:** Contains company's address and stock exchange symbol.

With the growth in narrative content comes the opportunity for 'spin' and unreasonable optimism on the part of the company. Investors need to be aware of this and satisfy themselves that management's evaluation of the company and its future prospects are consistent with the financial picture.

### Self-Assessment Question 9

1. What are the pros and cons of the growth in narrative content in the annual report?

## The accounts section

This part of the report is mandatory. It contains the:

- financial statements
- notes accompanying the statements
- directors' report
- auditor's opinion.

Although the OFR is not part of the accounts section, it may in time be considered as such despite the recent removal of its mandatory status.

## THE FINANCIAL STATEMENTS AND NOTES

We have discussed the financial statements at length and have found sufficient information to complete a financial analysis. However, there is only so much space on an A4-size sheet, and to avoid clutter, accountants provide additional disclosures in accompanying notes. The number of notes can run from twenty-five to in excess of sixty. It is generally agreed that during the boom economy of the late 1990s the notes were not as closely examined as they should have been. Companies such as Enron and Elan claimed that liabilities and the results of joint ventures were disclosed in the notes and that perhaps analysts did not bother to read them. A recommended approach to the notes is found in this recent observation by investment manager Alistair Hodgson (*Financial Times*, 17 September 2005): 'I almost look at the notes more than I look at the main figures at first. The notes tend to hold the key to anything that looks strange. I look to pick out things that the auditor has told the company to declare – the kind of thing they might not want to declare, but they have got to do so in order to make the accounts honest.' To put it succinctly, to ignore the notes is to do so at your peril.

## DIRECTORS' REPORT

This report must describe the:
- principal activities of the company
- any significant developments that occurred during the year.

Also attached to the report is a **statement of directors' responsibilities**, a legal requirement. As we mentioned in Chapter 10, the report includes details on directors' remuneration, as suggested by the combined code. Significant developments vary from company to company, but commentary usually covers:
- revenues and profits
- any exceptional items
- significant changes in activities
- existing borrowings and proposals to finance major expenditures with long-term debt
- employment policies
- research and development.

Deciding to enter new markets or exit existing ones would constitute a significant event.

## AUDITOR'S REPORT

We have dealt with this report under the audit process. However, it must be stressed that auditors, mindful of the growth in the narrative content, will state in their report that they have read other information contained in the annual report to determine any inconsistencies with the financial statements.

## Operational and financial review

Although the OFR is not required, shareholders will expect to see it. The statement has been a feature of the annual report for a number of years, ever since the combined code suggested the principle that 'the board should present a balanced and understandable assessment of the company's position and prospects' (D.1). This was reaffirmed in the revised code (Higgs 2003). By distinguishing it from the chairperson's and CEO's statement, the OFR minimises the element of 'spin'. It attempts to describe operations and the financial story associated with those operations. Accordingly, it enhances the image of good corporate governance at a company.

The items discussed in the OFR include:

- analyses of revenues and profits, with breakdown by region or continent (if an international company)
- capital expenditures
- financial risk management
- funding
- management of interest rate and foreign exchange risk
- significant events, such as the move to international accounting reporting standards (IFRS).

The Tesco OFR from 2004 states that one of the main financial risks faced by the group relates to 'the availability of funds to meet business needs'. This is followed by a paragraph on **funding and liquidity** stating that 'the objective is to ensure continuity of funding. The policy is to smooth the debt maturity profile, to arrange funding ahead of requirements and to maintain sufficient undrawn committed bank facilities.'

A good OFR provides this kind of insight into strategy and risk management.

### Self-Assessment Question 10

1. List the components of the annual report that you believe enhance corporate governance.

## CHAPTER REVIEW

The completion of an audit by external auditors is a requirement for all but the smallest of limited companies; it concentrates on examining and testing the company's internal control systems. The audit results in a financial report that issues an opinion on whether the financial statements give a true and fair view of the company's affairs. The report is given to the shareholders.

Testing systems is the primary activity of auditors and is pursued either by compliance testing, which tests controls, or by substantive testing, which involves actual tra... pursuing an audit trail from the genesis of the transaction right through to the statements. If compliance testing gives satisfactory results, then substantive testi... minimised.

The external auditor makes no guarantees that there are no errors or fraud. He or she must exercise due care, and as long as the audit procedures provide for a reasonable expectation of detecting material error or fraud, then the auditor is not liable for failing to detect immaterial error or fraud.

Certainly, an external audit underlines the users' confidence in the financial statements, and although they can be costly, regular audits provide management with the opportunity to receive timely advice to enhance efficiency.

The annual report has grown in size, with many reports exceeding eighty pages. There are essentially four components to the report: introductory content, operational reports and reviews, accounts section and shareholders' information. The accounts section is required by law. The growth in the narrative content is reasonable, as the numbers on their own are not sufficient. However, there is the danger that management may embellish the perception of the company and accordingly users must look very closely at the numbers, including the notes accompanying the statements.

# SELF-ASSESSMENT QUESTION ANSWERS

## SAQ 1
1. In the annual report to shareholders, auditors will state that they had access to all records and information that they considered necessary to complete the audit.

## SAQ 2
1. Key characteristics of an audit:
   - It must be carried out by an independent auditor.
   - The auditor must have access to all relevant records and information.
   - An opinion must be expressed on whether financial statements have been prepared in accordance with generally accepted accounting principles.
   - The statements must give a true and fair view of the entity's affairs.

## SAQ 3
1. There are four auditing concepts: credibility, audit process, reporting and standards of performance. Audit process has the 'roll up the sleeves' quality about it and involves the mechanics of pursuing the audit. Gathering evidence, understanding risk, applying materiality, using a sceptical mindset and the use of sound judgment are the nuts and bolts of the audit process.

## AQ 4

1. The auditor cannot look at every transaction and therefore is unable to guarantee that there are no errors or fraud. What is expected of the auditor is to be conscious of the possibility of fraud and error occurring. As long as the auditor plans for the reasonable expectation of material fraud and error, due care is considered to be exercised.

## SAQ 5

1. Compliance tests look at controls, whereas substantive tests are applied to account balances and transactions.

## SAQ 6

1. The physical inspection will firstly establish that the asset *exists*. This then will facilitate the *valuation* of those assets.
2. A positive evaluation of the internal control system will allow the auditor to restrict substantive testing.

## SAQ 7

1. (a) This is a scope limitation that is material and therefore the opinion will be qualified. If impact is relatively small, the opinion will begin with 'Except for'. If it is more extensive and the auditor is unable to issue an opinion, then it is a disclaimer.
   (b) Assuming that this is material and management does not agree to adhere to GAAP, then the opinion will begin with 'Except for' if the impact is not too severe. If the impact is extensive, then an adverse opinion will be given: 'the financial statements do not reflect the true and fair view.'
   (c) A scope limitation that could at a minimum require an 'Except for'. More likely, the auditor will disclaim giving an opinion.
   (d) If management agrees with the auditor's assessment and discloses the situation adequately, then an unqualified opinion preceded with a paragraph under the heading 'fundamental uncertainty' will be issued. Where management disagrees, the auditor will issue an adverse opinion.

## SAQ 8

1. Management is responsible for preparing the financial statements and establishing the internal control system. The external auditor is responsible for examining the financial statements and expressing an opinion on whether they fairly reflect the activities of the business in the period under review.

## SAQ 9

1. On the positive side, commentary provides insight to the numbers that reflect the

company's financial position and performance. It also allows the user to evaluate strategy and future prospects. The emergence of the OFR minimises 'spin' and forces management to give a positive picture without the aspirational sentiment.

The negative aspect to the growth in the narrative is that companies will tend to put a positive 'spin' on the company's performance. The sheer volume of pages, complete with colour photographs and graphics, runs the risk of crowding out pertinent information such as debt-equity structure or goals from prior years not attained.

## SAQ 10

1. The inclusion of a corporate governance statement is a welcome addition, as discussed in Chapter 10. The directors' report and the auditor's report being legal requirements should inspire confidence. The emergence of the OFR in recent years will provide users with useful insights and perhaps act as an antidote to any 'over the top' aspirations and claims of the chairperson and CEO.

# REFERENCES

American Accounting Association, Committee on Basic Auditing Concepts, Florida: AAA 1973.

Beasley, M. & Salterio, S., 'The relationship between board characteristics and voluntary improvements in the capability of audit committees to monitor', *Contemporary Accounting Research,* XVIII/4 (2001).

Bisk, N., *Auditing from CPA Comprehensive Exam Review*, Tampa, FL: Fox Gearty 1993.

DiPiazza, S.A. and Eccles, R.G., *Building Public Trust: The Future of Corporate Reporting*, New York: John Wiley & Sons 2002.

Financial Reporting Council, *The Implications of New Accounting and Auditing Standards for the 'True and Fair View' and Auditors' Responsibilities*, London: FRC 9 August 2005.

Higgs, D., *Review of the Role and Effectiveness of Non-executive Directors*, London: The Stationery Office 2003.

IFAC, *Handbook of International Auditing, Assurance and Ethics Pronouncements*, New York: International Federation of Accountants 2004.

Lee, T., 'The nature of auditing and its objectives', *Accountancy*, 81 (1970).

MacKenzie, W., 'Foreword' in E. Normanton, *Accountability and Audit of Governments*, Manchester: University Press 1966.

O'Regan, P., *Introduction to Accounting*, Limerick: The International Equine Institute, University of Limerick 1998.

O'Regan, P., *Financial Information Analysis*, Chichester: John Wiley & Sons 2001.

Porter, B., Simon, J. and Hatherly, D., *Principles of External Auditing*, 2nd ed., Chichester: Wiley 2003.

Smith, S., 'It pays to read between the lines', *Financial Times*, 17 September 2005.

Tesco plc, *Annual Report and Financial Statements 2004*, Registered Office: Tesco House, Delamere Road, Cashunt, Hertfordshire February 2004.

# Index